QUICK ESCAPES®
LAS VEGAS

Help Us Keep This Guide Up to Date

Every effort has been made by the author and editors to make this guide as accurate and useful as possible. However, many things can change after a guide is published—establishments close, phone numbers change, facilities come under new management, and so on.

We would love to hear from you concerning your experiences with this guide and how you feel it could be made better and be kept up to date. While we may not be able to respond to all comments and suggestions, we'll take them to heart, and we'll also make certain to share them with the author. Please send your comments and suggestions to the following address:

> The Globe Pequot Press
> Reader Response/Editorial Department
> P.O. Box 480
> Guilford, CT 06437

Or you may e-mail us at:
> editorial@globe-pequot.com

Thanks for your input, and happy travels!

QUICK ESCAPES®
LAS VEGAS

25 WEEKEND GETAWAYS IN AND AROUND LAS VEGAS

BY
HEIDI KNAPP RINELLA

The Globe Pequot Press

GUILFORD, CONNECTICUT

Text design by Nancy Freeborn
Maps created by Geografx © The Globe Pequot Press

All photos by the author except as follows: Pages 67, 77, 179, and 184, courtesy Nevada Commission on Tourism; page 141, courtesy Anaheim/Orange County Visitor and Convention Bureau; pages 208 and 213, courtesy Arizona Office of Tourism; and page 245, courtesy Tom Gentry, Flagstaff Convention and Visitors Bureau.

Library of Congress Cataloging-in-Publication Data is available.

ISBN 0-7627-2189-8

Manufactured in the United States of America
First Edition/First Printing

The information listed in this guidebook was confirmed at press time. We recommend, however, that you call establishments before traveling to obtain current information.

To my parents, Jean Knapp and the late Eugene Knapp, whose sense of wonder at the world's offerings encouraged my own undying wanderlust, and to my daughters, Aynsley and Aubrey, and husband, Frank, for their companionship as we were visiting the places in this book and their unlimited tolerance and understanding as I was writing it. I look forward to many more quick escapes with them.

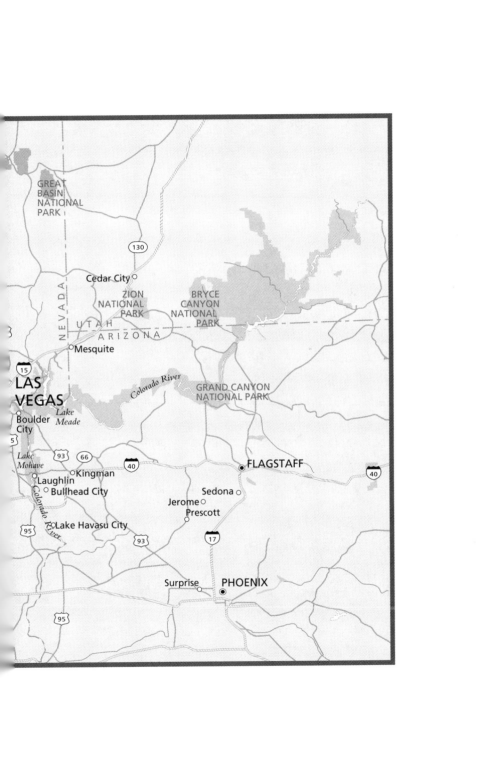

CONTENTS

Introduction xi

DESERT ESCAPES 1
1. Death Valley: Cool Fun in the Hottest Spot in the Country . . . 2
2. Mesquite: Escape From the Glitz 12
3. Lake Havasu City: A Desert Surprise 21
4. Laughlin, Bullhead City, and Kingman: A Desert Oasis 31
5. Palm Springs: A Resort in the Desert 42
6. Sedona: Red Rocks in the Sunset 52

MOUNTAIN ESCAPES 63
1. Reno: Gambling and the Great Outdoors 64
2. Lake Tahoe: Alpine Escape 74
3. Zion National Park: Rocks That Form a Temple of Beauty . . . 84
4. Bryce Canyon National Park: Tough for Farming,
   Great for Hiking 94
5. Cedar City: To the Mountains! 105
6. Big Bear Lake: An Active Resort Area Nestled in the Pines . . 115
7. Sequoia and Kings Canyon National Parks:
   Spend Time in the Timber 125

SEASIDE ESCAPES 135
1. Anaheim: What Walt Hath Wrought 136
2. San Diego: Centuries of Old-World Charm by the Pacific . . 147

3. Long Beach: An Escape Fit for a Queen 157
4. California Beaches: Surf's Up 167

OLD WEST ESCAPES 179
1. Virginia City and Carson City: Nevada History Lives On. . . 180
2. Grand Canyon: Get Acquainted with a Western Legend 190
3. Phoenix: Go West into History 200
4. Prescott and Jerome: A Look at Life in the Territory 210

HISTORICAL ESCAPES. 221
1. Boulder City and Lake Mead: Fun at the Dam and Lake . . . 222
2. Pasadena: Everything's Coming Up Roses. 231
3. Flagstaff: Where College Kids and Nature Lovers Can Get
   Their Kicks. 241
4. Barstow, Victorville, and Apple Valley: Chilling Out in the
   High Desert 251

Index 263
About the Author 273

Mesquite, Nevada

INTRODUCTION

L as Vegas is arguably one of the most exciting cities in the world, drawing more than 36 million visitors each year. Both visitors and year-round residents revel in the wealth of nightlife, nature spots, and other opportunities for entertainment and recreation that are offered in and around the valley.

But no matter how desirable a home city might be, sometimes its local folks want nothing more than to get out of town for a couple of days, and Las Vegas offers plenty of opportunities for that, too. In this case, it's the city's location in the southwestern United States that's so desirable; within a few hours, residents can travel deeper into the Mojave or Sonoran deserts of California and Arizona; explore the Utah mountains with their unmatched national parks and legendary powder for skiers; journey to the California shore to surf, walk on the beach or just take in the excitement of life in Southern California; or visit gen-u-ine Old West settlements, including a few ghost towns, just for fun.

You'll want to take a few items with you as you make your quick escapes:

Be sure to have good, up-to-date maps; you'll want those that are thorough enough to list old mining towns and recent enough to provide all of the routes in this fast-developing region.

If it's summer and you're going to be traveling in the desert, be sure to take plenty of water—about one gallon per person per day, plus more for your vehicle. Take a wireless phone, too, but be mindful that lots of places in the desert are without wireless service, so be sure someone knows where you're going and when you're due back. And remember that sunscreen.

Consider an annual pass to the National Parks System. It's currently $50 per year, but since admission to some national parks is $20 per vehicle and a great number of national parks are in close proximity, your pass will pay for itself in just a few quick escapes.

Oh, and one other thing: Have fun.

Happy wandering.

DESERT
ESCAPES

Death Valley

COOL FUN IN THE
HOTTEST SPOT IN THE COUNTRY

2 NIGHTS

Sightseeing • Golfing • Hiking
"20 Mule Team" history • Historic inn

Any baby boomer worth his or her P.F. Flyers will remember *Death Valley Days,* the TV show sponsored by "20 Mule Team" Borax.

You're also likely to think of Death Valley, California, in another way—as the site of the nation's high on many a summer day, temperatures that seem so hot, so unfit for sustaining human life, that it's abundantly clear how the region got its name. Indeed, Death Valley is known as one of the hottest places in the world; its record high of 134 degrees is eclipsed only by a temperature of 136 degrees once recorded in Libya.

Death Valley was named by pioneers looking for a shortcut to the California gold fields—prospectors who were grateful simply to leave the place. But the heat and relative lack of vegetation didn't stop many more from flooding to the valley in search of gold and silver. The precious metals weren't plentiful, but the mineral borax was.

Like lots of other locations in the world (think Iceland), Death Valley got a bit of a bad rap when it was named. There's a lot of beauty in them thar hills, and much of it stems from the hills themselves, or mountains, rather, whose barren state reveals their geological formations.

Death Valley is full of life as well. If you visit in early spring, you may find the valley floor afire with the color of desert flora. And there are few other

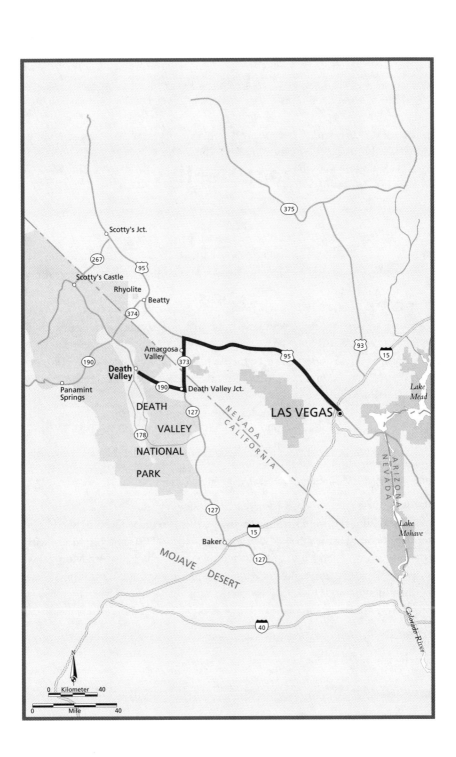

places where it's easy to spot coyotes scampering around. They're wary of humans, so don't worry about being approached; on the other hand, because they'd just as soon keep their distance, it's best to respect that and give them a wide berth.

Besides, in this park where visitors and workers seem like they're truly in love with the place, the coyotes are just about the only unfriendly creatures around. So quit worrying about turning into bleached bones and make a quick escape to Death Valley.

DAY 1

The east entrance to Death Valley National Park is about 130 miles from Las Vegas, an easy two-and-a-half-hour drive—and you're unlikely to encounter any traffic problems.

Take U.S. Highway 95 north from Las Vegas about 85 miles to Amargosa Valley and go south on Nevada Route 373 for about 15 miles, until it becomes California Route 127 when you cross the state line; then follow it for another 7 miles or so. Turn right (west) onto California Route 190 and follow it about 16 miles to the **Furnace Creek** area of **Death Valley National Park.**

At Furnace Creek, you'll find a little settlement of sorts. This area first became a resort in about 1927, when the Pacific Coast Borax Company decided to follow the lead of Palm Springs. The region was declared a national monument in 1935, and improved roads and such amenities as visitor centers followed; it was designated a national park in 1994.

DINNER: What better way to launch a visit to Death Valley National Park than by having dinner in the **Dining Room at the Furnace Creek Inn** (Highway 190 South, Death Valley, CA 92328; 760–786–2345). The big room, with its wrought-iron chandeliers and panoramic view of the Panamint Mountains, is the site of some decidedly upscale fare—continental with an emphasis on regional ingredients. There's a dress code in the dining room from October to mid-May. Expensive.

LODGING: There generally isn't room at the inn on a walk-in basis, so you'll have to plan ahead, but it'll be worth it to stay at this landmark resort (rates from $230 to $375; 760–786–2345 or www.furnacecreekresort.com) that recently was restored to its 1927 grandeur. Tucked against a mountainside, it's

A 20-mule-team borax wagon at Furnace Creek Ranch, Death Valley

genteel enough to offer daily afternoon tea. The inn has sixty-six rooms and two suites, plus lighted tennis courts and a spring-fed swimming pool that stays at a warm 85 degrees.

DAY 2

Morning

BREAKFAST: Mosey on over to the **Furnace Creek Ranch,** just around the corner from the inn, and the **Forty Niner Cafe** (760–786–2345) for some traditional breakfast fare and Mexican favorites. Moderate.

Might as well take your car when you go to the ranch for breakfast, because you'll need it to explore this park of 3.3 million acres—of which more than 3 million acres are wilderness.

One caveat before you strike out: This is a vast area, and while a half-million people visit each year, you're likely to find yourself alone at any given time. There's simply too much ground for rangers to cover any of it regularly, and visitors tend to spread out. So especially if it's summer—but really at any time of year—be sure your vehicle is in good repair, and take along enough water to sustain your party. The recommendation is one gallon per day per person, plus three gallons for your vehicle, although radiator water is available at several points throughout the park (marked on the park map). Be sure to read the safety precautions and regulations on the park map.

To get that map, begin your exploration of **Death Valley National Park** at the **Furnace Creek Visitor Center,** where you can also see a slide show, learn about borax and get a general orientation. The visitor center also has a bookstore if you'd like to learn more about the region.

Afterward, drop back in at the Furnace Creek Ranch for a tour of the little **Borax Museum** (760–786–2331). Be sure also to see the borax wagon at the ranch. Because the borax loads were so heavy, and had to travel so far to reach a railhead, 20 mules were needed to pull them; the wagons had wheels that were considerably larger in diameter than the height of the average person.

The Furnace Creek complex is toward the southern end of the park, so start your driving tour by heading south along California Route 190 to Dante's View, an overlook at 5,475 feet above sea level. From Dante's View, you'll be able to see the lowest point in the United States (282 feet below sea level) as well as the Panamint Range and the surrounding mountains. On a clear winter day—and most days are clear in Death Valley, which receives less than 2 inches of rain in an average year—you will be able to see Mount Williamson, which soars 14,375 feet in the Sierra Nevada to the north.

Take CA 190 back up to the Furnace Creek area and then head south on California Route 178 to explore the southernmost area of the park. If you're interested in ruins, drop about 45 miles south to what remains of Ashford Mill and loop back along the unpaved West Side Road past the remnants of the Eagle Borax Works.

About 12 miles south of Furnace Creek along CA 178 is the turnoff for the Devil's Golf Course, a grouping of interesting formations—jagged spikes of rock salt on the salt-pan surface.

A little farther north is Artists Drive, a one-way loop through colorful canyons and badlands. Nearby are Zabriskie Point, Twenty Mule Team Canyon, and the Golden Canyon Interpretive Trail, which is a good place for a hike as it meanders through a canyon filled with colorful rocks.

Another pleasant hike is the Harmony Borax Works Interpretive Trail just north of Furnace Creek. Harmony, vintage 1883, was the first successful borax plant in the valley.

LUNCH: Back at the ranch, stop in at the **19th Hole** at the adjacent **Furnace Creek Golf Course** (760–786–2301) and see barmaid Jan, who promises that her burgers are the best around. They're huge, juicy, and cooked on a big charcoal-fired grill. Best of all, you can have lunch overlooking the golf course, a field of green that seems like a mirage. Note the tall palms that dot the area—the remains of a failed date-farming venture. Inexpensive.

Afternoon

If you're a golfer, don't resist the novelty of playing a round 214 feet below sea level, on a course billed as the lowest grass course in the world. (Of course, you should know that as altitude, or lack thereof, affects the distance that the ball will travel, your drives will be shorter on this course.) The course was renovated by Perry Dye in 1997, and believe it or not, water plays a role on nine of the eighteen holes. Coyotes tend to play a role on all eighteen; they've been known to come out of the adjacent trees and roll around like puppies on the fairways. They have a special fondness for snatching balls and taking off with them, so be sure to bring plenty of extras.

Even if you don't play golf, you're likely to enjoy walking the course and reveling in this desert oasis. Or stop by the nearby pool, which, like the pool at the inn, has naturally heated spring water that's always at a comfortable 85 degrees.

Another option is to strike out for the ruins of the Keane Wonder Mill, reached via the Beatty Cutoff, which forks off of CA 190 about 10 miles north of the Visitor Center. From the cutoff you'll need to take a dirt road to reach the old mill (site of the gold strike that started the mining rush in the region) right up against Chloride Cliff and the Funeral Mountains. Unlike many old mining sites, this one has been stabilized to reduce the danger of injury, with grates placed across shaft entrances, so it's relatively safe to wander around. You'll see several shafts, plus the remains of an elaborate trestle structure that was used to move the minerals once they were removed from the cliff.

Farther up CA 190 is Stovepipe Wells Village, one of the resort complexes in the park. Nearby is the site of the original Stovepipe Well, where pioneers sunk a well that became a landmark for the tall pipe sticking up out of the valley floor, and the much-photographed Sand Dunes.

DINNER: The **Wrangler Steakhouse** at the Furnace Creek Ranch (760–786–2345) serves steaks, chops, chicken, and pasta and has a salad bar. Moderate.

Evening

If you have any energy left, drive out of the park along CA 190 to Death Valley Junction, home of the **Amargosa Opera House** (760–852–4441), truly a unique institution. The proprietress is Marta Becket, a former New York dancer who moved to the town with her husband in the late 1960s and renovated an old Pacific Coast Borax Company building, gradually creating the hotel and opera house. Becket, now in her seventies, and a sidekick still perform musical theater from October through mid-May at 8:00 P.M. on Saturdays. It's a little out of the way and some nights the house is empty or nearly so, so Becket painted an audience—a sixteenth-century Spanish audience—on the walls of her theater. The paintings alone are worth the drive.

LODGING: The Furnace Creek Inn and Ranch Resort (see above).

DAY 3

Morning

BREAKFAST: The Furnace Creek Inn is known for its Sunday brunch, which features glorious pastries and smoked salmon, among other things. Expensive.

After breakfast, head north on CA 190 to CA 267 to reach Ubehebe Crater, created during a volcanic eruption about 1,000 years ago. The crater is 2,400 feet across.

An awe-inspiring point of quite a different nature—and a fine way to cap your visit to Death Valley National Park—is **Scotty's Castle**, 8 miles from the crater in Grapevine Canyon. Construction on Scotty's Castle began in 1922 by wealthy industrialist Albert M. Johnson, and it was sort of gradually appropriated over the years by Johnson's friend, "Death Valley Scotty" (also known as Walter E. Scott), a colorful local character.

The "castle"—actually a huge and ornate house that would seem more at home in the forests of Europe than a Death Valley canyon—is complete with a Great Hall, music room with a 1,000-pipe organ, chimes tower with twenty-five carillon chimes, unfinished swimming pool, manmade stream, and more. Costumed interpreters assume identities of period characters to lead 50-

minute tours of the castle. After the tour, wander around the extensive grounds, and be sure to hike up the hill to see Scotty's grave, from which there's a sweeping view of the canyon. Scotty's Castle is open 9:00 A.M.–5:00 P.M. daily. Admission $8.00.

LUNCH: The snack bar at Scotty's Castle (760–786–2331) serves all manner of sandwiches, which can be enjoyed indoors or at some of the picnic tables on the castle grounds. Inexpensive.

Afternoon

To return to Las Vegas from Scotty's Castle, follow CA 267 through Grapevine Canyon to Scotty's Junction and then turn south on US 95. As you pass through the town of Beatty, Nevada, consider a side trip to the ghost town of **Rhyolite,** which was born after a 1904 gold strike. Between 1905 and 1912, the town had an estimated 3,500 to 10,000 residents, more than fifty mines, fifty-three saloons, eighteen grocery stores, and two churches. By 1919, nearly everyone was gone.

But not everything—the desert preserves things rather nicely. Nearly 100 years later, visitors still can see a 1906 house made primarily of bottles, plus the ruins of a three-story bank, two-story school, general store, and numerous other buildings.

THERE'S MORE

Pioneer Territory Wagon Tours, Crystal, Nevada (775–372–1717). Old West–style covered-wagon rides; day and overnight trips with chuck-wagon dinners and tours of Ash Meadows National Wildlife Refuge and Devil's Hole.

SPECIAL EVENTS

Beatty, Nevada

March. Rhyolite Resurrection Festival. Celebrates the ghost town and continuing preservation efforts. (775) 553–2424

May. Best of the West. NHPA-sanctioned horseshoe tournament. (775) 553–2424

July. Old-Fashioned Family Fourth of July. (775) 553–2225

September. Beatty Days. (775) 553–2424

October. Pitch and Witch Horseshoe Tournament. (775) 553–2424

Burro Races. (775) 553–2424

Beatty Grand Prix Off-Road Motorcycle Race. (775) 553–2424

Western Cup Cowboy Shooting Championship. (775) 553–2424

Death Valley, California

January. Furnace Creek Invitational Golf Tournament. (760) 786–2345

May. Death Valley to Mount Whitney Bike Race. Two-day race that draws more than 300 riders. (760) 786–2345

July. Badwater Ultramarathon. A 135-mile road run from 282 feet below sea level at Badwater to 8,300 feet on Mt. Whitney. (310) 312–1841 or (310) 283–1578

November. Death Valley 49ers Encampment, Furnace Creek and Stovepipe Wells. Includes Western art show, cowboy poetry, music, photography, campfires, sing-a-longs, and pioneer costume contest. (760) 786–2345

December. Holiday festivities at Furnace Creek. (760) 786–2345

OTHER RECOMMENDED RESTAURANTS AND LODGINGS

Amargosa Valley, Nevada

Longstreet Inn, Casino, RV Park, and Golf Club, NV 373; (775) 372–1777. Two-story, eighty-unit inn with pool, whirlpool, gazebo, and pond.

Beatty, Nevada

Exchange Club, 119 Main Street; (775) 553–2333. Motel with forty-four units, some with whirlpool.

Stagecoach Hotel Casino and RV Park, US 95 North; (775) 553–2419. Hotel with eighty rooms, pool, and whirlpool.

Death Valley, California

Panamint Springs Resort, Highway 190, 48 miles east of Lone Pine and 31 miles west of Stovepipe Wells; (775) 482–7680. Small Western-style resort.

Restaurant at Panamint Springs Resort, Highway 190, 48 miles east of Lone Pine and 31 miles west of Stovepipe Wells; (775) 482–7680. Steaks, lasagna, chili, spaghetti, and homemade soups; outdoor barbecues with a spectacular view of Panamint Valley at sunset.

Stovepipe Wells Village, State Road 190, 24 miles northwest of Furnace Creek Visitor Center; (760) 786–2387. Eighty-three rooms, restaurant and saloon, pool.

FOR MORE INFORMATION

Beatty Chamber of Commerce, 119 East Main Street, Beatty, NV 89003; (775) 553–2424.

Death Valley National Park, P.O. Box 579, Death Valley, CA 92328–0570; (760) 786–2331; www.npa.gov/deva.

Mesquite

ESCAPE FROM THE GLITZ

2 NIGHTS

Golf • Spas • Virgin territory • Valley of Fire

It's true that the residents of sparsely populated Nevada are pretty much con-
centrated in Las Vegas and Reno; beyond that, the state comprises mostly tiny
towns and federal government land. But there are a couple of burgeoning
resort towns out there, and one of them is fast-growing Mesquite, Nevada,
northeast of Las Vegas near the Utah border.

The proverbial three tries were needed to establish Mesquite as anything
more than another spot in the desert. All of these efforts were undertaken by
Mormon pioneers, who then were in the process of or already had established
thriving communities in Utah. An attempt by fifteen families to settle on the
shores of the muddy Virgin River near what is now Mesquite in 1882 was
thwarted when a flash flood wiped out the canals they had dug to irrigate
their crops. Another attempt in 1887, by a Mormon polygamist with fifty-one
children, failed for similar reasons. But Brigham Young's believers weren't
ready to give up yet. Six families returned in 1894, re-dug the canals and
planted the area with alfalfa. Mesquite was a reality.

Those agricultural roots served Mesquite well for several decades, and an
agrarian economy still is the backbone of the nearby Nevada communities of
Logandale and Overton, where sprawling ranches are visible from the highway and Future Farmers of America members show their livestock at the
annual Clark County Fair. Along the path to development, Mesquite also
became a dairy-farming center, supplying the growing communities around
it, most notably Las Vegas.

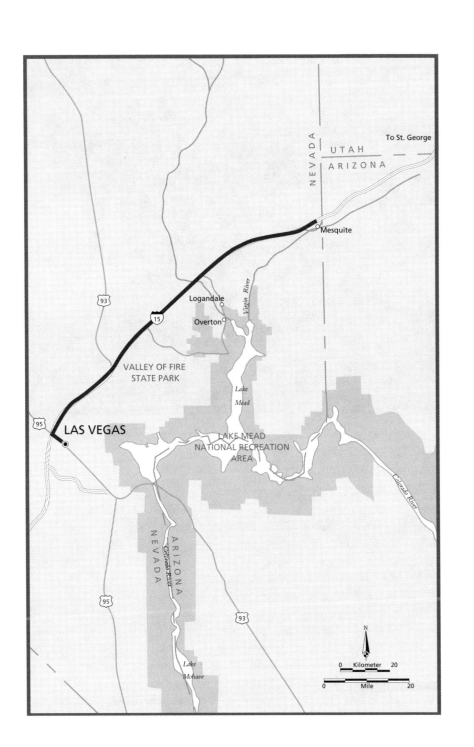

Gardens in front of the CasaBlanca Hotel-Casino, Mesquite

With the phenomenal growth of Las Vegas, tourism was coming to southern Nevada with a vengeance, and Mesquite wouldn't be left in the dust. The little farm town's location on the main route between Salt Lake City and Los Angeles, with Las Vegas in the middle, made it a popular stopping point for travelers, and businesses sprang up to fill their needs, which often have included a few minutes at a slot machine.

When Lake Mead was formed by the construction of Hoover Dam in the 1930s, its northern end was just to the southeast of Mesquite, which brought more and more boaters to the town over the next several decades. And once Interstate 15 came through, right along the side of Mesquite, the town's transformation from cow town to budding resort community was assured.

But don't get the idea that Mesquite is no longer quaint; a recent headline on the city's Web site read, "Mesquite Fire and Rescue Begins 24-Hour Day

DESERT

Coverage," and the estimated population stands at only about 15,500. It's a huge change from the traffic and tussles of Las Vegas. And for that reason, Mesquite—and its neighbors Logandale, Overton and Moapa—are great spots for a quick escape.

DAY 1

Evening

Mesquite is about 80 miles from Las Vegas, for a drive of about an hour and fifteen minutes, which means an evening departure will ensure a good start on your weekend. And the route's an easy one: Simply drive north on Interstate 15 to exit 122 and you'll be in Mesquite.

DINNER: Just off the interstate is the **CasaBlanca Hotel-Casino** (950 West Mesquite Boulevard, Mesquite 89027; 702–346–7529 or 800–459–PLAY; www.casablancaresort.com). Mesquite's resorts are known for the bargain prices that help them compete with their bigger brethren in Las Vegas, so you might start off your budget-saver Mesquite weekend with a meal at the **Purple Fez Cafe,** which offers a steak-and-lobster dinner for $12.99, twenty-four hours a day. Inexpensive.

LODGING: As soon as you approach it, you'll know the CasaBlanca aims to present itself as an oasis in the desert, with lush gardens and rushing waterfalls to welcome visitors. The CasaBlanca has 500 tower rooms (rates from $39 to $89), 200 kitchenette rooms and suites that are a block away, a golf course, a pool with waterslide and cascading waterfall, an arcade, and even an RV park if you'd rather bring your own accommodations.

DAY 2

Morning

BREAKFAST: The **Paradise Buffet** at Si Redd's Oasis Resort Casino (897 West Mesquite Boulevard, Mesquite 89027; 702–346–5232), just down the street from the CasaBlanca, has a lush Hawaiian theme and is a good spot to fill up on eggs with bacon or sausage, waffles, pancakes, and the like, to get ready for a day exploring the Virgin River region. Inexpensive.

Head south on I–15 to exit 75 toward Valley of Fire. When you get off the interstate you'll see **Moapa Tribal Enterprises** (702–865–2787), where the

Moapa band of the Paiute Indian tribe sells fireworks, tobacco products, and souvenirs, including Native arts and crafts.

Continue east on Nevada Route 169 and you'll come to **Valley of Fire State Park** (702–397–2088; www.state.nv.us/stparks/vf.htm). Nevada's largest state park is also its oldest, dedicated in 1935. There's much to see there, and most of it will require getting out of your car and doing a bit of walking, so be sure to wear comfortable shoes. You can pick up a guide map at the visitor center.

Valley of Fire is known for its rock formations—the park itself was named for the red sandstone that was formed from sand dunes some 150 million years ago—and there are various interesting formations to be seen, including Arch Rock, Piano Rock, the Three Sisters, and the Beehives, the sources of whose names will be obvious. Petrified logs also can be seen in two locations in the park, where they have been fenced to protect them from the feet of incautious visitors.

From about 300 B.C. to A.D. 1150, the region was home to the Basket Maker people and, later, the Anasazi Pueblo Indians, who came to the Moapa Valley to farm. These occupants may have been mere transients in the scheme of things, but they left behind an enduring sign of their existence in the petroglyphs that dot the area. At Valley of Fire, some of the most recognizable ancient petroglyphs are on the walls along the path approaching Mouse's Tank, the naturally formed hideout of an early twentieth-century renegade. And be sure to see Atlatl Rock, where a group of petroglyphs includes a depiction of an atlatl, a notched stick that the ancients used to help them propel their spears; it was sort of a forerunner to the bow and arrow. The petroglyphs at Atlatl Rock are high on a rock wall, but a stairway has been constructed for easy access.

Drive south on NV 169 and then follow it as it heads to the town of Overton. Stop for an ice cream at the **Inside Scoop** (395 South Moapa Valley Boulevard; 702–397–2055), then head to the **Lost City Museum** (721 South Moapa Valley Boulevard; 702–397–2193).

The museum was, in a way, another product of the construction of Hoover Dam. The National Park Service built it in 1935 because of fears that the ancient Anasazi sites that had formed the Pueblo Grande de Nevada would be covered by rising lake waters. Anasazi artifacts were excavated and brought to the museum, where they could be displayed to the public. The museum grounds also include a replica of an ancient pit house, a replica of a pueblo, and some actual pueblo foundations. Archeological work on the remaining

Lost City sites continues, and the museum features changing exhibits and various special programs. There's also a great gift shop here, offering visitors a chance to stock up on Indian crafts at quite reasonable prices.

After you leave the museum, drive north on NV 169 through the town of Logandale, which is sort of the agricultural heart of Clark County, of which Las Vegas is the county seat. The Clark County Fairgrounds are in Logandale, and depending on what time of year you visit, you may be able to stop in at a special event.

LUNCH: Panda Garden (10 Mesquite Boulevard, Mesquite 89027; 702–346–3028) is the real deal and offers all sorts of Chinese favorites, including the requisite egg rolls and fried won tons, plus such delights as Chinese chicken salad. Moderate.

Afternoon

After a morning touring the sites, take some time to relax. Both Si Redd's Oasis and the CasaBlanca have spas. The **Spa at CasaBlanca** (702–346–7529 or 800–459–PLAY) offers, in addition to regular Swedish massage, couples massages, Watsu, salt-glow, seaweed wrap and mudbath treatments, plus time in the soaking mineral pools and eucalyptus steam room.

Feel like doing some shopping? **Coyote Design** (171 East Mesquite Boulevard; 702–346–7330) is a microcosm of Southwestern spirit, with a lot of unique items imported from Mexico.

If something a little more active is what you had in mind, how about a round on one of the five championship courses in the Mesquite area? One of the best is the **Oasis Golf Club** at Si Redd's Oasis Resort (702–346–7820 or 866–992–4653), a challenging, Arnold Palmer–designed course that takes full advantage of the region's rugged beauty. If you're in need of a lesson or just want to brush up your skills a bit, contact the **Arnold Palmer Golf Academy** (702–346–7810) for instruction designed to work with your natural skills.

Si Redd's also offers its well-known **Ranch and Gun Club** (702–346–5232), which offers trap, sporting clays, and skeet. Horseback rides, hayrides, and ATV tours also can be arranged at the resort.

Hiking and biking are other options in the Mesquite area; contact local chambers of commerce for maps. Or strike out on the **Gold Butte Back Country Byway** (pick up a map, published by the federal Bureau of Land Management, at the Mesquite Chamber of Commerce office at 850 West

Mesquite Boulevard), a 62-mile route into the wilds around Mesquite. The route is laid out in a circle. Part of it is accessible only to high-clearance four-wheelers, but the route makes it easy to turn back when the road gets too rough for your vehicle, and you'll still see some amazing scenery—and maybe even some bighorn sheep or desert tortoises. The old mining area of Gold Butte is among the historic points on the route.

DINNER: Carollo's (561 Mesquite Boulevard, Mesquite 89027; 702–346–2818) is known for its barbecued ribs, but its steaks make it worthy of a stop as well, and fish, poultry, and pasta dishes also are available. Moderate.

LODGING: CasaBlanca Hotel-Casino (see above).

DAY 3

Morning

BREAKFAST: Here's the kind of deal that has made Mesquite a favorite of Las Vegans who've seen bargain buffet prices all but disappear: Sunday brunch at the buffet at the CasaBlanca is just $7.77—including champagne. All of the usual breakfast favorites are here as well as a few CasaBlanca signature dishes like Cherries Jubilee. And you're free to linger as long as you'd like. Inexpensive.

Don't linger too long, though, because there's still much to see. If you choose to head north, you can do some serious outlet shopping by driving north on I–15 to St. George, Utah, and the **Zion Factory Stores and Promenade at Red Cliff** (245 North Red Cliffs Drive; 800–269–8687 or 435–674–9800), with more than fifty-five stores.

On the way, I–15 passes through some of the most beautiful scenery in the area—and that's saying a lot—as it winds through the rugged beauty of the serpentine **Virgin River Gorge.** Even if you don't feel like shopping, the scenery alone is worth the drive.

If you're more into boating, **Overton Beach of the Lake Mead National Recreation Area** is just southeast of Overton, reached via Nevada Route 167. At Overton Beach you'll find boat rentals, a general store, and marine services. For boat-rental information, contact the **Overton Beach Resort** at (702) 394–4040. While you're in the area, if the lake levels are right, you might be able to spot parts of the ghost town of St. Thomas, which was covered with water when Lake Mead was formed.

Time to head back to Las Vegas, an easy 80-mile trip.

THERE'S MORE

Beaver Dam, Arizona

Beaver Dam Golf Resort, (520) 347–5111. Tree-lined nine-hole course 8 miles east of Mesquite.

Mesquite, Nevada

Cosmic Bowling Center Complex, Virgin River Hotel/Casino, 100 Pioneer Boulevard; (702) 346–7777 or (800) 346–7721. Open bowling available.

Desert Valley Museum, 31 West Mesquite Boulevard; (702) 346–5705. Local artifacts and memorabilia including 1936 slot machines, high-school basketball trophies from 1915 and 1916, switchboards from Mesquite's first phone system.

Mesquite Raceway, Hillside Drive; (702) 346–0727. BMX, drag, dirt oval, motocross, sand-drag, and mud racing.

Wolf Creek at Paradise Canyon, 401 Paradise Parkway; (866) 252–GOLF. Eighteen-hole, 7,018-foot course with features that include an eleven-story tee box and creek that winds through canyons.

SPECIAL EVENTS

Logandale, Nevada

April. Clark County Fair, Clark County Fairgrounds. (702) 398–3247.

October. Bluegrass Festival, Clark County Fairgrounds. (702) 398–3247.

Mesquite, Nevada

February. Annual Mesquite Chili and Arts Festival. (702) 346–2902.

May. Cinco de Mayo. (702) 346–2902.

Mesquite Days. (702) 346–2902.

July. Fourth of July Water Festival. (702) 346–2902.

September. Virgin Valley Car Show. (702) 346–2902.

October through April. Mesquite Concert Series. (702) 346–2902.

OTHER RECOMMENDED RESTAURANTS AND LODGINGS

Logandale, Nevada

VIP Restaurant, 3313 North Moapa Valley Boulevard; (702) 398–7722. Chinese and American cuisine.

Mesquite, Nevada

Eureka Hotel and Casino, 301 Mesa Boulevard; (702) 346–4600. Hotel with spa.

Virgin River Hotel Casino, 100 Pioneer Boulevard; (702) 346–7777. Rustic Western theme.

Overton, Nevada

Best Western North Shore Inn at Lake Mead, 520 North Moapa Valley Boulevard; (702) 397–6000. Close to Lake Mead and Valley of Fire.

José's Mexican Restaurant, 475 North Moapa Valley Boulevard; (702) 397–8400. Mexican favorites.

Sugar's Home Plate, 309 South Main Street; (702) 397–8084. Breakfast, lunch, and dinner served in a casual atmosphere amid sports memorabilia.

FOR MORE INFORMATION

Mesquite Area Chamber of Commerce, 850 West Mesquite Boulevard, Mesquite, NV 89027; (702) 346–2902; www.mesquite-chamber.com.

Moapa Valley Chamber of Commerce, P.O. Box 361, Overton, NV 89040; (702) 397–2160 or 800–519–2243; www.moapavalley.com.

DESERT

Lake Havasu City
A DESERT SURPRISE

2 NIGHTS

*London Bridge • Boating • Swimming • Waterskiing
Hiking • Cruising the river • Old-English atmosphere*

Hey, fella; wanna buy a bridge? How about a beach community—in the middle of the Mojave Desert?

Improbable as it sounds, the "beach community" description fits Lake Havasu City, which is deep in the Arizona desert. As you drive into town and pass marinas, boatyards, and beaches, you'll get the distinct feeling that you could be on the California coast—only without the crowds and without the high prices. Closer to Las Vegas than California coastal communities, it's a nice alternative for a weekend trip to a resort beach community. This oasis of sorts is a prime spot for all manner of water sports—or even just sunning on the beach.

Oh, and the bridge. That would be the London Bridge—the original London Bridge, built in 1831. How did it come to be transplanted to the Arizona desert? And how did this marine-oriented community come to be? These are the kind of questions that make a weekend in Lake Havasu City such a great escape from the glitzy lights and land-locked locales of Las Vegas.

One caveat before we get started: Although some city fathers like to point out that the average temperature in Lake Havasu City is 88 degrees, that's a little misleading. Average high temperatures June through September are above 100 degrees—in July and August the average high is 110. So if you visit during the summer, be prepared with plenty of water and lots of sunscreen.

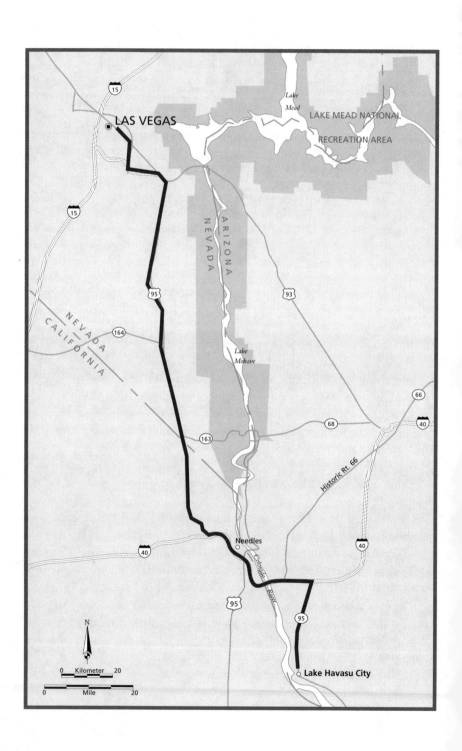

DESERT

DAY 1

Afternoon

Lake Havasu City is about 140 miles from Las Vegas, which makes it ideal for a Friday afternoon or early evening departure. From Las Vegas, head south on U.S. Highway 95 about 85 miles to pick up Interstate 40 near Needles, California. Travel east on I-40 for about 31 miles to exit 9, Arizona Route 95 South. Follow AZ 95 about 20 miles south to Lake Havasu City.

DINNER: As you enter the community, turn left onto Kiowa Boulevard and then right onto Lake Havasu Avenue. After a couple of hours on the road, you'll no doubt welcome the casual atmosphere of **Big John's Steak 'n Pub** (717 North Lake Havasu Avenue, at Acoma Boulevard, Lake Havasu City, AZ 86403; 520-453-5858). Big John's specializes in certified Angus beef, plus seafood, ribs, and pasta, and there's an adjoining sports lounge for the sports nuts in your crowd. Moderate.

LODGING: Take Acoma Boulevard back to AZ 95 and follow US 95 south to Swanson Avenue; you'll see the **London Bridge Resort** on the waterfront overlooking the bridge (1477 Queens Bay, Lake Havasu City, AZ 86403; 520-855-0888 or 888-503-9148; www.londonbridgeresort.com). A waterfront all-suite condominium resort, the London Bridge has two- and three-bedroom suites, three pools and a spa, restaurant and lounge. Rates are from $69 to $289.

DAY 2

Morning

BREAKFAST: Celebrities restaurant (141 Swanson Avenue, Lake Havasu City, AZ 86403; 520-453-1210) has fresh home-baked muffins, coffees, and more. Inexpensive.

Now it's off to check out the first reason most people come to Lake Havasu City these days: the **London Bridge** in all its glory. Four granite arches span a waterway and connect the mainland with a manmade island.

First, the question everyone asks: How did the London Bridge come to rest in this most unlikely of places?

London Bridge, rebuilt in Lake Havasu City in 1968

The history of the London Bridge—or maybe that should be the London Bridges—dates to A.D. 43, when the first of a succession of bridges was erected. Construction on the model that stands today in Lake Havasu City was begun in 1825, when the first piece of granite quarried in Dartmoor was laid by the lord mayor of London.

By the 1960s, however, the bridge was—you knew this was coming—falling down, and that's where Lake Havasu City comes into play. The British government, which was about to replace its relatively attractive and certainly historic bridge with one that was far more utilitarian, recognized the novelty value of others owning its bridge and began taking bids for its sale.

Enter Robert McCulloch Sr. You might say McCulloch was the father of Lake Havasu City; he'd purchased the abandoned Army Air Corps landing strip and rest camp in 1963 while looking for a site to test boat motors.

The land had no homes, which made it a little problematic as a site for a future community; McCulloch built a mobile-home park for his employees.

But a 45-mile-long lake—formed in 1938, through the construction of the Parker Dam, one of several dams erected to tame the mighty and unpredictable Colorado River—was too much of a novelty this deep in the desert to be overlooked. Gradually, businesses began drifting into town, then more and more residents and the homes for them to live in.

When the London Bridge went on the block, McCulloch saw it as the perfect centerpiece for his new planned community. He figured the cost of disassembling the bridge—$1,200,000—then doubled that and added $1,000 for every year of his life to arrive at a winning bid of $2,460,000. The bridge was disassembled, shipped across the ocean, and put back together again, with the lord mayor of London laying the cornerstone in 1968 in a tidy example of repeated history. Once the bridge was reconstructed, a channel was dredged in Lake Havasu, which is fed by the Colorado River, and water was diverted to pass under the bridge and form the island.

McCulloch's idea worked; today, Lake Havasu City has grown from no homes to more than 24,000 residents.

You'll want to walk across the bridge and back, of course, but it's best viewed from beneath, at the **English Village** (520–855–0888), a quaint little Tudor-style complex filled with the usual T-shirt and candy shops and some more offbeat offerings, like a shop that specializes in banners and windsocks in a really incredible variety you're not likely to see again soon. The **London Bridge Candle Factory** (520–855–9097) bills itself as the largest candle shop in the world. **Lotions and Potions** (520–453–OILS) has more than 175 fragrances that you can put into lotions, shampoo, or, in keeping with the beachy surroundings, suntan lotion.

If you do walk across the bridge to the island, be sure to take in the **Creative Cultural Center** (1350 McCulloch Boulevard; 520–855–7300). Open daily most of the year and on weekends October through March, the park features a Southwestern market, American Indian art and storytelling, nature walks, and Southwest ecology talks, craft expos, pottery making, and other events, sometimes with character re-enactors. There's evening activity as well; you can have a candlelight dinner while watching performances by Indian dancers, or maybe listen to a cowboy balladeer perform under the stars.

Also on the island is the appropriately named **Island Mall and Brewery** (1425 McCulloch Boulevard; 520–855–6274), which has a two-story enclosed mall with shops and a coffee house plus restaurants and a brewpub.

More shopping opportunities are available at **Main Street in the Uptown District** (2176 McCulloch Boulevard; 520–855–6246) with more than 200 shops, including antiques galleries, in the "historic downtown" of Lake Havasu City.

LUNCH: The Mermaid Inn (401 English Village, Lake Havasu City, AZ 86403; 520–855–3234) serves English-style fish and chips, plus hamburgers, cheeseburgers, icees, and Hawaiian shaved ice. Moderate.

Afternoon

Spend the afternoon exploring Lake Havasu—on the water—and you'll come to understand why so many regattas are staged here every year. A good start is the **Fun Center** (507 English Village; 520–453–4FUN), where you can rent bumper boats, aquacycles, paddleboats, personal watercraft and miniboats, or maybe try parasailing or watergliding. **Resort Boat Rentals** (502 English Village; 520–855–9194) rents pontoon boats, ski boats, and personal watercraft by the hour or by the day.

For some aquatic fun of another type, go to the **Lake Havasu City Aquatic Center** (100 Park Avenue; 520–453–8686). There's something there for just about all ages, including a wave pool, 250-foot water slide, kiddy lagoon, pirate slide, and two therapeutic pools.

For more active fun on dry land, the nearby **Rotary Community Park** (1400 South Smoketree Boulevard; 520–453–8686) has a skate park, playground equipment designed for various age groups (plus a special-needs playground area), bocce ball court, beach volleyball, horseshoe pits, jogging trails, and beach.

DINNER: Nicolinos Italian Restaurant (86 South Smoketree Avenue, Lake Havasu City, AZ 86403; 520–855–3545) has been a Lake Havasu City institution since 1988—a fairly long time in such a young town. Specialties include pizza, pasta, chicken, veal, and seafood, and—in a bit of a surprise—a full Mexican menu. Moderate.

LODGING: The London Bridge Resort (see above).

DAY 3

Morning

BREAKFAST: Sir James Midtown Cyber Cafe (2148 McCulloch Boulevard, Lake Havasu City, AZ 86403; 520–855–7669) has bagels, muffins, and Danish and a full coffee, tea, and espresso bar. Inexpensive.

Time to see more of the natural beauty that surrounds Lake Havasu City. **Topock Gorge,** part of the **Havasu National Wildlife Refuge**, is accessible only on foot or by boat, so the most pleasant option would naturally be to take a boat trip such as those offered by **Jetboat Tours** (501 English Village; 520–855–7171 or 888–855–7171). The 50-mile journey heads up the Colorado River through the refuge, winding around Blankenship Bend and Devils Elbow and bypassing interesting rock formations. Keep your eyes peeled and you might see bighorn sheep, coyotes, wild burros, or any of a number of birds, including some of the country's most rare birds, such as the Southwestern willow flycatcher or the Yuma clapper rail.

Another option is **Lake Havasu State Park and Windsor Beach** (699 London Bridge Road, 520–855–2784), the most-visited of all Arizona state parks. The park offers camping, hiking, a nature trail, and a boat launch, but the most popular attraction seems to be the beach area, which fills up early on weekend days when the weather is pleasant. Open daily, sunrise to 10:00 P.M.

LUNCH: London Arms Pub and Restaurant (422 English Village, Lake Havasu City, AZ 86403; 520–855–8782) is a brewpub with traditional Brit pub offerings such as Scotch eggs and fish and chips, plus prime rib, steaks, and fresh fish. There's also outdoor seating on a patio overlooking the London Bridge. Moderate.

Afternoon

Back to Las Vegas, via AZ 95, I–40, and US 95.

THERE'S MORE

Arizona Jet Ski Rentals, 655 Kiowa Avenue; (520) 453–5558. Daily and hourly rentals.

Bridgewater Links, 1477 Queens Bay; (520) 855–4777. Nine-hole executive course with lake and mountain views.

Cattail Cove State Park, 10 miles south of Lake Havasu City on AZ 95; (520) 855–1223. Beach, hiking trail, camping, and marina.

Dixie Belle River Party Boat, English Village; (520) 453–6776. Paddlewheel riverboat with daily tour schedule.

Havasu Island Golf Course, 1040 McCulloch Boulevard; (520) 855–5585. Eighteen-hole executive course, plus driving range and putting and chipping greens.

Havasu Speedway, south of Lake Havasu City on AZ 95; (520) 505–7223. Stock-car racing on Saturday nights from February through November.

Lions Dog Park, 1340 McCulloch Boulevard; (520) 453–8686. Fenced park complete with water feature and fire hydrants.

London Bridge Golf Club, 2400 Clubhouse Drive; (520) 855–2719. Two eighteen-hole championship courses, day and night driving range, putting green.

MBK Bikes, 76 North Lake Havasu Avenue; (520) 453–7474. Bicycle and in-line skate rentals; daily and weekly rates.

Outback Off-Road Adventures, 1350 McCulloch Boulevard; (520) 680–6151. Educational desert Jeep tours.

SPECIAL EVENTS

February. Annual Home Show; (520) 453–7755.

Annual Lake Havasu Winterfest Jamboree; (520) 855–4115.

Annual Lower Colorado River Regional Chili for Charity; (520) 855–6125.

March. Annual Juried Spring Art Show; (520) 855–8078.

St. Patrick's Day Parade and Street Fair; (520) 764–3776.

April. Annual International Hava-Salsa Challenge; (520) 680–0221.

Annual Lake Havasu Pro-Am Charity Bass Tournament; (520) 855–3474.

May. Cinco de Mayo Sailing Regatta; (520) 680–7845.

Annual Western Outdoor News Lake Havasu Striper Derby; (714) 546–4370, ext. 30.

August. Maxifli Ironman Golf Tournament, over fifty-four holes on three golf courses; (520) 855–5585.

September. Annual Campbell Boat Regatta and Boat Parade; (520) 855–2133.

September and October. Touch of Culture, with "Who Dunnit?" murder mystery, fine arts and Southwestern crafts displays, Indian dancing and cooking demonstrations, and reenactments depicting characters of Colorado River history; (520) 680–0221.

October. Annual Kids Fishing Derby; (520) 453–8686.

Annual London Bridge Square Dance Jamboree and Bridge Days; (520) 453–3444.

Skat-Trak World Championship personal watercraft races; (520) 680–0884.

November. London Bridge Invitational Sailing Regatta; (520) 680–7845.

London Bridge Seaplane Classic; (520) 680–9711.

November–early January. Festival of Lights with more than one million lights decorating English Village; (520) 680–0884.

December. Annual Boat Parade of Lights; (520) 855–8857.

Annual Christmas Tree Lighting Ceremony; (520) 453–8686.

Annual Soroptimist House and Garden Tour; (520) 680–7707.

Annual Toys for Tots Golf Tournament; (520) 453–3444.

OTHER RECOMMENDED RESTAURANTS AND LODGINGS

Banana Jones' Bar and Grill, 440 El Camino Way; (520) 505–4333. Casual Caribbean-theme restaurant specializing in Jamaican jerk-seasoned chicken wings.

Barley Brothers Grill, Island Mall and Brewery, 1425 McCulloch Boulevard; (520) 453–1400. Seafood, steaks, prime rib, pizzas.

Bridgewater Cafe and Lounge, London Bridge Resort, 1477 Queens Bay; (520) 855–0888. Steaks, ribs, and grill specials overlooking the London Bridge.

Havasu Travelodge, 480 London Bridge Road; (520) 680–9202. Lakeview rooms within walking distance of bridge.

Holiday Inn, 245 London Bridge Road; (520) 855–4071. Lakeview balcony rooms.

Howard Johnson Express Inn and Suites, 335 London Bridge Road; (520) 453–4656. Lakeview balcony rooms.

Island Inn Hotel, 1300 West McCulloch Boulevard; (520) 680–0606. Within walking distance of London Bridge and London Bridge Beach.

Krystal's Fine Dining, 460 El Camino Way; (520) 453–2999. Beef, seafood, ribs, and chicken.

Nautical Inn and Conference Center, 1000 McCulloch Boulevard; (520) 855–0888. Beachfront and lake views.

Red Robin, 70 Swanson Avenue; (520) 855–8555. Gourmet burgers.

FOR MORE INFORMATION

Lake Havasu City Chamber of Commerce, 314 London Bridge Road, Lake Havasu City, AZ 86403; (520) 855–4115; www.havasuchamber.com.

Lake Havasu Tourism Bureau, 314 London Bridge Road, Lake Havasu City, AZ 86403; (520) 453–3444 or (800) 242–8278; www.golakehavasu.com.

Laughlin, Bullhead City, and Kingman

A DESERT OASIS

2 NIGHTS

Watersports • Gambling • Exploring • Old West
Romantic weekends on the river

The Laughlin, Nevada–Bullhead City, Arizona–Kingman, Arizona region is that rare thing in the desert—an area whose residents actually can say that "a river runs through it."

That river is the Colorado, which was wild and unpredictable before the Hoover Dam was built roughly 70 miles upstream during the early 1930s. Hoover was followed in 1941 by Davis Dam (just 2 miles north of Kingman), which was designed to regulate releases from its big brother to the north. And so the Colorado that runs through the region today is a big, gentle ol' man, just rolling along.

Laughlin's primary reason for being today is casino gambling, and it does a thorough job of that, with eleven casino-resorts lined up along its decidedly downscaled version of the Las Vegas Strip. That laid-back feel has great appeal for a lot of people (an estimated 4.4 million of them a year) who choose to do their gambling in this town where it's difficult to get lost—or to find a traffic jam—and where the resorts are small enough to negotiate without a map.

Bullhead City, in Arizona just across the river from Laughlin, is a bedroom community of sorts. Bullhead City was named for a rock, shaped somewhat like a bull's head, that jutted out of the river, and got its first real growth spurt as a base for those who were working on Davis Dam, the completion of

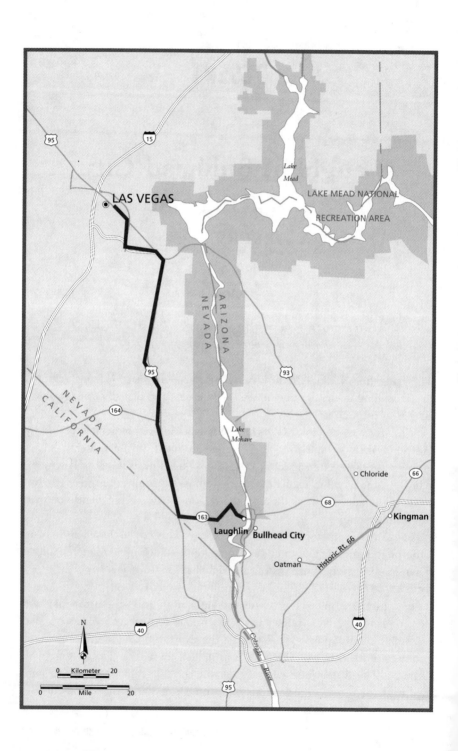

which, alas, was responsible for that namesake rock being submerged. Today, Bullhead City is a vacation community and a home to many workers in Laughlin's casinos.

Less than 30 miles to the east is Kingman, founded in the late nineteenth century as a railroad town and now the biggest community on the longest remaining strip of Route 66.

And sprinkled in and around the three larger towns are the tiny spots of Oatman and Chloride, Arizona—Oatman regarded as a ghost town come to life, Chloride as an Old West outpost and artists' retreat.

So this region has it all—gambling, history, art, and a giant dollop of the Old West. It's a great mixed bag of a quick escape from Las Vegas.

DAY 1

Afternoon

Laughlin is just 96 miles from Las Vegas, for an easy drive of about 1 and a half hours. It's an easy route: Just head south on U.S. Highway 95 for about 75 miles, then east on Nevada Route 163 to Laughlin.

You'll probably want to spend the first evening exploring some of the resorts on Casino Drive and the offerings inside. All of them have slot machines, video poker, and table games, of course, and some have keno, poker rooms, and race and sports books. But, in the entertainment-for-all tradition of Las Vegas, there are lots of non-gambling activities as well.

Don Laughlin's Riverside Resort Hotel and Casino (1650 South Casino Drive; 800–227–3849 or 702–298–2535) is home to a collection of more than eighty historic and classic vehicles, which can be viewed free of charge. The tropical atrium at the **Golden Nugget Laughlin** (2300 South Casino Drive; 800–950–7700 or 702–298–7111) is filled with more than 300 live plants from all over the world. The showroom at the **Flamingo** (1900 South Casino Drive; 800–FLAMINGO or 702–298–5111) regularly hosts top entertainment; call ahead or check the resort's Web site at www.laughlinflamingo.com. And at the railroad-themed **Ramada Express Hotel and Casino** (2121 South Casino Drive; 800–243–6846 or 702–298–4200), you can take a free ride on what's known as Laughlin's only working railroad. The train, dubbed "The Gambler," is a replica of The Genoa, which worked the Virginia and Truckee Line in northern Nevada a century ago. It makes a .75-mile circuit of the hotel's twenty-seven-acre property.

DINNER: The **Steakhouse at the Ramada Express** in Laughlin (702–298–4200, ext. 6375) features steaks and chops from its on-site butcher shop, plus seafood and pasta. Best of all, it's all served up in the atmosphere of a turn-of-the-century railroad. Moderate.

LODGING: Harrah's Laughlin (2900 South Casino Drive, Laughlin, NV 89029; 800–447–8700 or 702–298–4600; www.harrahs.com; rates from $15 to $83) has 1,657 rooms, two casinos (including one non-smoking, which is still a rarity in the casino world), a beach, health club, four restaurants, shops, a showroom, and an arcade.

DAY 2

Morning

BREAKFAST: There's lots to see in the region, so for an early start, stop in at **Club Cappuccino** at Harrah's Laughlin Casino-Hotel for a specialty coffee and a chocolate- or almond-filled croissant. Inexpensive.

Now it's time to explore the natural environment around these parts, whose beauty is responsible for drawing so many people to the area. A good way to start is to take a cruise of the Colorado River. **Laughlin River Tours, Inc.** (800–228–9825) operates two boats that ply the Colorado: The *Edgewater Belle* is docked at the Edgewater Hotel and Casino and the *Celebration* is docked at the Flamingo. Both boats are tricked out to look like old-fashioned paddlewheel steamers. The narrated cruises last about an hour and a half, and the *Celebration* now offers dinner cruises as well.

Off NV 163, about 10 miles west of Laughlin, you'll find a gravel road that leads to the trail head to **Grapevine Canyon**, which is adorned with ancient petroglyphs—the pictorial writing Native tribes used to communicate and to record their lives. Near Grapevine Canyon is **Christmas Tree Pass;** depending on the time of year you visit, you might find the surrounding plants adorned with impromptu Christmas decorations.

If you're interested in engineering, stop and take a look at **Davis Dam,** which can be reached from NV 163 to the east—not far from its intersection with Casino Drive. Davis Dam is an earth-and-rock embankment with a concrete spillway. The 200-foot-high dam also produces hydroelectric power.

If relaxing on the water is more your speed, drive to **Lake Mohave Resort** (Katherine Landing, Arizona; 520–754–3245) across the bridge near Bullhead City. The resort is on the shore of Lake Mohave (originally a stretch of the Colorado River), which is 67 miles long and only 4 miles wide at its widest point. The lake, formed by Hoover Dam to the north and Davis Dam to the south, is today a watersports mecca. If you have just a little time, consider renting a ski boat, patio boat, fishing boat, or personal watercraft. If you have more time to spend, rent a houseboat and really do some relaxing; houseboats that sleep as many as fourteen people are available.

Just north of the marina at Katherine Landing is the site of the old **Katherine Mine,** a gold-mining operation. A few structures from the mine remain if you're feeling adventurous. But if you do decide to do some exploring, tread carefully and stay away from any shaft entrances, which can be extremely dangerous.

In the same area—at Davis Camp, just north of the Laughlin Bridge—is the **Colorado River Museum** (520–754–3399), which has exhibits on gold mining, trapping, and steamboating in the area, as well as displays dedicated to local natives—and even early slot machines.

LUNCH: Towne's Square Cafe (about 3 miles south of the Laughlin Bridge at 1751 US 95, Bullhead City, AZ 86429; 520–763–2477) is a homey spot serving up sandwiches and more elaborate entrees. Moderate.

Afternoon

After lunch, continue south on US 95 to the turnoff for Historic Route 66 and head east on 66 to **Oatman,** Arizona, which bills itself as "an authentic Western ghost town and mining camp." It's also the spot where Clark Gable and Carole Lombard spent their wedding night March 29, 1939, at the Oatman Hotel, following their wedding in Kingman.

Oatman's advertising is accurate enough; there aren't many places where you'll see wild burros roaming the streets. Well, technically they're wild, but these burros are so accustomed to people that one or more is likely to wander up to you, looking for a handout.

Oatman also has a number of shops, restaurants, and saloons with live entertainment, but the best entertainment of all is the free shows on Route 66. More than 500,000 people visit Oatman each year, and the townspeople are happy to oblige them with staged gunfights.

Also near Oatman is the **Gold Road Mine** tour (Historic Route 66 2.5 miles east of Oatman; 520–768–1600; www.goldroadmine.com). The most thrilling thing about the Gold Road is that it's an actual gold mine that was in full production from 1996–1998, closing only when the price of gold dropped below $300 an ounce in 1998 and poised to reopen if prices rise again. This is a walking tour, with visitors going .125 mile into the mine on a tour that lasts about an hour.

Leaving Oatman, follow Historic Route 66 east to Kingman, Arizona, the biggest town and roughly geographical center of the longest remaining (at 158 miles) stretch of Route 66, which became legendary during the 1940s as the modern-day way west.

Today, the downtown historic district of Kingman is home to antiques stores, shops, and restaurants. For a look at the way things used to be, stop at the city's **Powerhouse Visitor Center** (120 West Andy Devine Avenue; 520–753–6106) for a map of a walking tour of downtown. The map covers twenty-seven downtown sites; Kingman has more than sixty buildings on the National Register of Historic Buildings.

For an even closer look at Old Kingman, tour the **Bonelli House** (430 East Spring Street; 520–753–3195), which is filled with antiques and heirlooms of the region—including a clock that once was the only one in Kingman.

More recent history can be spotted at **Locomotive Park** (First and Andy Devine Avenues; 520–753–6106), home to the last steam engine to run the Kingman line.

To return to Laughlin, travel west on Arizona Route 68.

DINNER: William Fisk's Steakhouse at Harrah's Laughlin offers such delights as sautéed crab cakes with papaya-basil sauce and blackened shrimp with spicy Cajun cream sauce. Moderate.

LODGING: Harrah's Laughlin (see above).

DAY 3

Morning

BREAKFAST: Have an early breakfast or a later brunch at the **Fresh Market Square Cafe** at Harrah's Laughlin. Moderate.

Now take some time to explore the Colorado River; you can rent WaveRunners and boats (as well as lounge chairs with umbrellas) at Harrah's, or venture to the **Bay Shore Inn** (1955 West Casino Drive; 702–299–9010) to rent personal watercraft or paddleboats.

Feel like doing some shopping? The **Horizon Outlet Center** (1955 South Casino Drive; 702–298–3033) includes fifty-eight stores, plus a food court and nine movie screens.

Then, head back to Las Vegas on a different route than the way you came. Travel east on AZ 68 to Kingman, then north on US 93 and branch off to the little town of **Chloride,** Arizona.

Chloride was once a silver town, with more than seventy-five mines. Today, it's mainly a historic spot. Stops that are worthy of note are the **Chloride Post Office,** the oldest continuously operated in Arizona, the **Old Jail,** and the **Playhouse,** which still is the site of old-time melodramas.

Chloride is also an artists' community these days, with more shops and galleries springing up all the time. Follow a dirt road 1.5 miles beyond Chloride (ask in town for directions) to the **Purcell Murals**, which miner and Southwestern artist Roy Purcell painted in 1966 on a number of rocky expanses.

LUNCH: Have lunch at **Shep's Mining Camp Cafe** (520–565–4251), which serves sandwiches, salads, burgers, and the like. Inexpensive.

Afternoon

Time to head back to Las Vegas. Return to US 93 and turn north; follow 93 right into the city.

THERE'S MORE

Bullhead City, Arizona

Chaparral Country Club, 1260 East Mohave Drive; (520) 758–3939. Nine-hole course in the center of town.

Desert Lakes Golf Course, 5835 Desert Lakes Drive; (520) 768–1000 or (520) 768–1070. Eighteen-hole championship course.

Kingman, Arizona

Hualapai Mountain County Park, Hualapai Mountain Road, 14 miles east of Kingman; (520) 757–0915. Heavily forested park that's a big contrast to the surrounding desert. Cabins, camping, hiking, and picnic areas.

Don Laughlin's Riverside Resort, Laughlin

Mohave Museum of History and Arts, 400 West Beale Street; (520) 753–3195. Re-created Mohave and Hualapai dwellings, exhibit on Mohave ranching, cowboy actor Andy Devine memorabilia, and local arti-facts bring history of northwestern Arizona into focus.

Willow Springs Ranch, 5000 Estrella Road, Golden Valley; (520) 565-4753. Horseback riding.

Laughlin, Nevada

Big Bend of the Colorado State Recreation Area, 5 miles south of Laughlin on the Needles Highway; (702) 298–1859. Swimming, fishing, picnicking, boat launching.

Forever Resorts at Cottonwood Cove, (800) 255–5561 or (702) 297–1464. Houseboat rentals by the weekend or week at Cottonwood Cove, one hour north of Laughlin on the shore of Lake Mohave.

SPECIAL EVENTS

Bullhead City, Arizona

January. Turquoise Circuit Rodeo; (520) 754–4121 or (800) 987–7457.

April. Route 66 Fun Run, starting in Seligman, Arizona; (520) 754–4121 or (800) 987–7457.

Chloride, Arizona

June. Old Miners Day; (520) 565–4803.

Kingman, Arizona

August. Hualapai Mountain Park Arts and Crafts festival; (520) 757–3545.

September. Mohave County Fair; (520) 753–2636.

Laughlin, Nevada

April. Laughlin River Stampede Rodeo; (702) 298–2214.

June. Laughlin River Days, Formula One racing; (800) 227–5245.

October. Laughlin Invitational Professional Bull Riders; (702) 298–2214 or (800) 227–5245.

Oatman, Arizona

January. Bed races; (520) 768–6222.

March. Gable/Lombard weekend; (520) 768–6222.

July. Annual Sidewalk Egg Fry; (520) 768–6222.

September. Oatman Gold Camp Days and Burro Biscuit Tossing Contest; (520) 768–6222.

OTHER RECOMMENDED RESTAURANTS AND LODGINGS

Bullhead City, Arizona

Best Western Bullhead City Inn, 1126 US 95; (520) 754–3000. Eighty-eight units plus pool and whirlpool.

Sunridge Hotel and Conference Center, 839 Landon Drive; (520) 754–4700. Quiet hillside location with 148 units.

Chloride, Arizona

Sheps Miners Inn, P.O. Box 100; (520) 565-4251 or (877) 565-4252. Bed-and-breakfast with twelve units.

Kingman, Arizona

Dambar Steakhouse, 1960 Andy Devine Drive; (520) 753–3523. Steaks, ribs, and salads.

Hotel Brunswick, 315 East Andy Devine Street; (520) 718–1800. Historic bed-and-breakfast inn on Historic Route 66.

Hualapai Mountain Lodge, Pine Lake Star Route; (520) 757–3545. Motel in rustic setting at 6,500 feet; activities include cross-country skiing and hunting.

Laughlin, Nevada

Colorado Belle Hotel Casino, 2100 South Casino Drive; (702) 298–4000. This resort, a giant replica of a nineteenth-century paddlewheeler, has 1,200 rooms, five restaurants, and two pools.

Edgewater Hotel and Casino, 2020 South Casino Drive; (702) 298–2453. Southwestern-themed resort with 1,450 rooms, pool, and whirlpool.

Jane's Grill, Golden Nugget Laughlin, 2300 South Casino Drive; (800) 950–7700 or (702) 298–7111. Mesquite-grilled burgers and chicken; wood-fired pizza.

Prime Rib Room, Don Laughlin's Riverside Resort, 1650 South Casino Drive; (800) 227–3849 or (702) 298–2535. Prime rib carved tableside; salad-vegetable-potato-dessert bar.

FOR MORE INFORMATION

Bullhead Area Chamber of Commerce, 1251 U.S. Highway 95, Bullhead City, AZ 86429; (520) 754–4121 or (800) 987–7457.

Kingman Area Chamber of Commerce, 120 West Andy Devine Avenue, Kingman, AZ 86402; (520) 753–6106; www.arizonaguide.com/visitkingman.

Laughlin Visitors Bureau, 1555 South Casino Drive, Laughlin, NV 89029; (702) 298–3022; www.visitlaughlin.com.

Oatman Chamber of Commerce, P.O. Box 423, Oatman, AZ 86433; (520) 768–6222.

DESERT

Palm Springs

A RESORT IN THE DESERT

2 NIGHTS

*Golf • Spas • Scenic tramway • Equestrian events
Romantic resorts*

OK, so you know people have been spending time in Palm Springs, California, for many years. But would you have guessed 10,000 years?

Those stone-age dwellers whose campsites have been studied in the region make Palm Springs one of the oldest settlements on the western part of the continent. The first recorded "discovery" of the area was in 1774, when Spanish soldiers who had prevailed in what now is southern California explored the boundaries of their new empire. But until the mid-nineteenth century, the Cahuilla Indians who inhabited the area saw few white people.

That all changed in 1853, when a government survey party came through and noted the 30-foot mineral pool bubbling out of the hot sand near modern-day Palm Springs. They established a wagon route through a nearby pass, and by 1882, Palm Springs was a stop on the stagecoach line between Prescott, Arizona, and Los Angeles. The Southern Pacific railroad later followed roughly the same route as it pushed westward, setting the stage for a novel sort of development that sometimes still can be seen in Palm Springs: By keeping the odd-numbered sections of land on either side of the track for itself and giving the even-numbered tracts to the Indians, the railroad company created a checkerboard effect of developed and undeveloped plots.

The first permanent white settler, the Honorable Judge John Guthrie McCallum, arrived from San Francisco in 1884, seeking a warm, dry climate for his tubercular son, and built an aqueduct to improve the water supply,

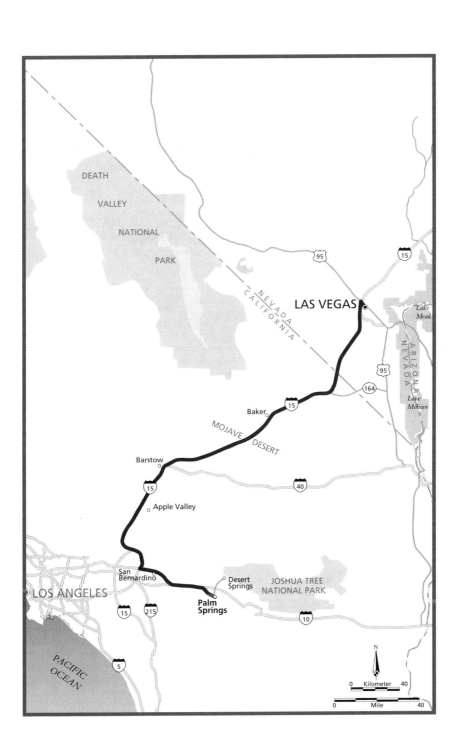

thereby setting the Coachella Valley's agricultural roots. It wasn't long before others followed and realized the area's potential as a tourist destination. The first Palm Springs Hotel was built in 1886; the Desert Inn—which later belonged to actress Marion Davies, in the 1950s—was established in 1909.

Practically the whole region was pressed into service during World War II, when Gen. George South Patton moved in tank corps here to train for the invasion of the North African deserts and the El Mirador Hotel turned into a hospital for those wounded in battle. An airfield also was established, which would eventually become Palm Springs Airport.

Once the war was over and Patton and his boys were gone, development in the area exploded. The area boasted just one golf course in 1945—a whole nine holes—but there are now more than ninety courses. The Palm Springs resort area is also home today to 600 tennis courts and 10,000 swimming pools.

OK, it's still the desert, but with a resort atmosphere like this, who wouldn't want to spend some time here? And that's what makes Palm Springs a top spot for a quick escape.

DAY 1

Afternoon

Palm Springs is about 275 miles from Las Vegas—driving time about four hours—meaning a Friday-afternoon departure is timely.

Head south on Interstate 15 for about 213 miles, then follow I–215 South for about 13 miles. Take Interstate 10 East and travel for about 40 miles, finally heading down California Route 111 south toward Palm Springs.

As you drive into town, you'll be on Palm Canyon Drive (also CA 111), the main drag and heart of the city, with shops, restaurants, and lounges lining both sides of the street.

DINNER: Thai Smile (651 North Palm Canyon Drive, Palm Springs, CA 92262; 760–320–5503) is right on the main drag—between Tamarisk and Alejo—which gives you a chance to check out the action. The restaurant has an extensive menu of Thai and other Asian favorites, including the familiar (five different styles of curry, which can be made with chicken, beef, pork, shrimp, duck, or tofu, the ubiquitous pad Thai and soups such as wonton and Tom-Kha-Kai) and the not-so familiar (Screaming Duck). Save room for the homemade coconut ice cream for dessert. Moderate.

Sweeping views of the Coachella Valley from the Palm Springs Aerial Tram

LODGING: A Holiday Inn doesn't sound very exotic in this desert wonderland, but this isn't your standard Holiday Inn. The **Holiday Inn Palm Mountain Resort** (1255 South Belardo, Palm Springs, CA 92262; 760–325–1301; www.palmmountainnresort.com; rates from $89 to $165) is 1 block from North Palm Canyon Drive, a convenient location because it's close enough to walk in this town where parking can sometimes be a problem. Additionally, the hotel has standard exterior entrance doors plus louvered doors (and windows) that open onto a central courtyard that looks more like the tropics than the desert, complete with bougainvillea and palm trees. Also in the courtyard is a pool, spa, and cabana bar.

DAY 2

Morning

BREAKFAST: You've got a lot to do today, so it'd be a good idea to get a hearty start. **Elmer's Pancakes and Steaks** (1030 East Palm Canyon Drive, Palm Springs, CA 92262; 760–327–8419) is so dedicated to the importance of a good solid morning meal, they even pontificate about it on the menu. And it's not just talk; breakfast offerings include corncakes or buckwheat cakes with sausage, sausage waffles with applesauce, and formidable German pancakes served with lemon wedges and powdered sugar. Moderate.

Thus fortified, you're ready for a day spent outdoors in the finest Palm Springs tradition.

For the best way to get oriented to the area—to really get the lay of the land, and an idea of the breathtaking scenery to boot—head back down Palm Canyon Drive to Tramway Road and then drive southwest. You'll travel up, up, up to the **Palm Springs Aerial Tram** in Chino Canyon (1 Tramway Road; 760–325–1449 or 888–515–TRAM; www.pstramway.com), probably the area's primary attraction (especially if you're not a golfer).

The tram takes passengers from the rocky landscape at its base station 2,643 feet above sea level 2.5 miles up to its Mountain Station at 8,516 feet, passing through five climate zones in the process.

There is, as you can imagine, a compelling view of the San Jacinto Mountains and the valley below. What you probably haven't imagined is that the two eighty-passenger cars actually rotate as they make their way up and down the mountain to provide 360-degree views.

At the top is **Mt. San Jacinto State Park and Wilderness Area** (760–325–1391 or 909–659–2607), with more than 54 miles of trails, plus primitive campgrounds (bring-your-own-everything) and a ranger station. The Adventure Center up top, which is open only from mid-November through mid-April, has cross-country ski rentals and lessons, plus snowshoe and tube rentals. In the Mountain Station is a restaurant, lounge, gift shop, and museum with a view of the history of the tramway.

Still feeling adventurous? **Tahquitz Canyon** (500 West Mesquite Avenue, just north of Palm Canyon Drive downtown; 760–416–7044; www.tahquitzcanyon.com) on the Agua Caliente Reservation has educational, cultural, and scenic exhibits, including artifacts, a theater room with a video on the legend of Tahquitz Canyon, rock art, ancient irrigation systems, and a 60-foot waterfall.

Another perspective is available at **the Palm Springs Desert Museum** (101 Museum Drive; 760–325–7186; www.psmuseum.org), which—you guessed it—is just a block from Palm Canyon Drive. The museum, which was established in 1938, offers a journey through several centuries of art, including Native American art, Western art, nineteenth-century American and European art, and twentieth-century contemporary works.

LUNCH: Vintage Marketplace (105 South Palm Canyon Drive, Palm Springs, CA 92262; 760–320–9000) is a combination restaurant–patio bar–wine shop–pasta shop. Lunch offerings include burgers, salads, vegetable lasagna, tri-color tortilla pie, omelets, and pastas. Moderate.

Afternoon

If you play golf, you'll certainly want to take to the links in Palm Springs. **Canyon South Course** (1097 Murray Canyon Drive; 760–327–2019) and the **Tahquitz Creek Golf Resort** Legends or Resort courses (1885 Golf Club Drive; 760–328–1005), all of which are open to the public, are among the possibilities.

If you don't play or just aren't in the mood, consider a Jeep tour. One company that offers trips is **Desert Adventures** (888–440–JEEP or 760–324–JEEP), which regularly schedules several "adventures," including the Indian Cultural Adventure, Lost Legends of the Wild West Adventure, and Mystery Canyon Adventure (the latter of which includes a chance to sample freshly picked dates and cross the San Andreas Fault as you take the "hike of death").

If you'd rather do things the old-fashioned way, take a horseback ride into the desert. The guides at **Smoke Tree Stables** (2500 Toledo Avenue; 760–327–1372) lead hourly or day-long rides.

DINNER: The landmark **Cedar Creek Inn** (155 South Palm Canyon Drive, Palm Springs, CA 92262; 760–325–7300) features steaks and such entrees as mixed grill, rack of lamb, salmon, and trout, all served with superb side dishes and an array of salads and soups in an airy, casual atmosphere. Expensive.

LODGING: The Holiday Inn Palm Mountain Resort (see above).

DAY 3

Morning

BREAKFAST: Might as well keep up the hearty theme and go to **Billy Reed's**

(1800 North Palm Canyon Drive, Palm Springs, CA 92262; 760–325–1946), where breakfast specialties include calves liver with onions and eggs, Portuguese sausage and eggs, custom or pre-designed omelets, pancakes, waffles, and biscuits and gravy; if they're in season, you can even get a date milkshake. Moderate.

Time to go shopping. Lots of stores, boutiques, and tiny jewel-box shops are tucked between the restaurants and clubs that line Palm Canyon Drive. Or, drive a few miles down CA 111 to Palm Desert and the **Gardens on El Paseo** (877–735–7273), which has more than 100 upscale stores, including Saks Fifth Avenue.

If you're a really hard-core shopper, **Desert Hills Premium Outlets** outside of town (48400 Seminole Drive, Cabazon; 909–849–6641) offers 120 stores, with a shocking proportion of designer names including Burberry, Dana Buchman, and Judith Leiber—just the place to stock up on souvenirs from your Palm Beach weekend to return to Las Vegas in style.

Return to downtown Palm Springs for lunch.

LUNCH: Hamburger Hamlet (123 North Palm Canyon, Palm Springs, CA 92262; 760–325–2321) has been beloved since 1950 for dishes such as onion soup fondue; chicken pot pies; sautéed chicken with tangy apple chutney; chocolate fudge cake with ice cream, fudge sauce and whipped cream; and— good Lord!—all manner of burgers. Moderate.

Now it's time to retrace your route and return to Las Vegas.

THERE'S MORE

Indio, California

General Patton Memorial Museum, Chiriaco Summit; (760) 227–3483. Museum on site of the General George South Patton Desert Training Center.

Joshua Tree, California

Joshua Tree National Park, 6554 Park Boulevard; (760) 366–3448. More than one million acres of Mojave and Colorado Desert landscape, including the unique Joshua trees.

Mira Loma, California

Galleano Winery, 4231 Wineville Road; (909) 685–5376. Wine tastings and tours.

Palm Desert, California

The Living Desert Wildlife and Botanical Park, 47-900 Portola Avenue; (760) 346–5694. Animals, botanical gardens, and trails.

Wind Farm Tour, 46205 Portola Road; (760) 251–1997. Tours (in an electric vehicle, of course) through a forest of windmills.

Palm Springs, California

Moorten Botanical Gardens, 1701 South Palm Canyon Drive; (760) 327–6555. More than 3,000 varieties of desert plants from around the world; also a bird sanctuary.

Oasis Waterpark, 1500 Gene Autrey Trail; (760) 327–0499. Wave pool and waterslides for kids of all ages.

Offroad Rentals, 59511 Highway 111; (760) 325–0376. All-terrain vehicle rentals for beginning or skilled riders.

Uprising Outdoor Adventure Center, 1500 South Gene Autry Trail; (760) 320–6630 or (888) CLIMB–ON. Rock climbing for the whole family.

Riverside, California

Castle Park, 3500 Polk Street; (909) 785–3000. Amusement rides, miniature golf, and games.

SPECIAL EVENTS

Indian Wells, California

March. Tennis Masters of Indian Wells, first in a new series of nine tournaments; (800) 999–1585.

Indio, California

January through March. Indio Desert Circuit Horse Show. More than 200 hunter, jumper, equitation and pony show jumping events in six weeks; (760) 775–7731.

February. National Date Festival and Riverside County Fair, with midway, vendors, camel and ostrich races, daily concerts, and Arabian Nights festivals; (800) 811–FAIR.

La Quinta, California

March. La Quinta Arts Festival, featuring paintings, sculpture, and ceramics, plus jazz and classical music, hosted by La Quinta resident Merv Griffin; (760) 564–1244.

Palm Springs, California

January. Bob Home Chrysler Classic. Five-day golf tournament on four desert courses; (760) 346–8184 or (888) MRBHOPE.

Nortel Networks Palm Springs International Film Festival, with a mix of more than a hundred feature films; (760) 322–2930 or (800) 898–7256.

February. Frank Sinatra Celebrity Golf Tournament, an event known for easy access to celebrity players; (800) FS–STARS.

March. Nabisco Championship, Ladies Professional Golfers Association Circuit, with more than one hundred top women golfers; (760) 324–4546.

April. Desert AIDS Walk, raising funds for the Desert AIDS project; (760) 323–2118, ext. 262.

August. Palms Springs International Festival of Short Films, featuring live-action and animated features of thirty seconds to forty minutes; (760) 322–2930 or (800) 898–7256.

OTHER RECOMMENDED RESTAURANTS AND LODGINGS

Palm Springs, California

Estrella Inn and Villas, 415 South Belardo Road; (760) 320–4117 or (800) 237–3687. Rooms, suites, and villas on three acres of gardens a block from downtown.

Great Wall Chinese Restaurant, 362 South Palm Canyon Drive; (760) 322–2209. Standard offerings plus a number of house specials.

Korakia Pensione, 257 South Patencio Road; (760) 864–6411. Moroccan villa built in 1924.

Le Vallauris, 385 West Tahquitz Canyon Way; (760) 325–5059. Fine dining; tree-shaded patio.

Otani: A Garden Restaurant, 266 Avenida Caballeros; (760) 327–6700. Sushi, tempura, and teppan.

The Willows Historic Palm Springs Inn, 412 West Tahquitz Canyon Way; (760) 320–0771. Restored 1927 Mediterranean villa.

Palm Desert, California

Ristorante Mama Gina, 73-705 East Paseo; (760) 568–9898. Northern Italian cuisine.

Tres Palmas Bed and Breakfast, 73-135 Tumbleweed Lane; (760) 773–9858. Southwest decor and architecture within walking distance of El Paseo.

FOR MORE INFORMATION

Palm Desert Chamber of Commerce, 73-710 Fred Waring Drive, Suite 114, Palm Desert, CA 92260; (760) 346–6111; www.pdcc.org.

Palm Springs Chamber of Commerce, 190 West Amado Road, Palm Springs, CA 92262; (760) 325–1577; www.pschamber.org.

Palm Springs Tourism, 333 North Palm Canyon Drive, Suite 114, Palm Springs, CA 92262; (800) 34–SPRINGS; www.palm-springs.org.

DESERT

Sedona

RED ROCKS IN THE SUNSET

2 NIGHTS

Mystical red rocks • Hiking • Backcountry touring
Ancient ruins • Romantic bed-and-breakfasts

Las Vegas may have its own impressive red-rock formations—at Red Rock National Conservation Area, on the western outskirts of the city—but they're no match for the majesty of the formations that surround Sedona, Arizona. On all sides of this little resort town are towering crags with names like Two Nuns, Bell Rock, Courthouse Butte, and Cathedral Rock.

There's a coolness factor in Sedona, too; in July, when afternoon highs often reach 115 degrees in the Las Vegas valley, the average high is a comparatively comfortable 95 in Sedona.

The first Europeans to "discover" the region were Spanish explorers who were looking to plunder Indian mines in 1583. The first permanent settlers didn't arrive until 1876; the settlement had grown to twenty families by 1902. It was Theodore Schnebly, who had petitioned for the first post office, who gave the settlement its name: Sedona was named for his wife.

The region was known for its apple orchards and other agriculture until tourism took hold. In 1950, surrealist painter Max Ernst moved to town and the artist-colony tradition that remains today was off and running.

Oh, and Sedona is famed for one other thing: its concentration of vortexes that supposedly release psychic energy or power from the Earth. Those who believe say the sites of the vortexes are Cathedral Rock, Bell Rock, Boynton Canyon, and Table Top Mountain.

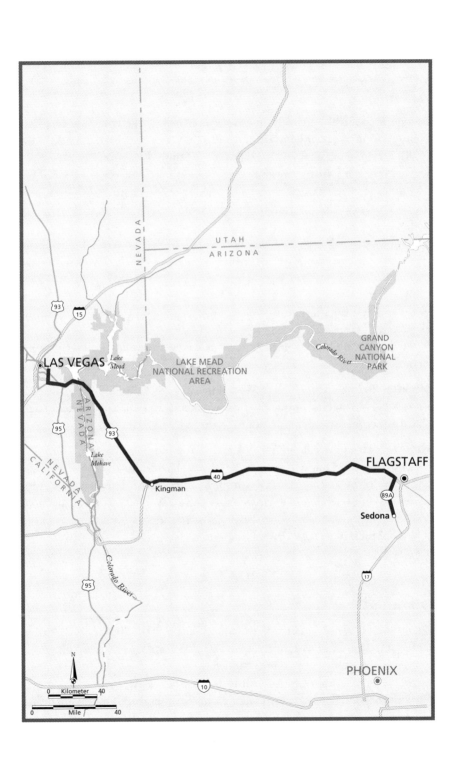

DAY 1

Afternoon

Sedona is about 275 miles from Las Vegas. Much of the trip is by interstate highway, so it takes a little over four hours.

To reach Sedona, take U.S. Highway 93 South for about 80 miles, picking up Interstate 40 East near Kingman. Continue east on I–40 for about 145 miles to exit 195A near Flagstaff, then take Interstate 17 South a short distance to exit 337, Arizona Route 89A South, and follow AZ 89A into Sedona.

If you left Las Vegas early enough that it's still light out when you get to AZ 89A—an easy thing to do in the summer—you'll find yourself on an exceptionally scenic road that winds through the beauty of Oak Creek Canyon. Stop along the way at scenic overlooks—they fill up quickly on Saturday and Sunday afternoons—to get an up-close-and-personal view of the creek and the canyon.

Follow AZ 89A through Sedona to its western edge to get the lay of the land.

DINNER: Prime Cut (2250 West Highway 89A, Sedona, AZ 86339; 520–282–2943) serves prime rib, steaks, seafood, and salads in a moderately casual atmosphere, with limited outside seating. Moderate.

LODGING: Head back along AZ 89A and turn south onto Arizona Route 179 to **The Inn on Oak Creek** (556 Highway 179, Sedona, AZ 86339; 520–282–7896 or 800–499–7896; rates from $130 to $225). The inn, an eleven-room bed-and-breakfast that extends over the creek, offers views of the creek and its canyon, and all rooms have gas fireplaces and private baths with whirlpool tubs; most have private outdoor decks.

DAY 2

Morning

BREAKFAST: Have breakfast at the Oak Creek Inn or at **The Secret Garden Cafe** (at the entrance to Tlaquepaque; 520–203–9564), which has homemade pastries and fresh organic coffees. Moderate.

Then it's back up AZ 89A to **Slide Rock State Park** (within Oak Creek Canyon; 520–282–3034), which was developed around a 70-foot natural rock

The towering red cliffs of Sedona

waterslide. There's a pioneer homestead there as well, plus one of the region's few remaining apple orchards, but the slide's the draw for most of the families who flock into the park on hot days. Try to get there in the morning, or you might find a sign stating that the parking lot is full.

For an incomparable view of **Oak Creek Canyon**, drive farther up AZ 89A to the state-maintained overlook. On weekends, local Indian tribes have a market in the park, selling jewelry, pottery, and other folk items such as dreamcatchers. The overlook also is, of course, the best place to view the canyon and the creek and road that snake along on its floor. You'll see pines clinging to impossibly small rock outcroppings and look down into dense forests so inaccessible on the 1,200-foot-high canyon walls that they no doubt remain untouched by man.

Speaking of man: To get a look at the way early peoples expressed themselves, visit the **V-Bar-V Ranch Petroglyph Site** (Forest Road 618;

520–282–4119). To get there, head south on AZ 179 until it passes beneath I–17; proceed under the highway to Forest Road 618 and on to the site.

V-Bar-V, which has been opened to the public through a joint effort of the Coconino National Forest, Friends of the Forest, and Verde Valley Archeological Society, showcases more than 1,000 petroglyphs—images produced by the ancient Sinagua people.

LUNCH: Shake off the red dust at **Canyon Breeze** (300 North Highway 89A, Sedona, AZ 86339; 520–282–2112), advertising "refreshing food and drink" that translates to Sonoran-style cuisine such as Sonoran chips and salsa and a Sonoran rice and bean burrito, plus an eclectic selection including a mesquite bacon and Swiss burger, an albacore tuna wrap, and pepperoni pizza. Moderate.

Afternoon

More dust, but you'll no doubt agree that it's worth it—especially if a visit to the V-Bar-V Ranch left you wanting more information about the first peoples who inhabited the Sedona area.

If you'd rather leave the driving to someone else, take a trip with **Pink Jeep Tours** (294 North Highway 89A; 520–282–5000 or 800–873-3662). Pink Jeep offers a variety of tours in and around (and sometimes over) the red rocks of Sedona in—you guessed it—pink Jeeps; the company also offers "ancient expeditions" tours in forest-green Jeeps. The hour-and-a-half Canyon West tour takes in such formations as Lizard's Head and Balancing Rock; the two-and-a-half-hour Ancient Ruins tour takes passengers through canyons to a 700-year-old Sinaguan cliff dwelling.

You can do the tour yourself, as well. Four-wheel-drive vehicles are necessary for only a few routes; for most, a vehicle with a relatively strong suspension will get you there just fine. If you'd like, you can rent a Jeep from one of several companies in the area, among them **Sedona Jeep Rentals** (Sedona Airport, on Airport Road off West Highway 89A; 520–282–2227 or 800–879–JEEP) and **Desert Jeep and Bike Rentals** (75 Bell Rock Plaza, Suite 3; 520–284–1099 or 888–464–5337). Either way, be prepared: You'll be riding along some bumpy, dusty dirt roads as you travel back through the centuries.

But there's much to see. Many formations, including Capitol Butte, Sugar Loaf, and Coffee Pot Rock, can be spotted from AZ 89A or roads that branch off of it. **Chapel of the Holy Cross** (Chapel Road, off AZ 179; 520–282–4069) was built in 1956 between two towering red-sandstone formations; a ramp leads to its entrance and the design is dominated by a 90-foot cross. Nearby is Two Nuns; Bell Rock and Courthouse Butte can be viewed from farther down AZ 179; take Rock Boulevard off 179 to get up close and personal to Cathedral Rock.

For a look at some Sinagua ruins, go to the **Honanki** site (520–282–3854). Take AZ 89A West 9 miles from the Y in Sedona to Forest Road 525. Turn right onto FR 525 and follow the dirt road about 10 miles; the ruins and rock art site are at the foot of Loy Butte.

The **Palatki Ruin and Red Cliffs Rock Art Site** (520–282–4119) is in the same general vicinity, except that you follow FR 525 to Forest Road 795 to the site, where the pictographs are in rock alcoves accessible by walking trail.

Red Rocks State Park (off West Highway 89A and Lower Red Rock Loop Road; 520–282–6907) highlights the ecology of Oak Creek. Nature hikes, bird walks, and other programs are offered.

DINNER: Spices Restaurant (2545 Highway 89A, Sedona, AZ 86339; 520–204–9117) has a menu that leans heavily to Italian with offerings such as toasted ravioli, Pescatora, and Four Seasons Fettucine, but also includes certified Angus beef and seafood. Moderate.

LODGING: The Inn on Oak Creek (see above).

DAY 3

Morning

BREAKFAST: Have breakfast at the Inn on Oak Creek, or try the **Hitching Post Restaurant** (269 North Highway 89A, Sedona, AZ 86339; 520–282–7761). You'll understand the Hitching Post's homey mission when you note that biscuits and gravy is the first thing on the menu, but the fare includes omelets and pancakes as well. Moderate.

Even if you don't consider shopping a participatory sport, you won't escape noticing that it's big in Sedona, which has a huge selection of shops and galleries.

Uptown Sedona, where the Hitching Post is located, is a prime shopping area right on the main road through town, with a Christmas shop, gift shops, T-shirt shops, fudge shops, and ice-cream shops.

Another prime shopping spot is the **Tlaquepaque Arts and Crafts Village** (near the intersection of AZ 89A and AZ 179; 520–282–4838; www.tlaq.com). There, in a shaded setting of Spanish Colonial decor, you'll find galleries such as **Aguajito del Sol** (520–282–5258) with its ceramics and watercolors and the **Bear Cloud Gallery** (520–282–4940) with its original American Indian spiritual artwork; jewelry stores such as the **Gold Door Gallery** (520–282–3370) with its gold and silver designs by Arizona artists and **Ninibah** (520–282–4256) with Indian jewelry, baskets, and kachinas; gift shops such as **Environmental Realists** (520–282–4945) with its mixed-metal jewelry, handcrafted knives, and wood accessories and **Esteban's** (520–282–4686) with its functional and decorative pottery; and clothing shops such as **I Am One of a Kind** (520–282–5711) with minerals, clothing, antiques, and jewelry.

LUNCH: And restaurants. While you're at Tlaquepaque, have lunch at **El Rincon** (520–282–4648), where the Mexican and Southwestern offerings include Navajo pizzas, rellenos, tostadas, and enchiladas (moderate), or the more elegant **Rene** (520–282–9225), with its pheasant salad, crepes Pompadour, or eggs Benedict (expensive).

It'll be tough to leave the beauty of the red rocks for the drive home along I–17 and I–40 and US 93, but at least Las Vegas has a miniature version of Sedona's splendor.

THERE'S MORE

Arizona Helicopter Adventures, Sedona Airport, on Airport Road off West Highway 89A; (520) 282–0904 or (800) 282–5141. Narrated tours of the Sedona area, including Indian ruins at Boynton Canyon.

Dahn Too Meditation Center, 1615 West Highway 89A; (520) 282–3600. Holistic healing, retreats, massage, tai chi, yoga.

A Day in the West, 252 North Highway 89A; (520) 282–4320 or (800) 973–3662. Horseback rides, Jeep tours, and cowboy cookouts.

Northern Light Balloon Expeditions; (520) 282–2274. Daily sunrise flights in the Sedona red-rock area.

Rainbow Trout Farm, 3500 North Highway 89A; (520) 282–3379. "Hook 'em" from artesian springs and "cook 'em" in barbecue pits on the grounds.

Red Rock Balloon Adventures, 295 Lee Mountain Lane; (800) 258–3754. "Aerial nature walks" and champagne picnics; video of flight.

DESERT

Red Rock Biplane Tours, Sedona Airport, on Airport Road off West Highway 89A; (520) 204–5939 or (888) TOO–RIDE. Flights over red-rock country of Sedona and other locations, with videotape of trip.

Sedona Red Rock Jeep Tours, 270 North Highway 89A; (520) 282–6826 or (800) 848–7728.

Sedona SuperVue Theater, Prime Factory Outlets in the Village of Oak Creek; (520) 284–3214. Film trip through red-rock area via helicopter, balloon, train, Jeep, and horseback.

Skydance Helicopters, Sedona Airport, on Airport Road off West Highway 89A; (800) 882–1651 or (520) 282–1651. Helicopter tours of area.

SPECIAL EVENTS

March. Sedona International Film Festival; (800) 780–2787 or (520) 203–4TIX.

St. Patrick's Day Parade; (520) 204–2390.

May. Annual Sedona Chamber Music Festival, ten-day event at various locations; (520) 204–2415.

June. Annual Sedona Taste, food and wine-tasting event to benefit Boys and Girls Club, Los Abrigados Resort; (520) 282–7822.

Annual Shakespeare Sedona Outdoor Theatre; (520) 284–2080.

Annual Western Art Exhibition and Sale, Sedona Cultural Park; (520) 774–8861.

July. Annual Fourth of July Celebration; (520) 282–4126.

September. Fiesta de Tlaquepaque, Hispanic and Southwest American Indian music, dancing, food, and art; (520) 282–4838.

Annual Pops at Poco, classical and pops music at Poco Diablo Resort; (520) 282–6649.

Annual Sculpture Walk, invitational art show at Los Abrigados Resort; (520) 282–3809.

Annual Sedona Jazz on the Rocks Festival, Sedona Cultural Park; (520) 282–1985.

Sedona EcoFest, performing arts event to promote ecological causes, Sedona Cultural Park; (520) 282–0747.

October. Annual Carnaval de Mascaras, festival with jugglers, magicians and mimes, Tlaquepaque; (520) 282–4838.

Annual Sedona Arts Festival and Artist Invitational, Red Rock High School; (520) 204–9456.

November through January. Annual Red Rock Fantasy, with displays designed and built by Arizona families; (520) 282–1777.

December. Festival of Lights with 6,000 luminaria, music, and holiday-themed activities, Tlaquepaque; (520) 282–4838.

OTHER RECOMMENDED RESTAURANTS AND LODGINGS

Bell Rock Inn and Suites, 6246 Highway 179; (520) 282–4161 or (800) 881–7625. Suites with fireplaces, two-story suites, bunkhouse rooms.

Best Western Arroyo Roble Hotel and Creekside Villas, 400 North 89A; (520) 282–4001 or (800) 7–SEDONA. Hotel rooms with red-rock views and two-bedroom villas.

Briar Patch Inn Bed and Breakfast, 3190 North Highway 89A; (520) 282–2342 or (888) 809–3030. Private cottages on eight-and-a-half acres on banks of Oak Creek.

Dahl and DiLuca Ristorante Italiano, 2321 West Highway 89A; (520) 282–5219. Italian veal, poultry, pastas, and grilled items.

Doubletree Sedona Resort, 90 Ridge Trail Drive; (877) 2–REDROCK. All-suite hotel with spa and championship golf course.

McDonald's, 2380 West Highway 89A; (520) 282–6211. World's only teal-green arches.

Mesquite Grill and BBQ, 250 Jordan Road in Uptown Sedona; (520) 282–6533. Smoked baby-back ribs, barbecued beef or pork, sandwiches.

Oaxaca, 321 North Highway 89A; (520) 282–4179. Southwestern specialties including Red Rock Enchiladas and Blue Mesa Trout.

DESERT

Robert's Creekside Cafe and Grill, 251 Highway 179 in Creekside Plaza; (520) 282–3671. Known for peach cobbler; also offering beignets, omelets, seafood, and prime rib.

A Territorial House Old West Bed and Breakfast, 65 Piki Drive; (520) 204–2737. Shaded property; rooms decorated in Arizona Territory decor.

FOR MORE INFORMATION

Sedona–Oak Creek Canyon Chamber of Commerce, Forest Road and Arizona Route 89A, P.O. Box 478, Sedona, AZ 86339; (520) 282–7722 or (800) 288–7336; www.sedonachamber.com.

MOUNTAIN
ESCAPES

MOUNTAIN

Reno

GAMBLING AND
THE GREAT OUTDOORS

2 NIGHTS

Bright lights • Casinos • Museums
Outdoor adventures • Basque cuisine

Reno's wholesome moniker of "biggest little city in the world"—emblazoned across Virginia Street for all to see—belies the fast that this resort town has long been beloved by a fast crowd who sought it out for its hot gambling and quickie marriages (and divorces).

Reno beat Las Vegas to the dice-and-cards punch, legalizing gambling soon after the state approved the practice in 1931. During the 1940s, it was known as a favorite vacation spot for Hollywood types. In the 1960s, no less an illustrious figure than Frank Sinatra owned the nearby Cal-Neva resort, which straddles the state line near Reno, furthering the city's image as a source of fast fun.

It seems Reno has provided comfort to travelers since its earliest days. The first recorded exploration by white settlers in the Reno area was in 1844, when a band of pioneers stumbled upon what is now known as Pyramid Lake. Long regarded as a special place by the native Northern Paiute Indians who appreciated its ample supply of trout, the lake had to be a welcome sight for the explorers who had just traveled through the barren deserts to the north. The lake got its name from the pyramid-shaped rock formation stretching some 400 feet above the surface; explorer John C. Fremont later wrote that it was he himself who named it.

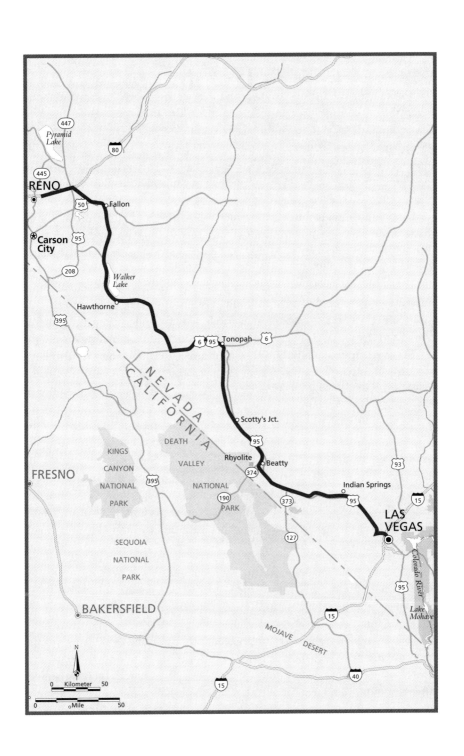

The same year Fremont's party passed through the area, 1844, another group of immigrants came in search of a route across the Sierra Nevada to California. A local Indian diagrammed a river and possible pass for them; when they found the river they named it for him in gratitude—the Truckee River, because they thought his named sounded like "Truckee." They did indeed find a pass, and became the first white party to follow it over the mountains. The pass was renamed three years later when the tragic story of the Donner party became known, but the river retained the name; there's also a town named Truckee today.

By the mid-nineteenth century, the rush to the gold and silver mines on the Comstock Lode at Virginia City to the south brought more settlers through the area; it's estimated that 22,500 prospectors passed through Truckee Meadows in 1849, 45,000 in 1850, and 52,000 in 1852.

The settlement at Reno began with a toll bridge erected to help all those folks cross the river. A tavern, inn, and gristmill followed; what is today Virginia Street, the main drag through modern Reno, once was the road that connected the California Trail with the Comstock Lode near Virginia City.

The train arrived in 1867 and with it a name change; the original name of Lake's Crossing was just too long for railroad schedules. Reno's new name would honor Gen. Jesse Lee Reno, a Civil War soldier who had been killed in Maryland.

Today, with the approval of casino gambling on Indian lands just over the border in California—home to many of Reno's most devoted visitors—many people have predicted doom for the big little city. But its location amid the staggering beauty of the Sierra Nevada and the resourcefulness of city leaders, many of whom trace their roots to pioneer stock, helps ensure its future as a vacation spot for years to come. "There's a little cowboy in all of us, a little frontier," Louis L'Amour wrote, and that becomes obvious during a quick escape to Reno.

DAY 1

Morning

Reno is about 450 miles from Las Vegas and can be reached in about six hours of solid driving. Much of the route is two-lane highway, but most of it is lightly traveled as it passes through desert areas. Be mindful, too, that airlines offer lots of bargain fares between Las Vegas and Reno; round trips often can

Reno's famous arched sign on Virginia Street

be had for $60 or so, which makes Reno a popular weekend destination for Las Vegans.

If you're driving, head out first thing Friday morning, or leave the night before and stop in Beatty, Tonopah, or Hawthorne, where there are motels. It would be difficult to get lost along the way, because you'll be following U.S. Route 95 North for about the first 400 miles. When you get to U.S. Highway 50 in Fallon, head west for about 9 miles until the road becomes US 50A, then follow that for about 10 miles to Interstate 80 West. Follow I–80 West about 30 miles to Reno and exit at Virginia Street (Business Route 395).

LUNCH: While you're passing through Fallon, stop at **Bob's Root Beer Drive In** (4150 Reno Highway; 775–867–2769) for some homemade root beer and food including burgers, hot dogs, spaghetti and meatballs, fish and chips, or grinders. Inexpensive.

Afternoon

For an orientation of Reno, what better place to start than those famous casinos? Most of them are along Virginia Street, which functions as a Main Street
for the town and is the site of the famous neon-lit "biggest little" sign that
arches across the street near **Fitzgeralds Casino-Hotel** (255 North Virginia;
800–535–LUCK; www.fitzgeralds.com/reno). If you're a gambler, the casinos
offer plenty to do; all have slot machines, video poker, and table games and
some have keno and poker rooms.

But even if you're not into gambling, there are plenty of attractions. At the
Reno Hilton (2500 East Second Street; 775–789–2000; www.renohilton.
com), for example, you'll find the Bunker, an indoor golf simulator that lets
you "play" thirty-two championship courses; the Ultimate Rush, which combines the sensations of hang-gliding, bungee jumping, and sky diving from a
185-foot tower; the Hilton Bay Aqua Golf Driving Range; a bowling center;
movie theaters; a health club and spa; and a 40,000-square-foot amusement
center.

Circus Circus (500 North Sierra Street; 775–329–0711; www.circusreno.
com) offers free performances by circus acts from all over the world on its Circus Stage. Performances begin at 11:15 A.M., seven days a week. Also on the
Midway are more than a hundred video and carnival games.

The Family Fun Center at the **Boomtown Hotel and Casino** (Boom-
town/Garson Road; 877–726–6686; www.boomtowncasinos.com) has a 3-D
motion theater, antique carousel, Covered Wagon Ferris Wheel, Rodeo Rider,
nine-hole indoor miniature golf course, and more than 150 games.

DINNER: The **Rapscallion Seafood House and Bar** (1555 South Wells
Avenue, Reno, NV 89504; 3 miles south of the Wells Avenue exit of I–80;
775–323–1211 or 877–932–3700) has a selection of the standard and the offbeat, the latter including a prawn cocktail with cucumber salsa and lemon;
pecan-roasted salmon; a mixed grill of salmon, crabcake, and prawns; a stew of
fish, prawns, scallops, and clams; plus steaks, pastas, and burgers. The restaurant
also is the winner of *Wine Spectator* magazine's Award of Excellence. Moderate.

LODGING: The **Peppermill Hotel Casino** (2707 South Virginia Street,
Reno, NV 89504; 775–648–6992 or 800–282–2444; www.peppermillcasinos.
com; rates from $54 to $124) has to be seen to be believed: It's neon-meets-
space-age-meets-Southern-plantation-excess, and is known for its suites,
which it has in great variety. There are 1,070 rooms, including 185 whirlpool

and other suites, with views of the Peppermill's waterfall pool, the Sierra Nevada, or the lights of Reno.

DAY 2

Morning

BREAKFAST: Time to get out and explore all that Reno has to offer. Have breakfast at **Heidi's Family Restaurant** (2450 South Virginia Street, Reno, NV 89504; 775–826–3336), where locals like to go for the lucky thirteen varieties of omelets on the menu. Inexpensive.

Just off Virginia—2 blocks east and 1 block south of the arch—is the **National Auto Museum** (10 Lake Street, 775–333–9300; www.automuseum. org), which showcases more than 220 antique and special-interest vehicles, some of which have appeared in movies. To put the collection in perspective, the museum has constructed four street scenes from various eras in the twentieth century that help visitors travel through time. There's also a gallery of changing exhibits, and visitors can chat with mechanics in the Automotive Shop.

More history is showcased at the museum of the **Nevada Historical Society** (1650 North Virginia Street; 775–688–1190), where the permanent collection is divided into five sections that each tell the story of a major element in the formation of Nevada: "Living on the Land," "Riches From the Earth," "Passing Through," "Neon Nights," and "Federal Presence." The themes are illuminated through the use of photographs and artifacts including documents. "Federal Presence," for example, which explains that 87 percent of Nevada's land is owned by the federal government, contains a large number of military-related artifacts and information on federal projects. "Passing Through" explains the importance of the early pioneers who came through "on their way to somewhere else," as museum staff say, many of whom stuck with it to settle the young state. The museum also has a research library and museum store, and a gallery of changing exhibits.

If you'd prefer an outdoor alternative to the museums, consider a stroll along the (Raymond I.) **Smith Truckee River Walk** (775–334–2417). Start at **Wingfield Park** (on the river between South Sierra Street, which is 1 block west of Virginia, and Arlington Avenue) in downtown Reno and you can walk about as far as you'd like in either direction. If you walk east, you'll pass the spot where, legend has it, thousands of divorcees over the years have pitched their no-longer-needed wedding rings into the Truckee.

You'll also likely see waterbirds and maybe a fisherman or two trying his or her luck. Along the walk is a public-art installation that features a number of panels depicting animals native to the region. It's not a static exhibit, however; water runs down the panels and even out of the mouths of several of the figures.

LUNCH: Luciano's (719 Virginia Street, Reno, NV 89504; 775–322–7373) is a cozy spot just south of downtown where even the spaghetti and meatballs is special. And save room for the truly inspired tiramisu. Moderate.

Afternoon

The **Wilbur D. May Center** (Rancho San Rafael Regional Park, 1502 Washington Street; 775–785–5961; www.maycenter.com) is a different sort of attraction—museum, aboretum, and outdoor family adventure in one. The museum houses the artifacts of May's life as a pioneering Nevada rancher and world traveler. The arboretum has twelve acres of trees and gardens, including courtyards and wetlands habitats. And the family-fun area—geared to kids ages two to twelve and dubbed the "Great Basin Adventure"—has a petting ranch, an area where kids can ride ponies or take flume rides, and the Discovery Room, where they can pan for gold, climb on dinosaurs, or explore teepees— and, most importantly, touch whatever they want.

Another option for family adventure can be found just to the east in Sparks, where **Wild Island** (250 Wild Island Court; 775–359–2927) has ten outdoor water rides, a wave pool, and other play areas.

DINNER: Louis' Basque Corner (301 East Fourth Street, Reno, NV 89504; 775–323–7203) is a cornerstone of Reno's Basque tradition—a remnant of the time when Basque sheepherders flooded the region during the Gold Rush. Sit down at one of the restaurant's long tables (reminiscent of that era's boardinghouse tradition) with a Picon punch or two ("two are the Picon and three is the punch"), which is Picon orange liqueur, grenadine, soda, and a brandy float, and move on to pass-around dishes of soup, salad, oxtail stew, and beans, with lamb, steak, sweetbreads, or salmon. Oh, and have a wedge of dry Jack cheese for dessert. Moderate.

LODGING: The Peppermill Hotel Casino (see above).

DAY 3

Morning

BREAKFAST: Stop in to eat under the flowering tree in the Peppermill's purple-and-blue **Coffee Shop,** where you'll find the usual breakfast favorites, including fluffy Belgian waffles, fresh fruit, and egg dishes. Moderate.

Then, consider a drive to **Pyramid Lake,** off Nevada Route 445 about 35 miles northeast of Reno (775–574–1000). Now part of a Paiute Indian reservation, the lake is considered among the state's best recreation areas for boating and for fishing (for trout as large as forty pounds). Contact the ranger about fishing or boating permits; camping, picnicking, and water sports also are available.

Then it's back to I–80 to retrace your steps for a return to Las Vegas. If you didn't stop on the way up at the ghost town of Rhyolite, near Beatty, consider a stop on the way back.

THERE'S MORE

Fallon, Nevada

Lahontan State Recreation Area, 16799 Lahontan Dam; (775) 867–3500. Picnicking, camping, boat launch, swimming, and fishing.

Reno, Nevada

ArrowCreek Golf Club, 2905 ArrowCreek Parkway; (775) 850–4653. Two eighteen-hole courses, one designed by Arnold Palmer and one by Fuzzy Zoeller and John Harbottle, that are open to the public.

Fleischmann Planetarium, University of Nevada, Reno; (775) 784–4811. Star shows, SkyDome films, museum, and observatory.

W. M. Keck Museum, University of Nevada, Reno, School of Mines; (775) 784–4528. Silver collection, mining artifacts, exhibits of rocks, minerals, and fossils.

Nevada Museum of Art, 160 West Liberty Street; (775) 329–3333. Exhibits range from contemporary to historic.

Sheppard Fine Art Gallery, University of Nevada, Reno, Department of Art; (775) 784–6658. Changing exhibits featuring works by regional and national artists.

Sierra Safari Zoo, 10200 North Virginia Street; (775) 677–1101. More than 200 animals representing more than forty species.

SPECIAL EVENTS

May. Asian Festival, with culture exhibits and entertainment, Silver Legacy Club; (800) 687–7733.

June. EuroFest, with exhibits and entertainment, Rail City Casino; (775) 954–2233.

Reno Rodeo, Reno Livestock Events Center; (775) 329–3877 or (775) 688–5751.

July. ARTown; (775) 332–1538.

Reno Basque Festival, Wingfield Park; (775) 787–3039.

August. Hot August Nights, Reno, Sparks, and Lake Tahoe; (775) 356–1956.

Nevada State Fair, Reno Livestock Events Center; (775) 688–5767.

September. The Great Reno Balloon Race, Rancho San Rafael Park; (775) 826–1181.

National Championship Air Races, Stead Airport; (775) 972-6429.

Late November through the end of December. Reno's River Holiday, Wingfield Park; (775) 334–2414 or (775) 337–3044.

OTHER RECOMMENDED RESTAURANTS AND LODGINGS

Incline Village, Nevada

Haus Bavaria, 593 North Dyer Circle; (775) 831–6122 or (800) 731–6222. European-style bed-and-breakfast on north shore of Lake Tahoe.

Reno, Nevada

Atlantis Casino Resort–Reno, 3800 South Virginia Street; (775) 825–4700. Marine-themed hotel complex.

Bed and Breakfast–South Reno, 136 Andrew Lane; (775) 849–0772. Bed-and-breakfast with two rooms.

Pimparel's La Table Francaise, 3065 West Fourth Street; (775) 323–3200. Casual restaurant with French cuisine.

Silver Legacy, 407 North Virginia Street; (775) 329–4777. Old-Nevada theme; headliners and comedy club.

Steak House, Harrah's Hotel and Casino, 210 North Center Street; (775) 788–2929. Top-notch service includes tableside preparations.

White Orchid, Peppermill Hotel, 2707 South Virginia Street; (775) 689–7300. Gourmet room in elegant setting.

Sparks, Nevada

John Ascuaga's Nugget Hotel Tower, 1100 Nugget Avenue; (775) 356–3300. Modern hotel complex with periodic headliner entertainment.

Windsor Inn, 60 East Victorian Avenue; (775) 356–7770 or (800) 892–3506. Smoke-free bed-and-breakfast.

FOR MORE INFORMATION

Nevada Commission on Tourism, 401 North Carson Street, Carson City, NV 89701; (800) NEVADA–8; www.travelnevada.com.

Reno–Sparks Convention and Visitors Authority, 4590 South Virginia Street, P.O. Box 837, Reno, NV 89504; (775) 827–7366 or (800) 367–7366; www.rscva.com.

MOUNTAIN

Lake Tahoe

ALPINE ESCAPE

2 NIGHTS

Skiing • Watersports • Hiking • "Bonanza"
Cozy inns • Gourmet restaurants

World-class skiing. An endless variety of watersports. Hiking and camping in the awesome beauty of the Sierra Nevada. A vast variety of resorts, from family-oriented mom-and-pop operations to those that dedicate themselves to the ultimate in luxury. Casino gambling across the border in Nevada.

Lake Tahoe, California, has it all, as resort areas go. But none of it would be there if it weren't for the lake itself, that sparkling-blue alpine jewel surrounded by reach-to-the-sky mountains that seem to rise from the lake's very shores. That lake has been good to the people of the region, and most of them can tell you at least something about its origins.

It was the endless shifting of the geologic faults that formed the Tahoe Basin some five to ten million years ago. As the land shifted, part of it rose to become the Sierra Nevada, which has some of the region's highest peaks. The land that sank in turn created a V-shaped valley. Volcanic activity, glaciers, and lots more movement over the next few eons, and voila! Lake Tahoe.

Lake Tahoe is not only beautiful, but massive. Its average depth is 989 feet—*average*. The deepest point is 1,645 feet below the surface of Crystal Bay, and the lake holds more than thirty-nine *trillion* gallons of water—enough to cover an area the size of the state of California 14 inches deep. That's an apt comparison, because if the water that evaporates from the lake could somehow be collected, it would be adequate to satisfy the water demands of the city of Los Angeles. Lake Tahoe never freezes, because of its huge volume, but

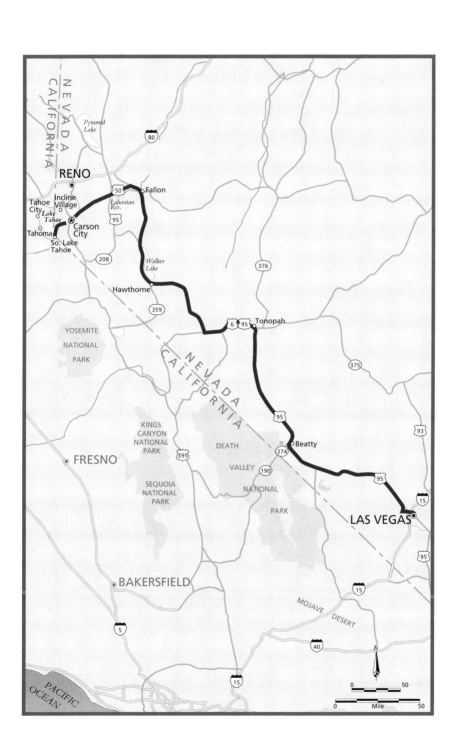

it's chilly. The surface water temperature ranges from 41 to 68 degrees, and below 600 feet the temperature is a constant 39 degrees.

But you're no doubt more interested in spending time at Lake Tahoe than in learning about its origins, and you're certainly not the first. Human habitation on the lake's shores has been traced to the Washoe Indians (who wintered in the Carson Valley) some 10,000 years ago.

The first sighting of the lake by a non-native was in 1844, when the party of explorer John C. Fremont, guided by the legendary Kit Carson, came through the area. The nearby Comstock lode silver-mining boom and attendant logging boom of the 1860s–1880s brought the first big influx of white people to the region, but they nearly deforested it, and the natural habitats still are recovering, more than 125 years later.

Despite the excessive practices of the loggers, the region had sufficient natural beauty that by the 1890s a resort economy had been born, fueled by visitors from San Francisco, Sacramento, and Virginia City, which was then a silver boomtown. And it's a resort area that Lake Tahoe remains today.

DAY 1

Morning

Lake Tahoe is about 475 miles from Las Vegas, but its beauty and reputation as the ultimate resort make it a popular destination for valley residents. Bargain airfares between Las Vegas and Reno, the closest major airport, can commonly be had for as little as $60 per person, round trip.

If you decide to drive, you'll likely want to get an early start on Friday morning. The trip takes about six hours, owing to the barren desert wilderness and the 75-miles-per-hour speed limits over much of the route. Be mindful of speed, though, when you're passing through towns along the way.

From Las Vegas, drive north on U.S. Highway 95 about 385 miles to the city of Fallon, passing through Beatty, Tonopah, and Hawthorne. Fallon is Pony Express Territory (keep an eye out for signs that commemorate the route) and today is home to the Navy's Top Gun flight school. Farmers in the region grow award-winning cantaloupes.

LUNCH: You'll no doubt be hungry by Fallon, cantaloupes notwithstanding, so stop at **Bob's Root Beer Drive In** (4150 Reno Highway; 775–867–2769) and cool off, no matter the weather, with a frosty homemade root beer and a burger, hot dog, or fish and chips. Inexpensive.

Lake Tahoe and the Sierra Nevada

Afternoon

From Fallon, head west on U.S. Highway 50 to Carson City and follow it into South Lake Tahoe, where US 50 becomes Lake Tahoe Boulevard.

DINNER: Evans American Gourmet Cafe (536 Emerald Bay Road, South Lake Tahoe, CA 96150; 530–542–1990; www.evanstahoe.com) lives up to its name, with appetizers such as scallop quenelles with sherry-lobster cream, port-glazed fillet of beef with porcini mushroom–green peppercorn sauce, and roast Cervena venison with balsamic roast cherries and lacquered root vegetables, served in a cozy cabin nestled in the pines. For dessert, how about a classic tarte tatin—or maybe Chocolate Obsession? Expensive.

LODGING: You're here to see the lake, aren't you? Many of the rooms and suites at **Inn by the Lake** (3300 Lake Tahoe Boulevard, South Lake Tahoe, CA 96150; 530–542–0330; www.innbythelake.com; rates from $98 to $325) have private balconies overlooking the lake, and some have private spas. There's also a terraced pool and spa area outdoors. Various packages are available, and your room comes complete with continental breakfast and use of bike or snowshoes, depending on the season.

DAY 2

Morning

BREAKFAST: Have breakfast at the Inn by the Lake, or head east on Lake Tahoe Boulevard to the intersection with Ski Run Boulevard, where you'll find **Hot Gossip** (530–541–4823), which serves great morning pick-me-ups from its espresso bar, plus a variety of pastries. Inexpensive.

Continue up Ski Run Boulevard to the **Heavenly Tram** (775–586–7000), to take a seven-minute tram ride some 2,000 feet above the level of Lake Tahoe for a sweeping view of the lake. If you're feeling ambitious, there are hiking trails nearby.

Then, to really get the lay of the land, embark on a 72-mile drive around the lake, stopping as often as you like. Head west from South Lake Tahoe on US 50, eventually turning onto California Route 89, which makes its way along the shoreline, then turn onto California Route 29 just north of Tahoe City, which continues around the lake and into Nevada; you'll need to turn onto US 50 South near Glenbrook to return to South Lake Tahoe.

As you travel, you'll pass various overlooks that offer amazing views of the lake and the Sierra Nevada; stop now and then to take it all in or snap a few pictures. **Emerald Bay** is one of the most attractive spots. Park at the Vikingsholm parking lot off CA 89 (parking is limited, so it's best to go in the morning) and find the 1-mile trail to **Vikingsholm** (530–525–7277; www.vikingsholm.org), which is at the head of the bay. The trail is steep, but you'll be rewarded by the chance to explore something that those gazing on it from the lakeshore can only imagine. Vikingsholm (which also is accessible by boat) is a thirty-eight-room re-creation of an ancient Nordic fortress and is the former home of Lora Josephine Knight, who commissioned it in Scandinavian style partly because of the fjord-like location of Emerald Bay.

A little farther north on CA 89, between Emerald Bay and Meeks Bay, you'll find **D. L. Bliss State Park** (530–525–7277), which offers naturalist programs and a sandy beach.

Still farther north, at Tahoma, is the **Ehrman Mansion** in **Sugar Pine Point State Park** (530–525–7982). The house, built by a San Francisco businessman in 1903 and originally called Pine Lodge, is an example of the grand tradition of early summer homes on Lake Tahoe. Owned today by the California State Park system, it has eight bedrooms and eight bathrooms, plus servants' quarters and lots of extra rooms given over to specialized purposes, such as a sewing room and storage rooms for all those trunks; the house had a live-in staff of twenty-seven. There also are various outbuildings, including a caretakers' cottage, children's house by the lake, maids' and butlers' houses, coach house, and boat houses.

LUNCH: All of this opulence has no doubt made you hungry, so go a little farther north to Tahoe City and **Jake's on the Lake** (780 North Lake Boulevard, Tahoe City, CA 96145; 530–583–0188), a waterfront grill with a seafood bar and lakefront deck, for a fresh fish sandwich or burger. Moderate.

Afternoon

If you visit Lake Tahoe during summer, you'll want to take advantage of watersports. **Tahoe City Marina** (700 North Lake Boulevard; 530–583–1039) offers boat rentals, fishing charters, and water-ski lessons; the **High Sierra Water Ski School** at Sunnyside (1850 West Lake Boulevard; 530–525–1214) is a water-ski and sailing school that offers personal watercraft, kayak, and canoe rentals as well. **Tahoe Paddle and Oar** at Kings Beach (7860 North Lake Boulevard; 530–581–3029) offers guided kayak tours of Crystal Bay and pontoon boat charters in Emerald Bay and Sand Harbor.

If it's winter, you'll find skiing at **Alpine Meadows** (California Route 89, Tahoe City; 800–441–4423 or 530–583–4232; www.skialpine.com), **Diamond Peak** (1210 Ski Way, Incline Village; 775–832–1177 or 775–831–3211; www.diamondpeak.com), **Homewood Mountain Resort** (5145 West Lake Boulevard, Homewood; 530–525–2992 or 530–525–2900; www.skihomewood.com), **Northstar-at-Tahoe** (Highway 267 at Northstar Drive, Truckee; 800–466–6784 or 530–562–1010; www.skinorthstar.com), **Squaw Valley USA** (1960 Squaw Valley Road, Olympic Valley; 800–401–9216 or 530–583–6955; www.squaw.com) and **Sugar Bowl** (Interstate 80 at the Norden exit, Norden; 530–426–9000 or 530–426–1111; www.sugarbowl.com).

DINNER: Back in South Lake Tahoe, **The Dory's Oar Restaurant** (1041 Fremont Avenue, South Lake Tahoe, CA 96150; 530–541–6603 or

866–541–6603) serves appetizers such as iced blue prawns with Jack Daniel's cocktail sauce and crème fraiche or blackened tiger shrimp with passionfruit and raspberry butter and entrees including Pacific swordfish topped with sweet orange and dry sherry cream or asparagus wrapped in filo pastry with Stilton, crushed herbs, and walnuts, all in a replica of a sixteenth-century Tudor English house. There's also Celtic harp music on selected evenings. Moderate.

LODGING: The Inn by the Lake (see above).

DAY 3

Morning

BREAKFAST: Check out of the inn early and head for Incline Village and breakfast at the **Ponderosa Ranch** (100 Ponderosa Ranch Road, Incline Village, NV 89451; 775–831–0691; www.ponderosaranch.com). Baby-boomers will remember the Ponderosa as the site of much of the filming of the *Bonanza* TV series.

The Ponderosa Ranch offers a hayride breakfast that sets out each morning during the summer, leaving between 8:00 and 9:30 A.M. aboard a haywagon that carries you up, up to a hilltop affording a gorgeous view of Lake Tahoe. Then the feeding begins, with a buffet breakfast of pancakes, scrambled eggs, sausage, and beverages under the pines. After breakfast, board the wagon for the trip back down the hill or make the hike on a broad paved path. Moderate.

There's much to see at Ponderosa Ranch, including the house where—in the TV world, at least—Pa, Adam, Hoss, and Little Joe made their home. There's also periodic entertainment and a Wild West village that houses a wagon collection, museums, church, saloon, shooting gallery, gold-panning creek—you name it.

Afterward, take Nevada Route 28 south to US 50 and take US 50 East, retracing your steps to return to Las Vegas.

THERE'S MORE

Lake Tahoe's East Shore, Nevada

Whittell Estate, Nevada State Park; (775) 687–1693. Shoreline estate with faux-medieval French château, boathouse, and lighthouse.

Olympic Valley, California

Squaw Valley Cable Car, 1960 Squaw Valley Road, Olympic Valley; (530) 583–6985. Provides sweeping view of Lake Tahoe and Squaw Valley. Ice skating and swimming also available.

South Lake Tahoe, California

Hornblower Cruises Lake Tahoe; (530) 541–3364. Day and evening cruises.

Tallac Historic Site, California Route 89 north of Camp Richardson; (530) 573–2600 or (530) 573–2674. Three historic summer estates built during the late nineteenth and early twentieth centuries.

Tahoe City, California

Gatekeeper's Log Cabin Museum, California Route 89; (530) 583–1762. Displays about history of Lake Tahoe region and its pioneers.

Watson Cabin Museum, 560 North Lake Boulevard; (530) 583–1762. Exhibits in oldest building in Tahoe City depict life at the turn of the twentieth century.

Truckee, California

Donner Memorial State Park, Donner Pass Road; (530) 583–7892. This park of 353 acres is near the site where the Donner party was stranded during the winter of 1846–47, losing nearly half of the eighty-nine-person group to death and resorting to cannibalism. Videotape details their ordeal; the Emigrant Trail Museum highlights the history of the region.

Zephyr Cove, Nevada

The MS *Dixie II*, departing from Zephyr Cove Resort, U.S. Highway 50; (775) 588–3508 or (775) 882–0786. Two-hour narrated sightseeing cruise around lake on paddle-wheeler.

SPECIAL EVENTS

Crystal Bay, Nevada

December through January. Sierra Fantasy holiday light show, Cal-Neva Resort; (775) 832–4000.

Lake Tahoe's West Shore, California

May. West Shore Jazz Festival, various locations; (530) 525–1973.

North Lake Tahoe, California

April. Tahoe International Film Festival. Independent films, documentaries, parties, various locations; (530) 583–FEST.

October. Lake Tahoe International Film Festival, various locations; (530) 583–FEST.

South Lake Tahoe, California

June. Valhalla Renaissance Festival, with crafts, fair, and entertainment in Elizabethan setting, Camp Richardson Resort; (530) 542–4166.

Tahoe City, California

February. Annual Snowboard Festival, Hacienda del Lago; (530) 583–0358.

July. Trans-Tahoe Sailboat Race, Tahoe Yacht Club; (530) 581–4700.

August. Lake Tahoe Summer Music Festival, various locations; (530) 583–3101.

Truckee, California

May. Windows on History, celebrating Truckee's history; (530) 587–2757.

October. Annual Donner Party Hike, guided hike along the Emigrant and Donner Trails; (530) 587–2757.

OTHER RECOMMENDED RESTAURANTS AND LODGINGS

Crystal Bay, Nevada

The Soule Domain, 9983 Cove Avenue; (530) 546–7529. Creative American cuisine served in a log cabin.

South Lake Tahoe, California

The Swiss Chalet, 2544 Lake Tahoe Boulevard; (530) 544–3304. German and Swiss cuisine, plus steaks and seafood.

Tahoe Chalet Inn, 3860 Lake Tahoe Boulevard; (530) 544–3311. Themed rooms with fireplaces and in-room spas.

Sunnyside, California

Cottage Inn at Lake Tahoe, 1690 West Lake Boulevard; (530) 581–4073. Themed knotty pine cottages with fireplaces, set among pines.

Tahoe City, California

Mayfield House Bed and Breakfast, 236 Grove Street; (530) 583–1001 or (888) 518–8898. English Tudor (circa 1930s) with featherbeds and stone fireplace.

Pfeifer House, 760 River Road; (530) 583–3102. Continental cuisine.

Sunnyside Restaurant, 1850 West Lake Boulevard; (530) 583–7200. Lakefront "Old Tahoe" restaurant specializing in fresh seafood.

Truckee, California

Hania's Bed and Breakfast Inn, 10098 High Street; (530) 582–5775 or (888) 600–3735. Southwestern decor with log furnishings and mountain views.

FOR MORE INFORMATION

Incline Village–Crystal Bay Chamber of Commerce, 969 Tahoe Boulevard, Incline Village, NV 89451; (775) 831–4440; www.laketahoechamber.com.

Lake Tahoe Visitors Authority, 1156 Ski Run Boulevard, South Lake Tahoe, CA 96150; (530) 544–5050 or (800) AT–TAHOE; www.virtualtahoe.com.

North Lake Tahoe Chamber of Commerce, P.O. Box 884, Tahoe City, CA 96145; (530) 581–6900.

South Lake Tahoe Chamber of Commerce, 3066 Lake Tahoe Boulevard, South Lake Tahoe, CA 96150; (530) 541–5255; www.tahoeinfo.com.

Zion National Park

ROCKS THAT FORM
A TEMPLE OF BEAUTY

2 NIGHTS

*Rock formations • Hiking • Horseback riding
Scenic drives • Bed-and-breakfasts*

The Paiute Indians weren't crazy about Zion Canyon and refused to stay there after dark, but to the Mormons who settled in the area, its towering red and white cliffs—some as high as 3,800 feet—made it a special place; the cliffs reminded them of places of worship and so they dubbed it Little Zion.

Today, the canyon is Zion National Park in Utah, 229 square miles that include the largest natural arch in the world (Kolob Arch, with a span of 310 feet) and wildlife including golden eagles, mountain lions, and mule deer that often can be spotted among the rocky outcroppings. Its natural beauty may not be as flashy as that of Bryce Canyon National Park, its neighbor to the east, but Zion is deeply appreciated nonetheless—by nearly two-and-a-half million people during 2000.

DAY 1

Afternoon

Zion National Park is about a three-and-a-half-hour drive from Las Vegas—about 170 miles—putting it in easy distance for a weekend trip at any time of year. And the heavily forested hills, towering rock spires, snow in the winter,

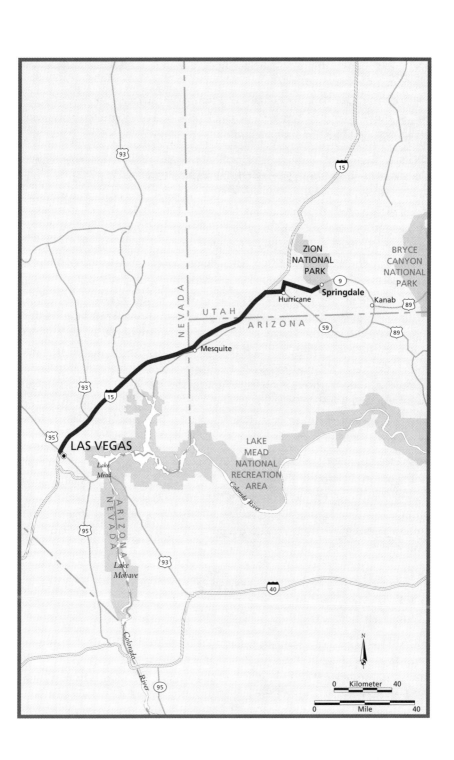

and comparatively mild climate during the summer add to its considerable allure as a weekend getaway.

To reach Zion National Park, head north on Interstate 15 for about 135 miles into Utah, taking exit 16 (Utah Route 9, Hurricane/Zion National Park). Follow UT 9 for about 35 miles to the park.

DINNER: As you pass through the hamlet of Hurricane, consider stopping for dinner and a show at the **Bar G Chuckwagon Cowboy Supper and Live Western Show** (55 North 3700 West; 435–635–5800—call ahead for reservations; www.bargchuckwagon.com). Dinner is chuckwagon style, appropriately enough, where customers holding tin plates line up in the chow line for fare that might include barbecued beef, baked ranch beans, cold chunky applesauce, spice cake, coffee, and lemonade. After dinner, restaurant employees whip off their aprons and climb onstage for an hour-long show with music, Western tricks, and, of course, plenty of cornball cowboy humor. Moderate.

As you approach the park entrance you'll pass through the little town of Springdale. If it's early enough, make a stop at the **Springdale Fruit Company** on Zion Park Boulevard, just 3 miles from the park gate (435–772–3222; www.springdalefruit.com), which is a woodsy market tucked into the middle of an apple orchard. Among the rows of offerings at Springdale Fruit, you'll find various types of produce—some organic, some exotic—plus juices, trail mixes, and various types of fresh-baked breads. Consider picking up the provisions for a park picnic lunch the next day.

LODGING: Bed-and-breakfasts and resort motels abound, but a logical choice is the **Zion National Park Lodge** (435–772–3213; for reservations, call 303–297–2757 or log on to http://www.nps.gov/zion; rates range from $90 to $114.50). The historic lodge, tucked at the foot of one of the park's signature majestic cliffs, has cabins with gas fireplaces and private porches and motel rooms with private porches or balconies.

DAY 2

Morning

BREAKFAST: There's a restaurant right in the lodge (435–772–3213) that offers everything from oatmeal to eggs Benedict, with eggs, pancakes, and the like in between. Moderate. Then it's off for a day of exploring Zion National Park.

For a good orientation tour of the park, follow the map you received at the entrance gate and take a scenic drive, stopping at overlooks and checking

The towering cliffs of Zion National Park

out trails for future reference. The entrance gate also is a good place to pick up a schedule of ranger programs offered seasonally. Programs may include short talks on history, animals, or geology, guided walks, or evening lectures.

If you visit Zion National Park during the months of November through March, you'll be able to make the scenic drive in your own vehicle. Be aware, though, that longer recreational vehicles can't make it alone through the tunnel on the Zion–Mount Carmel Highway (leading to Checkerboard Mesa, which looks remarkably like its name) and that their drivers must pay a fee for an escort.

If you visit during the warmer months when park attendance is at its peak, you'll be required to take a shuttle along the Zion Canyon Scenic Drive; there's no fee for the shuttle beyond the $20 park admission fee. Actually, there are two shuttles—one that makes nine stops in Zion Canyon, another that stops at six spots in Springdale. The two are connected by a footbridge near the **Zion Canyon Visitor Center,** so you can park either at the visitor center or in Springdale. You can get on and off the shuttles as often as you like; round trip on the canyon shuttle takes about one and a half hours.

The scenic drive is on the floor of the canyon, the park's famous cliffs rising in sheer, spectacularly colored walls on either side. The beauty starts even before you reach the visitor center, from which Bridge Mountain and its natural arch are visible. The Great White Throne, just beyond the lodge, is colored by both the red and white rock that characterize the canyon. Much of the drive follows the Virgin River, which we have to thank for all of this natural grandeur. This river, which the National Park Service likes to say has "the looks of a creek and the muscle of the Colorado," has been carving the canyon for more than thirteen million years.

Be sure to get out of your vehicle as often as possible. Don't miss the Court of the Patriarchs viewpoint, which overlooks the canyon at the foot of the Three Patriarchs—Abraham at 6,890 feet, Isaac at 6,825 feet, and Jacob at 6,831 feet. Near the northern end of the scenic drive is the Temple of Sinawava, a natural amphitheater centered by strong pillars known as The Altar and The Pulpit. No wonder those early Mormons thought this canyon looked churchlike!

LUNCH: It's time for lunch, and choices are many. Try a stop at the lodge, tuck into that packed picnic, or head back into Springdale for lunch at **Zion Park Gift and Deli,** which serves thick sandwiches on fresh-baked bread, ice cream, and baked goods (866 Zion Park Boulevard, Springdale, UT 84767; 435–772–3843). Inexpensive.

Afternoon

After lunch, it's time to get out of the car, now that you've got the lay of the land. Put on those comfortable shoes you had the foresight to bring along and explore the miles of trails mapped out in the park for all levels of fitness and energy. Novices might enjoy the Riverside Walk, which takes about an hour and a half and follows the river up to Zion Canyon Narrows, through hanging gardens of wildflowers during the spring and summer.

The Canyon Overlook Trail is an easy one-hour, 1-mile walk that ends at a particularly spectacular view of Zion Canyon and Pine Creek Canyon.

For something a little more strenuous but shorter—about an hour— consider the Emerald Pools Trail. This trail has two routes, with the lower ending at a pool and three waterfalls, the upper at a larger pool at the base of some pretty impressive cliffs.

For the truly fit—and somewhat brave, because there are steep cliffs and sheer drop-offs at times—Angels Landing shouldn't be missed. This hike takes about four hours but its summit is high above the canyon floor.

If **Kolob Arch** interests you, drive back out UT 9 to I–15 and head north to exit 40 and the park's Kolob Canyons entrance, where you'll find the **Kolob Canyons Visitor Center** and the Kolob Canyons viewpoint. This part of the park isn't as crowded as the Zion Canyon area—even at peak times—so you'll avoid the crowds. Particularly rewarding is a hike along the Kolob Arch Trail, which descends almost 700 feet to the base of Kolob Arch. Bear in mind, though, that this is a strenuous hike, very hot on a summer midday; figure about nine hours for its 14-mile length.

While you're hiking, keep an eye peeled for the abundant wildlife in the area, particularly birds; Zion National Park is home to 271 species (pick up a guide at the visitor center).

Another option is to bring along your bike or rent one at **Bike Zion** (1458 Zion Park Boulevard, Springdale; 435–772–3929; www.bikezion.com) and hit the **Pa'rus Trail,** which is both paved and free of vehicles. The Pa'rus Trail also is a great option for pedestrians, parents with strollers, and people who use wheelchairs.

DINNER: With all of this activity you'll no doubt work up a healthy appetite for dinner. The **Spotted Dog Cafe** at Flanigan's Inn (428 Zion Park Boulevard, Springdale, UT 84767; 435–772–3244; www.flanigans.com) offers local trout, Utah lamb, seafood, Black Angus beef, salads, and options for vegans. Moderate.

LODGING: Zion National Park Lodge (see above).

DAY 3

Morning

BREAKFAST: Have breakfast at the Zion National Park Lodge, or perhaps enjoy bumbleberry pancakes with bumbleberry syrup (we're still not sure what bumbleberries are, only that they're said to make you giggle) at the **Bumbleberry Inn** (897 Zion Park Boulevard, Springdale; 435–772–3522; www.bumbleberry.com). Inexpensive.

Then it's time to head back into Zion National Park for anything you may have missed the day before—perhaps the museum that's scheduled to open in 2002 with human history exhibits and a video presentation.

If you're interested in a way to catch anything you may have missed without adding insult to the injuries you inflicted on those poor sore muscles, stop by the **Zion Canyon Giant Screen Theatre** (145 Zion Park Boulevard, Springdale; 888–256–FILM; www.zioncanyontheatre.com) and its six-story screen, where you'll feel as though you're hanging from a 2,000-foot cliff.

Or, if you've had your fill of rocks for a little while, explore the little towns that surround the park. In Hurricane, which is west of Zion National Park on UT 9, you'll find the **Hurricane Valley Heritage Park, Pioneer and Indian Museum** (35 West State Street, 435–635–3245), which has displays about the Indians and early white settlers of Hurricane, including the first house in Hurricane, which was built as a granary.

Another option is to visit the ghost town of **Grafton.** To get there, take UT 9 through Springdale to Rockville, then turn south onto Bridge Lane, a side road that crosses the Virgin River on an old iron bridge. After the pavement ends, continue on and in 2 miles the road curves south; make a right turn there and continue parallel to the river to the ghost town. Among the sights are an old cemetery, its grave markers telling the poignant truth of life on the frontier in the 1860s, and a church/schoolhouse built in 1886.

Or spend more time in Springdale, with its truly surprising variety of galleries, gift shops, bookstores, and rock shops. Among them is the **Driftwood Gallery** (1515 Zion Park Boulevard; 435–772–3262), which features paintings, photography (including images of Zion Canyon by award-winning photographer David Pettit), and sculpture by local and regional artists, and **Fatali Gallery: Photography of the Southwest,** including the Zion Photographic Collection, (868 Zion Park Boulevard; 435–772–2422).

And if you really haven't gotten your fill of rocks, stop by **Zion Rock and Gem** (416 Zion Park Boulevard; 435–772–3436) for a few specimens from a collection including local rocks, gems, and fossils as well as exotic minerals—even amber with insects.

LUNCH: If the weather's pleasant (or even if it's not), consider having lunch al fresco at the **Switchback Grill** (1149 Zion Park Boulevard, Springdale, UT 84767; 435–772–3700; www.skybusiness.com/switchback/index.html), which offers dining indoors and out and specializes in flame-grilled cuisine, fresh fish, wood-fired pizza, and rotisserie chicken. Moderate.

After lunch, it's a leisurely three-and-a-half-hour drive from the canyons of Utah to the lights of Las Vegas. Just follow UT 9 West to I–15, take I–15 South and you're home.

THERE'S MORE

Cane Beds, Arizona

North Rim Cattle Co., HC-65, Box 420; (520) 875–8243. Guided tours and dude ranch, plus wild-West roundups. Guide service for photography and hunting.

Kanab, Utah

Best Friends Animal Sanctuary at Angel Canyon, U.S. Route 89; (435) 644–2001. At 350 acres, one of the largest sanctuaries in the country for abandoned and mistreated pets; set in a Jurassic-era canyon. Van tours of Dogtown, Catland, etc.

Moqui Cave, U.S. 89; (435) 644–2987. Dinosaur tracks (brought to the cave from their original site) and other artifacts.

Springdale, Utah

Bumbleberry Playhouse, 897 Zion Park Boulevard; (435) 772–3611. Cabaret-style melodramas with variety show following. Seasonal.

Zion National Park, Utah

Dixie College/O.C. Tanner Amphitheater Twilight Concert Series, on Zion Park Boulevard just outside park entrance; (435) 652–7994. Saturday night concerts in 2,000-seat outdoor amphitheater surrounded by the cliffs of Zion National Park. Memorial Day through Labor Day.

SPECIAL EVENTS

Springdale, Utah

Mid-March. St. Patrick's Day Parade and the Famous Green Jell-o Sculpture Contest, plus Celtic and Irish music; (888) 518–7070.

July. Fourth of July celebration, with flag ceremony, parade, Lions Club pancake breakfast, and fireworks show; (888) 518–7070.

Pioneer Days, celebrating pioneer heritage of Utah, with old-fashioned entertainment; (888) 518–7070.

October. Canyon Fest, with parade of arts and music festival; (888) 518–7070.

November. Butch Cassidy 10K Run and 5K Walk; (888) 518–7070.

December. Christmas Crafts Fair; (888) 518–7070.

Christmas parade through Valley of the Lights; (888) 518–7070.

OTHER RECOMMENDED RESTAURANTS AND LODGINGS

Springdale, Utah

Best Western Zion Park Inn and Conference Center, P.O. Box 800; (435) 772–3200 or (800) 934–7275.

Bit and Spur Mexican Restaurant and Saloon, 1212 Zion Park Boulevard; (435) 772–3498. Garden or indoor dining; specializes in Mexican cuisine.

Cliffrose Lodge and Gardens, 281 Zion Park Boulevard; (435) 772–3234 or (800) 243–8824. Five acres with lawns, gardens, and large pool.

Flanigan's Inn, 428 Zion Park Boulevard; (435) 772–3244. Rustic wood lodge with views.

Mean Bean Coffee House, 932 Zion Park Boulevard; (435) 772–0654. Coffees and fresh pastries.

Novel House Inn at Zion, 73 Paradise Road, P.O. Box 188; (435) 772–3650. Ten guest rooms, each themed to a well-known author.

Pioneer Lodge, 838 Zion Park Boulevard; (888) 772–3233. Thirty-nine rooms plus one- and three-bedroom apartments. Heated pool, indoor hot tub.

Red Rock Inn, 998 Zion Park Boulevard; (435) 772–3139. Five guest cottages; in-room whirlpool tubs or suite with private outdoor hot tub.

The Theatre Deli, 145 Zion Park Boulevard; (435) 772–2400. Sandwiches, soups, frozen yogurt; movie specials.

Watchman Cafe, 445 Zion Park Boulevard; (435) 772–3678. Coffees, pastries, soups, sandwiches.

Zion Canyon Campground, Market and Motel, 479 Zion Park Boulevard; (435) 772–3237. Full-service RV park/campground with pool, laundry, and motel.

Zion Pizza and Noodle Company, 868 Zion Park Boulevard; (435) 772–3815. Pizza, pastas, and salads, with microbrews on tap.

Virgin, Utah

Snow Family Guest Ranch Bed and Breakfast, 633 East Highway 9, P.O. Box 790190; (435) 635–2500 or (877) 655–7669. Twelve-acre horse ranch in shadows of Zion National Park.

FOR MORE INFORMATION

Hurricane Valley Chamber of Commerce, 95 South Main Street, P.O. Box 101, Hurricane, UT 84737; (435) 635–3402.

Zion Canyon Chamber of Commerce, P.O. Box 331, Springdale, UT 84767; (888) 518–7070.

Zion National Park, Springdale, UT 84767-1099; (435) 772–3256; www. nps.gov/zion.

Bryce Canyon National Park

TOUGH FOR FARMING,

GREAT FOR HIKING

2 NIGHTS

Hoodoos and hiking • Scenic rock formations
Horseback riding • Romantic getaway

They're called "hoodoos," these fanciful, pillar-shaped formations of stone, and they give Bryce Canyon—and, by extension, Bryce Canyon National Park—its unique character.

Actually, Bryce isn't a canyon at all, but a series of horseshoe-shaped natural amphitheaters that Mother Nature, working in collusion with the Paria River, carved in the Paunsaugunt Plateau. The canyon (we'll call it that to make things a little easier) encompasses an amazing array of colors: red, yellow, brown—even lavender—thanks to the iron oxides in the rock.

But it's the hoodoos and other rock formations that prompt most of our fascination with Bryce Canyon, the smallest of Utah's national parks at just 35,835 acres. For one man—Ebenezer Bryce, the Mormon settler for whom the canyon was named—that fascination was more like frustration. Trying to farm and raise cattle in this crazy canyon with its almost mazelike nature prompted Bryce to comment that it was "a hell of a place to lose a cow."

True enough, but you won't have to worry about that, will you? And with the breathtaking scenery, temperate climate, and wealth of recreational opportunities in the Bryce Canyon area, it seems that for Las Vegans, it's a heck of a place for a quick escape and an easy trip from Zion National Park, profiled in this chapter in Escape Three.

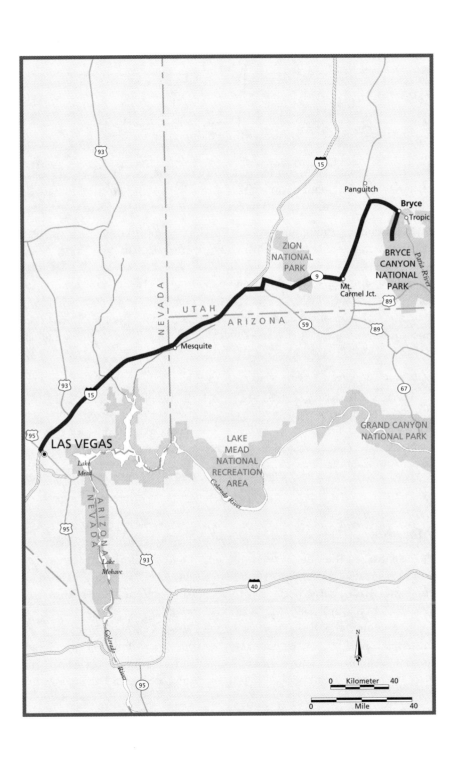

93

15

Panguitch

Bryce

Tropic

ZION
NATIONAL
PARK

9

BRYCE
CANYON
NATIONAL
PARK

Paria River

Mt.
Carmel Jct.

89

NEVADA

UTAH

ARIZONA

59

89

Mesquite

93

15

67

95

LAS VEGAS

Lake
Mead

LAKE
MEAD
NATIONAL
RECREATION
AREA

Colorado River

GRAND CANYON
NATIONAL PARK

ARIZONA
NEVADA

95

Lake
Mohave

93

40

Colorado River

95

N

0   Kilometer   40

0   Mile   40

DAY 1

Afternoon

Bryce Canyon is about 250 miles—around a four-hour drive—from Las Vegas, which makes it a great weekend getaway; plan on a Friday afternoon departure.

Take Interstate 15 North for about 125 miles to exit 16. Then take Utah Route 9 West for about 57 miles, then U.S. Highway 89 North for about 43 miles. Last, take Utah Route 12 West to Utah Route 63 to the park entrance.

DINNER: Before turning off onto UT 12, continue north 6 miles to the town of Panguitch and stop at the **Cowboy's Smokehouse** (95 North Main; 435–676–8030) for barbecue that includes mesquite-smoked brisket, ribs, chicken, and turkey, served up among Western artifacts and stuffed game trophies. Moderate. Consider grabbing enough takeout for a box lunch as you tour the park the following day, or pick up sandwiches from **C-Stop Pizza and Deli** (561 East Center; 435–676–8366), which sells tacos, pizzas, and salads as well as deli sandwiches.

LODGING: **Bryce Canyon Lodge** (435–834–5361; www.amfac.com; rates from $90 to $99) has 114 rooms in a fairly rustic (read: no TVs) restored 1924-era building that's on the National Historic Register. The lodge is furnished with reproduction hickory furniture and is within walking distance of a rim overlook. Suites and cabins also are available; the cabins have gas fireplaces. Reservations should be made well in advance during the busy summer season.

DAY 2

Morning

BREAKFAST: You'll no doubt want to spend the day exploring Bryce Canyon National Park, so a convenient spot for breakfast is the **Dining Room at Bryce Canyon Lodge** (435–834–5361). Selections include skillet breakfasts, omelets, a buffet, and flapjacks with Bryceberry compote. Moderate.

If you didn't stop the night before at the **Visitor Center** (435–834–5322), make that a priority now. It's a good place to get oriented to the park through general information, a slide show, a museum, and printed brochures. (The **Sunrise Nature Center**, open during the summer, also has information and exhibits.)

If you visit Bryce Canyon between late May and late September, consider taking one of the park's shuttles, which serve to reduce both the amount of traffic in the canyon and the pollution that traffic inevitably brings. While you'll have to wait for a shuttle occasionally, you're more likely to have to wait for a parking space if you drive your own vehicle and visit during peak periods, as there's an average of one parking space for every four vehicles that enter the park. The park entrance fee is $20 per vehicle or $15 if you take the shuttle.

Leave your car outside the park at the Shuttle Staging Area at UT 12 and UT 63; the Blue Line shuttle will take you to the Visitor Center inside the park. Transfer to a Red Line shuttle to take in the most famous viewpoints and most scenic trailheads in the Main Amphitheater section of the park. (The Green Line shuttle tours the south part of the park, providing access to backcountry trailheads; reservations for it must be made in advance at the Visitor Center.)

The shuttle stops at canyon viewpoints every ten to fifteen minutes. If you're taking a shuttle or making the drive yourself—the latter especially during the late-fall to late-spring months—there are numerous viewpoints you won't want to miss, including Fairyland Point; Sunset, Sunrise, and Paria Points (which ring Bryce Amphitheater, the largest in the park) and Rainbow Point, the southernmost point, from which it's possible to see 90 miles on a clear day.

If you're driving, a good way to see the park is to make the 18-mile drive to Rainbow Point and stop at the rest of the thirteen viewpoints on the way back.

LUNCH: Time for that box lunch you packed the night before; there are picnic tables at Rainbow Point, Sunset Point and Sunrise Point. If you didn't pack one and choose not to leave the park for lunch, your only option is the **Dining Room at the Bryce Canyon Lodge** (435–834–5361), but rest assured that the lunch offerings there are interesting, such as jalapeño hummus with chips, mozzarella and tomato salad with fresh basil, Bryce beef stew, and a broiled tuna sandwich. Moderate.

Afternoon

For a closer look at the canyons, hike the Amphitheater trail, an easy 1-mile round-trip section of the Rim Trail extending between Sunset and Sunrise Points. If you're feeling a little more ambitious—and have sufficient health and physical condition to be up to the challenge—take a longer section of the

Arch Rock, Bryce Canyon National Park

Rim Trail, which stretches more than 5 miles between Bryce and Fairyland Points. Be aware that this section of the trail is pretty steep.

There are also a number of trails that wind down through the rock formations below the canyon rims; remember, though, that what goes down must also come up, and the return trip can be strenuous, so be sure to wear sturdy hiking boots and carry lots of water. The Navajo Loop is 1.5 miles round-trip, Queen's Garden is just short of 2 miles, the Peekaboo Loop (which is also a horse trail) has 5- and 7-mile options, and the Fairyland Loop is 8 miles round-trip.

If you're really ambitious, there's the 23-mile **Under-the-Rim Trail** between Bryce and Rainbow Point, which has eight backcountry campsites, and the 9-mile Riggs Spring Loop Trail with four backcountry campsites; backcountry permits are required for these hikes.

If it's winter, consider cross-country skiing (bring your own equipment or rent it outside the park) or snowshoeing. Snowshoes are loaned at the Visitor Center at no charge whenever the snow is 18 inches deep or more.

If you're not feeling quite so ambitious but would like to get a closer look at the canyon, you might try a horseback ride led by a wrangler (Bryce Canyon Lodge, 435–834–5500 or contact **Canyon Trail Rides,** 435–679–8665). Available during mornings or afternoons April through October, the two-hour rides go to the floor of Bryce Canyon and loop back along the rim, winding through rock formations. Half-day trips also are available.

DINNER: The Dining Room at Bryce Canyon Lodge (435–834–5361) has a far more creative menu than you might expect in a national park lodge. Dinner entrees might include Utah red trout with lemon *beurre blanc,* pork loin with Bryceberry-sage sauce, and Yovimpa pork rellenos. Moderate.

LODGING: Bryce Canyon Lodge (see above).

DAY 3

Morning

BREAKFAST: Have breakfast at **The Hungry Coyote** (World Host Bryce Valley Inn, 200 North Main Street, Tropic, UT 84776; 435–679–8822), where you'll find traditional favorites.

Then continue along UT 12 to **Grand Staircase–Escalante National Monument** (435–826–4291; www.ut.blm.gov/monument). Stop in at the **Escalante Interagency Visitor Center** (755 West Main Street; 435–826–5499) for information on touring.

The nation's newest national monument is 1.7 million acres and includes Escalante Natural Bridge, which is 130 high and 100 feet across (and reached via a 2-mile hike along the Escalante River), and Grosvenor Arch, which isn't an arch at all but a group of them. Various areas of the national monument feature other rock formations, cliffs, and red-rock canyons, and major archeological and paleontological sites, including fossils, petrified wood, rock art, and prehistoric dwellings. One fairly recent development was the discovery of fossil skin impressions on a hadrosaur dinosaur skeleton—an extremely rare find. More contemporary wildlife frequently seen in the area include bighorn sheep, bears, mountain lions, bald eagles, peregrine falcons, and hundreds of other species of birds.

If you go north on UT 12 to US 89 and then south on Utah Route 143, you'll find **Panguitch Lake.** *Panguitch* means "big fish" in Paiute, and the lake is known for its rainbow, brook, cutthroat, and German brown trout. The lake also is a place to find boat and mountain-bike rentals, boat ramps, and campgrounds; hiking, cross-country skiing, and photography are popular pastimes here as well.

LUNCH: The **Flying M Restaurant** (614 North Main Street, Panguitch, UT 84759; 435–676–8008) serves hot and cold sandwiches, salads, and homemade pies in a casual, family-oriented atmosphere. Inexpensive.

Time to return to Las Vegas. Leave by early Sunday afternoon, follow UT 143 and Utah Route 14 back to I–15 South, and you should arrive home by early evening.

THERE'S MORE

Boulder, Utah

Boulder Mountain Ranch, Hell's Backbone Road; (435) 335–7480. Dude ranch with trail rides.

Escalante Canyon Outfitters, P.O. Box 1330; (435) 335–7311. Walking trips (supplied by horse) through local canyons.

Bryce, Utah

B Bar D Covered Wagon Co., 1089 West Main Street; (435) 254–4452 or (435) 834–5202. Horse-drawn covered wagon ride, cowboy dinner, country music and dance show.

Bryce Canyon Scenic Tours, P.O. Box 640025; (800) 432–5383 or (435) 834–5200. One-hour, three-hour, one-day, and three-day ATV tours, plus bus tours.

Cannonville, Utah

Kodachrome Basin State Park, 9 miles south of Utah Route 12; (435) 679–8562. Panorama of tall sandstone chimneys, rocks, and coves in 2,240-acre park.

Escalante, Utah

Escalante Petrified Forest State Park, off Utah Route 12; (435) 826–4466. State's highest concentration of accessible petrified wood; also boating, fishing, swimming.

Hatch, Utah

Daughters of Utah Pioneer Museum, U.S. 89; (435) 735–4207 or (435) 735–4296. Open by appointment, the museum displays antiques and relics of local pioneers.

Panguitch, Utah

Paunsagunt Western Wildlife Museum, 250 East Center Street; (435) 676–2500. More than 400 mounted North American animals (some shown in natural habitat) plus specimens from Europe, Africa, and India, as well as American Indian artifacts.

Scenic Rim Trail Rides, P.O. Box 58; (435) 679–8761 or (800) 679–5859. Hourly and day rides in Bryce Canyon region.

SPECIAL EVENTS

Antinomy, Utah

June. Rockin' R Ranch Authentic Cattle Drive; (801) 733–9538; www.rocknrranch.com. Cattle are rounded up, branded, and driven onto Boulder Mountain (return roundup in **August**).

Bryce, Utah

January. Utah Winter Games X-C Ski Marathon; (800) 444–6689 or (435) 676–8826.

February. Bryce Canyon Winter Festival, with ski races, ski archery, snowshoe tours and races, kids' events, entertainment, and more; (435) 834–5341 or (800) 468–8660.

June–September. Bryce Canyon Country Rodeo; (800) 444–6689 or (435) 676–8826.

August. Bryce Canyon Rim Run; (435) 834–5341, ext. 198 or (800) 468–8660. 5-mile trail run/walk is one of Utah's most scenic races, overlooking Bryce Canyon and passing through forests of ponderosa pines.

Cannonville, Utah

July. Annual Old Time Fiddlers & Bear Festival; (800) 444–6689 or (435) 676–8826. Includes dinner and fiddlers concerts.

Escalante, Utah

May. Escalante Center Festival and 10K Run; (435) 826–4556.

June. Annual Wide Hollow Fishing Derby at Petrified Forest State Park; (435) 826–5499.

July. Soap Box Derby and Pancake Breakfast; (435) 826–4889.

October. Potato Festival/Harvest Days/Art in the Park; (435) 826–4889.

Panguitch, Utah

June. Annual Quilt Walk Festival; (435) 676–8585. Quilt show, classes, theater.

Pioneer Home Tour; (435) 676–8585. Town-wide event.

Chariots in the Sky Balloon Festival; (435) 676–8585. Includes Saturday Evening Glow.

Horse races; (800) 444–6689 or (435) 676–8826.

July. Fourth of July Celebration; (435) 676–8585. Parade, barbecue dinner, games, youth rodeo, dance, fireworks.

Pioneer Day Celebration; (435) 676–8585. Parade, barbecue, children's races, High School Invitational Rodeo.

August. Garfield County Fair; (435) 676–8585. Carnival, rodeo, barbecue dinner, entertainment.

Bryce Valley/Panguitch High School Rodeo; (435) 676–8585.

December. Christmas in the Country; (435) 676–2418. Christmas home tours, parade, Christmas tree-lighting program, Santa visit.

Tropic, Utah

July. Fourth of July Celebration; (800) 444–6689 or (435) 676–1160. Includes races and dance.

Pioneer Day Celebration; (800) 444–6689 or (435) 676–1160. Parade, races, and more.

OTHER RECOMMENDED RESTAURANTS AND LODGINGS

Bryce, Utah

Best Western Ruby's Inn, Utah Route 63; (435) 834–5341. Rooms (some with whirlpool) and suites in casual Western atmosphere; family-owned and -operated since 1916.

Panguitch, Utah

Bryce Way Motel, 429 North Main Street; (800) 225–6534 or (435) 676–2400. One- and two-bedroom units and pool.

Buffalo Java, 47 North Main Street; (801) 676–8900. Veggie sandwiches, bagels, and coffees.

Color Country Motel, 526 North Main Street; (435) 676–2386 or (800) 225–6518. Newly refurbished motel with new pool and spa.

Grandma Tina's Spaghetti House, 523 North Main Street; (435) 676–2377. Italian food and a "secret" spaghetti sauce; children's and seniors' menus.

Panguitch Inn, 50 North Main Street; (435) 676–8871. Twenty-four rooms in restored building that dates to 1920s.

Tropic, Utah

Bryce Canyon Inn, 21 North Main Street; (435) 679–8502 or (800) 592–1468.

The Canyon Livery Bed and Breakfast, 50 South 660 West; (888) 889–8910 or (435) 679–8780. Homemade foods; windows overlooking Bryce Canyon. Horse boarding available.

Fox's Bryce Trails Bed and Breakfast, 1001 West Bryce Way; (435) 679–8700. Six rooms in contemporary-styled building.

Francisco Farm Bed and Breakfast Inn, 51 Francisco Lane; (435) 679–8721. Three rooms in homey log home in scenic area with farm animals.

The Hungry Coyote, World Host Bryce Valley Inn, 199 North Main Street; (435) 679–8822. Western-style food; indoor or outdoor dining.

FOR MORE INFORMATION

Bryce Canyon National Park, P.O. Box 170001, Bryce Canyon, UT 84717-0001; (435) 834–5322; www.nps.gov/brca.

Garfield Country Travel Council, P.O. Box 200, Panguitch, UT 84759; (800) 444–6689 or (435) 676–8826; www.brycecanyoncountry.com.

MOUNTAIN

Cedar City

TO THE MOUNTAINS!

2 NIGHTS

Skiing • Hiking • Bed-and-breakfasts • Shakespearean theater

Ask any group of Las Vegans of more than a few years' residence about the best place to go skiing in winter or escape the heat in summer, and you'll hear a common refrain: Cedar City.

Cedar City is in southwestern Utah, and at an elevation of more than 6,000 feet, it's almost always 15 to 20 degrees cooler than Las Vegas. Brian Head ski resort, Utah's highest Alpine resort at 9,600 feet, opens for business in mid-November most years—sometimes even earlier—and averages an astounding 450 inches of Utah powder each year.

Like much of the West, Cedar City's settlement by Europeans occurred fairly late by eastern standards. In 1851, a group of Mormon-convert miners arrived from Parowan, 20 miles away, to establish an iron works in the area. The men built small log homes, situating them in the manner of a fort, and brought their families from Parowan. The settlement was on its way.

But not so fast. There were a few problems to deal with in the early years, like the Walker Indian War of 1853, which prompted the settlers to move to a new site on the other side of Coal Creek. That site, as it turned out, was in the creek's flood plain; another move was in order. By 1855, the pioneers finally had settled in on the current Cedar City town site.

Oh, but more changes awaited them. The iron works was defunct by 1858, though iron mining in the area continued until the 1980s. Losing their main industry, the settlers turned to agriculture, which suited them just fine for about fifty years. But the 1928 arrival of the railroad in the area, which exposed the rest of the world to the glories of Utah's nearby national parks,

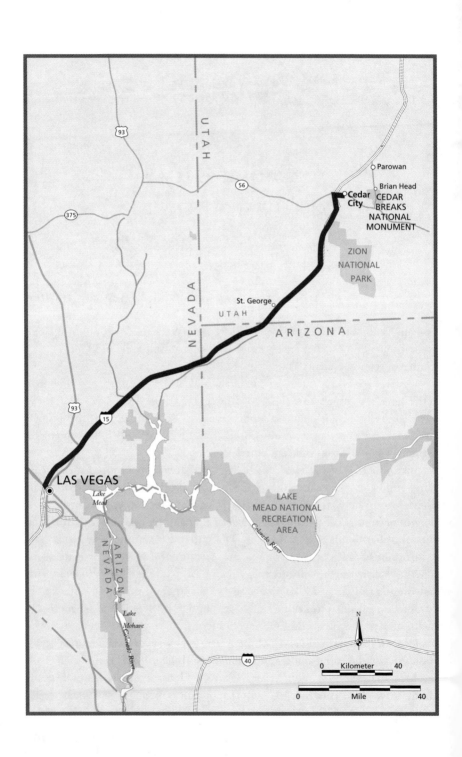

93

UTAH

56

375

NEVADA

93   15

LAS VEGAS

Lake
Mead

Lake
Mohave

Colorado River

ARIZONA
NEVADA

40

○ Parowan

○ Brian Head
Cedar   CEDAR
City   BREAKS
        NATIONAL
        MONUMENT

ZION
NATIONAL
PARK

St. George ○

UTAH

ARIZONA

LAKE
MEAD NATIONAL
RECREATION
AREA

Colorado River

N

0   Kilometer   40

0   Mile   40

Bryce Canyon and Zion, enabled Cedar City to re-invent itself once again, as the "Gateway to the Parks."

Today, tourism remains Cedar City's Number 1 industry, and a first-time visitor is quick to figure out why: Its small-town charm, prodigious natural beauty, cool climate, and variety of activities make Cedar City a top choice for a quick escape.

DAY 1

Afternoon

Cedar City is about 170 miles from Las Vegas, straight up Interstate 15 North, for a driving time of less than three hours—another reason it's such a popular destination for Las Vegas residents.

DINNER: Cedar City's not exactly what you'd call urban, but to escape even more into the pine forests that surround it, drive just 2 miles east on Utah State 14 to **Rusty's Ranch House** (435–586–3839), which serves steak, seafood, chicken, and ribs in a Western setting that features big, open rooms decorated with mounted game. Moderate.

Evening

If it's summer or fall, plan ahead and get tickets for the **Utah Shakespearean Festival** (351 West Center Street; (435–586–7878 or 800–PLAYTIX; www.bard.org), which presents works by William Shakespeare and other playwrights during its summer season from June through early September and non-Shakespearean works from mid-September through late October.

The festival, which won a Tony Award in 2000 for Outstanding Regional Theater, is presented in three venues during the summer—the open-air Elizabethan-style Adams Shakespearean Theater, the traditional Randall L. Jones Theatre and the smaller Auditorium Theatre. During the fall season, just the Randall L. Jones Theatre is used.

The festival always combines the classic and popular; a recent summer season included *The Tempest, The Two Gentlemen of Verona, Julius Caesar, The Pirates of Penzance, Arsenic and Old Lace,* and *Ah, Wilderness,* while a recent fall season featured *The Fantasticks* and *Around the World in 80 Days.*

Another option for dinner is the festival's **The Royal Feaste** (435–586–7878), between matinee and evening performances, which is part theater, part dinner.

LODGING: It's called **The Big Yellow Inn Bed and Breakfast,** and it's indeed both big and yellow. The sprawling Georgian-revival home a block from the Utah Shakespearean Festival (234 South 300 West, Cedar City, UT 84720; 435–586–0960; www.bigyellowinn.com; rates from $89 to $180) has eleven air-conditioned rooms with private baths and a 900-square-foot gable suite. A grand staircase, eight fireplaces, three sitting rooms, porches, and balconies all add to a feeling that somehow blends grandeur and comfort. And you can walk back to the inn after the play.

DAY 2

Morning

BREAKFAST: The Big Yellow Inn provides a full breakfast, so stock up; you've got a full day ahead of you.

If you attended the Shakespearean festival the night before, you spent some time in a theater; now you can spend some time in an amphitheater—a natural venue more than 2,000 feet deep and more than 3 miles in diameter. To reach **Cedar Breaks National Monument** (435–586–9451; www.nps.gov/cebr) from Cedar City, take a short drive east on UT 14 and north on Utah Route 148 (if the weather's good and the roads are clear), or a slightly longer drive north on I–15 to Parowan and then south on Utah Route 143 (especially in winter).

It's been said that if Cedar Breaks were anywhere else, where it wasn't overshadowed by the nearby Zion and Bryce Canyon National Parks, it would be considered one of the world's scenic wonders, and it's true. Cedar Breaks is inevitably compared to its big brothers to the east, but this smaller park has its own distinctive (and breathtaking) beauty.

The amphitheater was eroded over millions of years out of the region's Pink Cliffs, with erosion and sedimentation forming its arches, spires, and columns, and mineral content contributing its characteristic reds, yellows, and purples.

Start your visit at the **Visitor Center,** which is off UT 148 toward the southern end of the park. There you'll find maps, brochures, and books that explain the history, geology, and flora and fauna of Cedar Breaks.

The 5-mile scenic drive that heads north through the park includes a number of overlooks providing various perspectives of the massive amphitheater, and there are hiking trails if you'd like to get out of the car and stretch your legs. The 2-mile **Alpine Pond Trail** is a circular route that leads hikers

The view from Brian Head Overlook, Cedar City

to a forest glade and a pond, while the **Ramparts Trail,** also 2 miles, passes ancient bristlecone pines and ends at an overlook. Camping and picnicking are other options, as is cross-country skiing during winter.

Another option for outdoor activity is **Brian Head** (435–677–2810 or 888–677–2810; www.brianheadutah.com) on UT 143 just north of Cedar Breaks. Brian Head primarily is known as a ski resort from November through April, but it is home to plenty of activity during the rest of the year, too. Scenic chair-lift rides are available from early July through late September, and mountain bikers can take a chair lift to access the on-slope trails at the Mountain Bike Park or use more than 60 miles of backcountry trails. Guided rides, bike rentals, and round-trip shuttle service are offered.

Brian Head also offers horseback riding from July through early September, Jeep tours, and fishing.

LUNCH: The **Mountain View Cafe** (508 North Highway 143, Brian Head, UT 84719; 435–677–2411) in Brian Head offers sandwiches, hamburgers, salads, and soups. Eat in, or consider packing a picnic and taking it along with you to one of the many scenic spots in the Cedar City area. Moderate.

Afternoon

You've had a good look at the scenic beauty of the Cedar City area; now get some insight into the region's history.

A good place to start is **Parowan,** a hamlet of about 1,900 people that's reached by taking UT 143 North out of Brian Head. For such a little town Parowan's got a surprising number of museums, among them the **Mountain View Museum** (10 South 600 West; 435–477–8100), a private collection on a working ranch where Belgian and Percheron horses are bred. The museum has restored wagons, coaches, and carriages, including a number of specialty vehicles—a hearse, a doctor's buggy, an Amish buggy, and a wedding carriage among them. There's a blacksmith shop and gun collection, too.

Also in Parowan you'll find the **Jesse North Smith Home Museum** (35 West 100 South; 435–477–8190), a two-story 1850s home of red adobe brick; the **Rock Church Museum** (Main Street on Town Square between Center and 100 South; 435–477–8190), an 1860s church inspired by the Salt Lake City Tabernacle that has also served as town hall, school building, and tourist camp; and the **Dr. Priddy Meeks Cabin Museum** (on 400 West, north of Center Street; 435–477–8190), home of the first doctor in southern Utah. (Note that these museums are open only Monday through Saturday from Memorial Day to Labor Day.)

Back in Cedar City (which you'll reach by taking UT 143 to I–15 and heading south) you'll find **Iron Mission State Park** (585 North Main Street; 435–586–9290; parks.state.ut.us/parks/www1/iron.htm), which has the largest collection of horse-drawn vehicles west of the Mississippi River and details the development of Iron County since the 1850s.

To see things the way the pioneers did, follow the walking trail at the **Coal Creek Trail/Cedar Canyon Park** (Utah Route 14; 435–865–9223), a 3-mile round-trip paved trail along the banks of Coal Creek up into Cedar Canyon. The trail provides benches and drinking fountains—something those pioneers no doubt would have appreciated.

DINNER: La Fiesta Mexican Restaurant and Cantina (890 North Main Street, Cedar City; 435–586–4646) bills itself as "the lively place across from the cemetery" and offers a full line of Mexican and Tex-Mex favorites. Inexpensive.

LODGING: The Big Yellow Inn Bed and Breakfast (see above).

DAY 3

Morning

BREAKFAST: Have breakfast at the Big Yellow Inn or maybe at **Sullivan's Cafe** (301 South Main Street; 435–586–6761), where the menu includes all-American favorites such as bacon and eggs or pancakes. Moderate.

Take in another part of southern Utah and head for home at the same time; drive south on I–15 to **St. George.**

The St. George area was dubbed "Dixie" by pioneers because it reminded them of the South—the climate was so mild. That was the source of the name of nearby **Dixie National Forest** (accessed off I–15; 435–865–3700; www.fs.fed.us/dxnf) and also inspired none other than Brigham Young, a leader of the Mormon Church, to make it the site of his summer home.

Visitors can tour **Brigham Young's Winter Home** today (200 North 50 West; 435–673–2517), seeing his parlor, bedrooms, and children's room, which contain some of his possessions, and stroll through his garden, complete with gazebo.

Also in the area is the **Jacob Hamblin Home,** just west of St. George in tiny St. Clara (west on Sunset Boulevard from St. George; 435–673–2161). Hamblin was a missionary to the local Indians in the 1860s, and built his home of rocks washed up by a flood. He later moved to Kanab with his wives—note the plural—and children.

North of St. George is the ghost town of **Silver Reef,** which can be found by taking I–15 North to the Leeds exit, then driving through town and following a dirt road for 2 miles. Silver ore was found in the sandstone at Silver Reef in the 1860s, and a town of 1,500 people and forty businesses sprang up, producing more than $10 million in silver before the mines closed at the turn of the century. The old Wells Fargo building (complete with small museum) remains, along with dilapidated mining and railroad equipment.

LUNCH: Have lunch or Sunday brunch at the **Fairway Grill** (430 East St. George Boulevard, St. George, UT 84770; 435–656-4448), where the food is homemade, including fresh-baked rolls and super chicken-fried steak. Moderate.

Then it's back down I–15 for the short trip back to Las Vegas.

THERE'S MORE

Cedar City, Utah

Cedar Ridge 18 Hole Golf Course, 200 East 900 North Street; (435) 586–2869. Clubhouse, driving range, and rentals.

Scenic Southern Utah Tours, 115 North Main Street; (435) 867–8690 or (888) 404–8687. Half- and full-day tours to area attractions.

Southern Utah University Special Collections, SUU Library, 351 West Center Street; (435) 586–7945. Rare books by regional authors, plus Cedar City memorabilia and Native arts and crafts.

St. George, Utah

Daughters of Pioneers Museum, 143 North 100 East Street; (435) 628–7274. Memorabilia from the era 1847–1870.

Snow Canyon State Park, Utah Route 18; (435) 628–2255. Black lava formations; pictographs. Camping available.

SPECIAL EVENTS

Brian Head, Utah

February. Brian Head Resort Fireworks and Torchlight Parade, celebrating President's Day holiday; (435) 677–2035.

Cedar City, Utah

March. Canyon Country Western Arts Festival, with potters, quilters, and other craftspeople, plus cowboy poetry and Western music; (435) 586–4484.

June. Paiute Restoration Gathering and Pow-Wow, plus vendors selling arts and crafts, parade, dinner, and talent night; (435) 586–1112.

Utah Summer Games, showcasing athletic talents of Utah residents, Cedar City and Parowan; (435) 865–8421.

July. Annual Mid-Summer Renaissance Faire, with food, vendors, games, exhibits, and entertainment; (435) 586–3711.

Parowan, Utah

April. Annual Spring Musical, showcasing talents of local residents; (435) 477–1032.

May. Walking Tour of Parowan, including Parowan Cemetery (is Butch Cassidy buried in the Parker family plot?); (435) 477–1032.

June. Summer Solstice Observation at Parowan Gap; (435) 477–1032.

August. Iron County Fair; (435) 477–8380.

September. Parowan Heritage Invitational, with draft-horse show competition, cowboy poetry, vendors, and a concert; (435) 477–1032.

OTHER RECOMMENDED RESTAURANTS AND LODGINGS

Cedar City, Utah

Adriana's Restaurant, 100 South 100 West; (435) 865–1234. Homebaked breads, Old-World charm.

Baker House Bed and Breakfast, 1800 Royal Hunter Drive; (435) 867–5695 or (888) 611–8181. Five bedrooms with private baths, whirlpool tubs, and gas fireplaces, plus top-level honeymoon suite.

Garden Cottage Bed and Breakfast, 16 North 200 West; (435) 586–4919. Home surrounded by English garden with climbing roses. Cottage has four air-conditioned rooms filled with antiques, and private baths.

Stratford Bed and Breakfast, 161 South 200 West; (702) 898–5704 or (877) 530–5280. Three-bedroom, two-bath bungalow with individually themed rooms.

Sulli's Steak House, 301 South Main Street; (435) 586–6761. Steaks, seafood, and pasta.

Willow Glen Inn B&B Conference and Reception Center, 3308 North Bulldog Road; (435) 586–3275. On the outskirts of Cedar City, on a ten-acre farm. Twelve rooms, some with kitchenettes.

Parowan, Utah

Adams Historic Home Bed and Breakfast, 94 North 100 East; (435) 477–8295. Restored 1870s home with three bedrooms with private baths, plus The Grainery with kitchenette.

St. George, Utah

Claim Jumper Steak House, 1110 South Bluff Street; (435) 674–7800. Steaks and seafood served in a cowboy atmosphere.

FOR MORE INFORMATION

Brian Head Chamber of Commerce and Visitor Services, 56 North Highway 143, Brian Head, UT 84719; (435) 677–2819 or (888) 677–2810; www.brianheadutah.com.

Cedar City Area Chamber of Commerce, 581 North Main Street, Cedar City, UT 84720; (435) 586–4484; www.chambercedarcity.org.

Iron County Tourism and Convention Bureau, P.O. Box 1007, Cedar City, UT 84720; (800) 354–4849; www.scenicsouthernutah.com.

Parowan Visitors Center, 73 North Main Street, Parowan, UT 84761; (435) 477–1032; www.parawan.org.

ESCAPE SIX

MOUNTAIN

Big Bear Lake

AN ACTIVE RESORT AREA

NESTLED IN THE PINES

2 NIGHTS

Pine forests • Filmmaking • Skiing • Mountain biking
Fishing • Hiking • Alpine slide • Quiet châteaux

Las Vegas has more than its share of natural beauty—soaring mountain peaks, red-rock formations, the majestic Lake Mead. But for the most part, "getting away from it all" in Las Vegas means going out into the desert. And that's exactly why a weekend getaway to Big Bear Lake, California, is so refreshing—in more ways than one.

Big Bear Valley's first known inhabitants were the Serrano Indians, more than 3,000 years ago. Thousands of years later, Benjamin D. Wilson was pursuing a different tribe of natives when, in 1845, he happened upon the valley and gave it its name. History records Wilson proclaiming that "the place was alive with bears!"

Time sure had its cycles in the Big Bear area. Fifteen years after Wilson's "discovery," William Holcomb was hunting some of those bears when he happened upon gold, launching Southern California's biggest gold rush. The gold rush brought people, of course, and change to the land. A dam constructed in 1884 prompted the construction of the first hotel in 1888.

It didn't take Hollywood filmmakers long to stake their own claim on the soaring pine-covered mountains that surround Big Bear Valley and its namesake lake. The first movie to be filmed there was *The Call of the North* in 1914; others included *Paint Your Wagon, The Parent Trap, Yukon Gold,* and *Dr. Doolittle.*

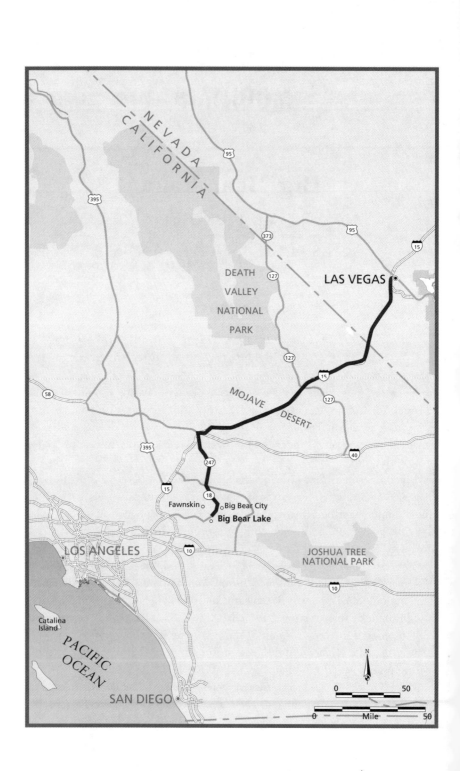

And even today, while you're in a restaurant waiting for your breakfast to arrive, you're likely to hear some guy on a cell phone working on a movie-development deal.

It's no surprise that Big Bear occasionally has been called upon to stand in for the forests of the Pacific Northwest, for it has much of the same scenic appeal. And just as it didn't take long for Hollywood to discover Big Bear as a filming opportunity, it didn't take Southern Californians long to discover it as a great place to literally chill out. It's no wonder that the Big Bear Lake Resort Association's slogan is, "It's cooler up here;" summer temperatures average 72 degrees during the day, 45 at night; winter temperatures average in the low 40s during the day and the mid-20s at night.

But as Big Bear is just three and a half to four hours from Las Vegas, we're always moved to ask: Why let Californians have all the fun?

DAY 1

Afternoon

At about 230 miles from Las Vegas, Big Bear Lake's relatively close proximity makes it great for a Friday afternoon departure. Head south on Interstate 15 about 180 miles into Barstow and follow the signs for California Route 247 South to California Route 18 South to California Route 38. Take the Stanfield Cutoff to Big Bear Boulevard and then turn left onto Moonridge Way, following that to Moonridge Road.

DINNER: The Captain's Anchorage (42148 Moonridge Road, Big Bear Lake, CA 92315; 909–866–3997) is a colorful spot serving steaks, prime rib, king crab, lobster, and desserts (including the whimsically named Shipwreck and its smaller version, the Baby Wreck). Opened in 1947, the Captain's Anchorage once was owned by actor Andy Devine and currently is occupied by a ghost named George. Moderate.

LODGING: The **Holiday Inn Big Bear Chateau** (42200 Moonridge Road, Big Bear Lake, CA 92315; 909–866–6666 or 800–232–7466; www.big bearinn.com; rates from $119 to $279) is a charming European-style hotel that's almost completely surrounded by pines—and 7,200 feet above sea level. Rooms have gas fireplaces that light at the touch of a switch, marble bathrooms, balconies, and some antiques; rooms with two-person spas also are available.

Big Bear Lake

DAY 2

Morning

BREAKFAST: Boo Bear's Den (572 Pine Knot, Big Bear Lake, CA 92315; 909–866–2162) serves all sorts of egg dishes (including eggs Benedict and huevos rancheros), omelets (including the Old Miner's Wish and the Skier's Dream), and pancakes and waffles. Inexpensive.

How you spend your day at Big Bear Lake will depend in large part on the time of year you visit—although, since the area averages more than 300 days of sunshine each year, the day will likely be sunny, no matter the season.

The Big Bear Valley is known as the only region in Southern California to offer four-season recreation. Skiing has been a popular winter activity here since the first ski resort opened in 1949; in the summer, this is a great place for swimming, hiking, and biking.

And don't forget that lake: Eight miles long and about a mile wide at its widest point, 72 feet deep at its deepest point and lined with 23 miles of shore, Big Bear Lake is a great spot for fishing (or ice fishing), swimming (or skating), boating, or just a leisurely bike ride along its trails or a walk along the water's edge.

There's plenty of wildlife to spot as well. By the 1890s, pioneers had pretty much killed off the grizzly bears that were native to the area, but black bears were introduced in the area during the mid-twentieth century. The region also is home to about thirty wintering bald eagles. As for plant life, among the pines and oaks are twenty-nine species of rare plants, ten of which are indigenous.

Probably the best place to get next to nature is the **Big Bear Discovery Center** of the **San Bernardino National Forest** (on CA 38 on the north shore of Big Bear Lake, 1.2 miles west of the Stanfield Cutoff; 909–866–3437; www.bigbeardiscoverycenter.org). The center offers guided tours, Nature Nights seminars by experts in various fields, canoe tours, campfire programs with entertainment, and hour-long talks on subjects such as high-altitude gardening or panning for gold. The center also has special events (such as a bald eagle display or evenings of musical entertainment) and information on boating, hiking, and camping in the forest.

A note about hiking: Black bears are far more tolerant of people than were their grizzly predecessors, but it's still advisable to hike in groups and make lots of noise to let them know you're there. A startled bear is an unhappy bear.

The Discovery Center also offers the Gold Fever Trail Guide, a map that'll guide you through a three-hour auto tour of fifteen sites of the 1860–1863 gold rush in the nearby Holcomb Valley.

LUNCH: North Shore Cafe (39226 North Shore Drive, Fawnskin, CA 92333; 909–866–5879) offers signature stir-fry dishes, grilled trout and grilled salmon, burgers, pancakes, waffles, and omelets. Moderate.

Afternoon

If it's winter, you'll no doubt want to hit the slopes for skiing, snowboarding, or tubing at **Snow Summit Mountain Resort** (880 Summit Boulevard; 909–866–5766; www.snowsummit.com) or **Big Bear Mountain Resort** (43101 Goldmine Drive; 909–585–2519; www.bearmtn.com). The snow-making equipment at both resorts enables them to have their runs open generally from late November through April, although the area does average 120 inches of snowfall each season.

Big Bear Mountain has twelve lifts serving thirty-three trails on 195 acres with a 1,665-foot vertical drop. For snowboarders, Big Bear Mountain offers its Outlaw Park and Quicksilver Terrain Park with railslides, fun boxes, and tabletops, and the first Super Halfpipe in Southern California, with 17-foot walls.

Snow Summit offers eleven chair lifts serving thirty-five ski runs spread across 230 acres and a 1,200-foot vertical drop. It also provides snowboarding with terrain parks and two half-pipes.

But when the snow's gone, the fun continues. Big Bear Mountain Resort has a nine-hole, high-altitude (which means your ball goes farther!) public golf course, complete with pro shop and driving range. And lately the ski resort has taken to covering the greens during the winter in an effort to protect them.

Snow Summit's a great place for hikers and bikers—that would be *bicyclists*—during the summer. The resort's Scenic Sky Chair carries bikes and riders through the San Bernardino Forest, and when they get to the top they can choose from a number of trails, from those geared to novices to a popular 9-mile loop and a longer route that covers 16 miles. Another option: trails on the resort's downhill runs.

DINNER: Stillwell's (Northwoods Resort Hotel, 40650 Village Drive, Big Bear Lake, CA 92315; 909–866–3121; www.northwoodsresort.com) serves steaks, seafood, vegetarian entrees, and more casual offerings in a rustic lodge setting. The restaurant was named for the first ballroom in the Big Bear Valley. Moderate.

LODGING: The Holiday Inn Big Bear Château (see above).

DAY 3

Morning

BREAKFAST: Old Country Inn (41126 Big Bear Boulevard, Big Bear Lake, CA 92315; 909–866–5600) is a rustic, faintly Swiss-style spot with some truly unique breakfast offerings, such as grilled rainbow trout and eggs, Rueben omelets, and French toast with apples and whipped cream. Moderate.

The **Magic Mountain Recreation Area** (Big Bear Boulevard; 909–866–4626; www.bigbear.com/alpineslide) is a popular year-round attraction. In winter, Magic Mountain's snowplay hill is nearly always covered with crowds of excited kids (and plenty of grownups, as well) hopping aboard tubes to make their way down the slippery slope—of fun. Magic Mountain makes its own snow and often is the first winter attraction to be ready in the fall. There's a conveyor belt–like device, the "Magic Carpet," that takes tubers up to the top of the hill where they can start their fun runs down. Families sometimes link arms and legs to form vertical chains down the hill. You can bring your own tube or use Magic Mountain's; either way, the pass is for all-day play.

But the alpine slide is Magic Mountain's biggest draw—not only in winter but also during the rest of the year. Riders take the chair lift to the top of the mountain, where the view of Big Bear Lake is just fantastic. Then they hop aboard sleds—either singly, or, especially in the case of younger kids, in pairs—and fly down the quarter-mile bobsled-style track. The sleds have controls so riders can manage their velocity, and with the sleds' Teflon runners and ball-bearing wheels, this is a great way to satisfy your need for speed. There also are two separate runs, with one designated for slower riders, and good spacing from an attendant at the top of the hill to ensure riders don't get hit from behind.

Magic Mountain also has a double water slide during the summer, go-carts, and a miniature golf course with breaking greens and water hazards.

Be sure to spend some time in **The Village,** several blocks of shops and restaurants near the intersection of Big Bear Boulevard and Pine Knot Avenue. The Village's more than seventy-five businesses includes such shops as the House of Jerky, *Der Weihnachts Markt* (Christmas and collectibles year-round), the Kite Factory, and the North Pole Fudge and Ice Cream Co.

LUNCH: Stop at the **Pine Knot Coffee House and Bakery** in the Village (535 Pine Knot Avenue, Big Bear Lake, CA 92315; 909–866–3537), where specialties include Dutch Oven Pancakes made in heavy iron skillets, breakfast croissants, waffles, and made-to-order deli sandwiches. Inexpensive.

Then it's out of the woods and back to Las Vegas, retracing the route that brought you to Big Bear.

THERE'S MORE

All Seasons Sports and Recreation Center Hang-Gliding Simulator, 42825 Big Bear Boulevard; (909) 585–8585. Actual flight; glider is tethered to a 700-foot cable that runs down a mountain.

Alpine Lakes Trout Fishing, Catalina Road; (909) 866–4532. No license required; equipment rental available.

Baldwin Lake Stables, East Shay Road; (909) 585–6482. One-hour to half-day trail rides, plus sunset rides, pony rides, and overnight camp rides. Petting zoo.

Big Bear Historical Museum, Big Bear City Park, Greenway Drive; (909) 585–8100. A walk through the history of Big Bear.

Big Bear Jeep Tours, 40977 Big Bear Boulevard; (909) 878–5337. Narrated ninety-minute to five-hour tours of off-road areas in the valley and surrounding mountains.

Big Bear Lake Scenic Boat Tour, Pine Knot Landing at the foot of Pine Knot Avenue; (909) 866–2628. Double-decker paddle-wheeler makes ninety-minute narrated cruises of Big Bear Lake.

Big Bear Marina, Paine Road at Big Bear Lake; (909) 866–3218. Pontoon boats, fishing boats, personal watercraft, fishing supplies.

Elevations Day Spa, 42007 Fox Farm Road Unit 1; (909) 866–7405. Massage therapy, facials, spa pedicures, and manicures.

Moonridge Animal Park, 43285 Goldmine Drive; (909) 866–0183. Injured or orphaned wildlife from grizzly bears to snakes.

Sierra Belle, 439 Pine Knot Avenue; (909) 866–BOAT. Narrated one-and-a-half-hour lake tours.

SPECIAL EVENTS

January. Bald Eagle Count, Big Bear Discovery Center; (909) 866–3437.

United States Amateur Snowboard Association (USASA) Events, Snow Summit and Big Bear Mountain; (909) 866–5766 or (909) 585–2519.

February. American Snowboard Tour, Big Bear Mountain; (909) 585–2519.

March. Special Olympics, Big Bear Mountain; (909) 585–2519.

TransWorld Snowboarding Team Challenge, Snow Summit; (909) 866–5766.

April. SpringFest 2001, Snow Summit; (909) 866–5766.

May. Annual Big Bear Jeep Jamboree; (909) 866–4607.

Peddlers' Market Antiques and Collectible Show, Elks Lodge; (909) 866–3557.

June. Annual Open Sky Music Festival; (909) 866–4607.

Bear Affair, Big Bear Lake traditional jazz festival; (909) 866–4607.

July. Boat Parade of Lights; (909) 866–4607.

Rotary Club BBQ and Fireworks over Lake; (909) 866–4607.

August. Annual Old Miners' Days trail ride, Cowboy Poetry and Music Festival, children's events, and parade; (909) 866–4607.

Annual Summit Classic Girls' Softball Tournament; (909) 866–4607.

September. Bear Fest International Film Festival; (909) 866–4607.

September through the end of October. Annual Oktoberfest; (909) 866–4607.

October. Big Bear Ultra 100 Mountain Bike Ride, 100 miles around Big Bear Lake; (909) 866–4607.

Halloween in the Village; (909) 866–4607.

November. Annual Christmas tree lightings; (909) 866–4607.

December. Christmas in the Village; (909) 866–4607.

Torchlight Parade, Snow Summit; (909) 866–5766.

OTHER RECOMMENDED RESTAURANTS AND LODGINGS

Big Bear Lake Inn, 39471 Big Bear Boulevard; (909) 866–3477 or (800) 843–0103. Mountain and lake views; oversized rooms with one or two king-sized beds.

Black Forest Lodge, 41121 Big Bear Boulevard; (909) 866–2166 or (800) 255–4378. Rooms with fireplaces or spas in Tyrolean setting.

The Blue Whale, 350 Alden Road; (909) 866–5514. Prime rib, seafood, game, and free-range fowl in lakeside setting.

Cowboy Express Steak House, 40433 Lakeview Drive; (909) 866–1486. Steaks, barbecued ribs, and chicken.

Forest Shores Inn, 40670 Lakeview Drive; (909) 866–6551 or (800) 317–9814. Lakefront mini-suites and suites with fireplaces.

Honey Bear Lodge, 40994 Pennsylvania Avenue; (909) 866–7825. All rooms with woodburning fireplaces, refrigerators, and microwaves.

Pong's Oriental Delights, 42104 Big Bear Boulevard; (909) 866–4400. Original and traditional Asian fare.

Southwest Station, 41787 Big Bear Boulevard; (909) 866–8667. Mexican foods, steaks, seafood, chicken, and ribs as well as specialty margaritas.

Thelma's Family Restaurant and Bakery, 337 Big Bear Boulevard; (909) 585–7005. Nightly dinner specials, full bakery.

Timberline Lodge, 39921 Big Bear Boulevard; (909) 866–4141 or (800) 803–4111. Lakeside cabins with fireplaces.

FOR MORE INFORMATION

Big Bear Lake Chamber of Commerce, 630 Bartlett Road, Big Bear Lake, CA 92315; (909) 866–4607.

Big Bear Lake Resort Association, 630 Bartlett Road, Big Bear Lake, CA 92315; (800) 4–BIG–BEAR; www.bigbearinfo.com.

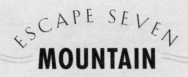

Sequoia and Kings Canyon National Parks

SPEND TIME IN THE TIMBER

2 NIGHTS

Towering trees • Rushing mountain streams
Forest idylls • Romantic inns

For the beauty of Sequoia and Kings Canyon National Parks, we have God, Mother Nature, and John White to thank.

You already know who God and Mother Nature are; depending on your personal beliefs, one or both of them is responsible for creating the sequoia trees that gave their name to these adjoining national parks in California and their majesty to our imaginations and sense of awe.

John White, you may not be as familiar with.

It seems that White was the parks superintendent who, in 1929, had the foresight to be concerned about the future health of his towering charges. "If we do not transfer the major part of the present activity away from the heart of Giant Forest," White said then, "the beauties of the area—already badly tarnished—will be further impaired." Indeed. If they were tarnished then, think what would've been left for us to see lo, these seventy-plus years later?

White was concerned, it seems, about the commercial development at the very roots of the giant trees; he knew it couldn't be a good idea to have a gas station, cabins, motels, a post office, and park buildings in the area, compacting and eroding the soil and damaging the roots of the giants themselves.

Clear heads sided with White, but turning things around was somewhat of an arduous process; it took until 2000 for the last buildings and asphalt to be removed from the sequoia grove.

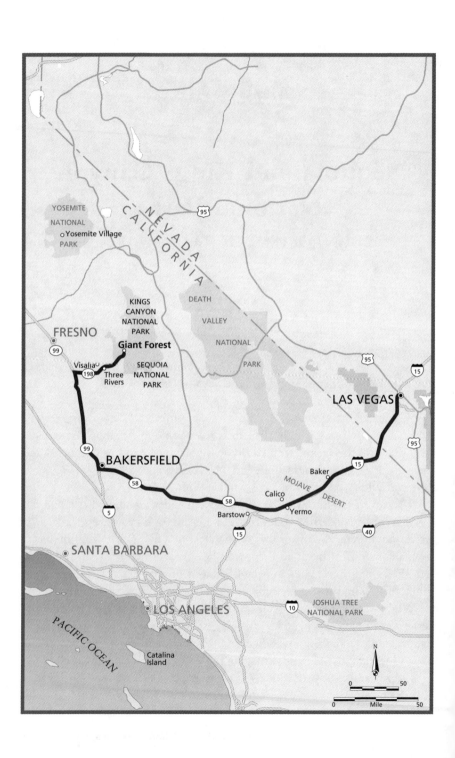

YOSEMITE
NATIONAL
Yosemite Village
PARK

NEVADA
CALIFORNIA

95

KINGS
CANYON
NATIONAL
PARK

DEATH

VALLEY

FRESNO

NATIONAL

99

Giant Forest

PARK

95

Visalia
198

SEQUOIA
NATIONAL
PARK

Three
Rivers

15

LAS VEGAS

95

99

BAKERSFIELD

58

Baker

15

5

58

Calico

MOJAVE

DESERT

Barstow

Yermo

15

40

SANTA BARBARA

LOS ANGELES

10

JOSHUA TREE
NATIONAL PARK

PACIFIC OCEAN

N

Catalina
Island

0   50

Mile   50

Today, though, Sequoia and Kings Canyon National Parks jointly form a shady, serene escape from our speed-infected world. This trip is a nice step back, a refreshing jaunt into nature. A great quick escape.

DAY 1

Afternoon

Sequoia and Kings Canyon National Parks are just over 400 miles from Las Vegas, for a drive of about six hours, so you'll want to schedule an afternoon departure.

Drive south on Interstate 15 to Barstow, then pick up California Route 58 and follow it west for about 125 miles to Bakersfield. From there, take California Route 99 north about 63 miles into Visalia. At Visalia, follow signs that will direct you along California Route 198 about 40 miles through Three Rivers to the park gate.

DINNER: A few miles after you pass through Three Rivers on your way into the park, stop at the **Gateway Restaurant and Lodge** (45978 Sierra Drive/Route 198, Three Rivers, CA 93271; 559–561–4133) on the right-hand side of the road. The Gateway has a tiered deck that overlooks the Kaweah River, with the sounds of the splashing water making for a particularly restful dinner of such dishes as trout, steaks, poultry, pastas, and salads. (As a side note, the restaurant and lodge gained some measure of notoriety as the site of a weekend getaway by actor Robert Blake and his wife, Bonny Lee Bakley, not long before she was murdered in Los Angeles.) Moderate.

LODGING: Wuksachi Village and Lodge (888–252–5757; www.visit sequoia.com; rates from $80 to $185) is in Lodgepole, the spot on the northwestern edge of the park where many park services have been relocated. They're far enough away to mitigate damage to the sequoias, but close enough so that guests feel shaded by the big trees; visitors also can see Mount Silliman and Silver Peak. The lodge has a dining room, lounge, gift shop, and conference facilities; the 102 rooms are in three buildings and are themed to the park.

DAY 2

Morning

BREAKFAST: From Wuksachi Village, strike out about 2 miles east to the Lodgepole Visitor Center and Village, where you'll find the **Lodgepole Snack Bar** (559–565–4070) serving breakfast beginning at 8 or 9 most mornings, depending on the season. Inexpensive.

At Lodgepole, you'll also find the National Park Service's **Visitor Center** (559–565–3782). While you're at the Visitor Center, pick up a *Sequoia & Kings Canyon National Parks Visitor Guide* if you didn't get one at the Ash Mountain Entrance or nearby Foothills Visitor Center when you entered the park from the Three Rivers Area the night before. The visitor centers (there are others at Grant Grove in the northwestern section of the park, Cedar Grove in the northeastern section, and Mineral King in the southeastern section) are great places to find exhibits, slide programs, books, and maps on the geology and forest life within the parks.

There's much to see and a fair amount of driving involved; the parks encompass 868,741 acres at elevations ranging from 1,500 to 14,494 feet above sea level. Most of the sites that are most desirable to visitors, though, are clustered in the Lodgepole and Giant Forest areas.

At the Lodgepole or Foothills Visitor Center, purchase tickets to tour **Crystal Cave.** Depending on availability, you should be able to get tickets for a specific time to fit your schedule. The half-mile trail from the parking lot to the cave entrance is steep, and on the way to the cave it's almost all downhill, which means it's almost all uphill on the way back! Your efforts will be rewarded, however, with a truly wondrous experience. (It'll also be a cool experience; the temperature in the cave is a steady 48 degrees, so be sure to bring a jacket.)

The cave was discovered in 1918 when two park employees fishing in the nearby Cascade Creek felt a cool breeze over their shoulders. Investigating, they found a cavernous area with stalactites, stalagmites, and various other formations—including curtains and "bacon strips" formed by water dripping through limestone over thousands of years.

In the following decades, pathways were constructed through the cave to improve visitor access; lighting is used effectively to highlight some formations. After visitors enter the cave's Spider Web Gate, the forty-five-minute tour takes them through the various rooms of the cave, crossing streams lined

Sequoia National Park

with natural marble, as a guide explains the formations and tells how old many of them are estimated to be. The guide also discusses the potential effects of an earthquake on the cave (not much, since it's in bedrock, although you'd hear a ringing sound from the rock formations) and at one point extinguishes a light so visitors can see the cave from the viewpoint of its natural inhabitants, including bats and insects.

After their tour, visitors are invited to linger a bit in the lovely creekside glade outside the cave's entrance. Benches and picnic tables make things all the more inviting, and there are a number of waterfalls in the area.

Now that you've sent the netherworld of Sequoia/Kings Canyon, how about exploring the park from a loftier perch? **Moro Rock** is near the point where the Crystal Cave entrance road intersects with Generals Highway, the main road through the park. At 6,725 feet, the rock is lower than some points in the park, but still dominates the landscape around it.

You'll need to be in good physical condition for this walk; the path to the top of the rock rises 300 feet in about ¼ mile through a series of stairways, steep paths, and steps cut into the rock. It's quite a climb, but when you get to the summit you'll likely feel as though you're king (or queen) of the world; the narrow, railing-lined path atop the rock provides spectacular views of the Great Western Divide and the western section of the park.

Or, if you'd prefer to get some great views of the park on four legs instead of two, consider horseback riding, anything from a one-hour trip to a back-country pack trip. A number of stables are listed in the Visitor Guide; closest to the Lodgepole and Giant Forest area are the stables at Wolverton (559–565–3039 during the summer and 520–855–5885 during the off-season); there are also stables at Cedar Grove, Grant Grove, Mineral King, and the appropriately named Horse Corral, which is between Grant Grove and Cedar Grove.

LUNCH: Stop back at the Lodgepole Snack Bar for burgers, pizza or ice cream, or drop by the **Lodgepole Market and Deli** and put together a picnic lunch of sandwiches and salads, snacks, fruits, and beverages to enjoy at any of the many picnic areas spread throughout the park. Inexpensive.

Afternoon

You wouldn't want to go all the way to Sequoia and Kings Canyon National Parks without seeing the world's largest tree, would you? That would be the **General Sherman Tree**, so named by a Civil War veteran (we're guessing he was Union) in 1879. It's not the world's tallest (at 274.9 feet), it's not the world's broadest (with a base circumference of 102.6 feet), but the two dimensions combined give it the largest volume of any tree in the world.

The General Sherman tree is reached via a trail that snakes up from the parking area. It's an easy walk and the effort is well worth it; this is a *very* impressive tree, stretching impossibly high. And you can get up-close-and-personal to the tree, so you even can take one of those tourist photos with your arms stretched around it—if not very far around it.

Speaking of those tourist photos: There are two other good photo ops near the General Sherman Tree, both of which are a lot of fun and both of which can involve your vehicle, providing it's not too large. You can drive through the **Tunnel Log,** which is a fallen sequoia that has been tunneled for auto traffic. And you can drive onto the **Auto Log,** another fallen log that's so large, you can drive right out onto it.

As you make your way through Giant Forest, you'll find that it's aptly named; some of the biggest trees in the world are found here. Many can be seen from the road (you'll find yourself oohing and aahing, "Look at that one. Look at *that* one. Look at that cluster of three!") and many more from the various trails in the area, which vary in length and intensity. Among them are the Little Baldy Trail, which climbs 700 vertical feet in 1.7 miles to a rocky summit with a spectacular view; it's a three- to four-hour trip. Another is the Tokopah Falls Trail, which takes about two and a half to four hours as it extends 1.7 miles among the Marble Fork of the Kaweah River to the granite cliffs and waterfall of Tokopah Canyon.

DINNER: All of this activity no doubt will work up a fearsome appetite. The glass-enclosed restaurant at the **Wuksachi Lodge** (reservations required; call 559–565–4070, ext. 608) provides impressive views of majestic trees and mountain peaks. The food's nearly as impressive, with appetizers such as goat cheese tamale with *guijuillo mole* or rock shrimp flautas with two salsas, and entrees such as ricotta-stuffed eggplant with wild mushroom ragout or grilled salmon with curried *guijuillo* orange sauce and basmati rice. And you can tuck into some *crème brulee* before you tuck yourself into bed. Moderate.

DAY 3

Morning

BREAKFAST: To explore another part of the park, head northeast to Grant Grove or northwest to Cedar Grove; you'll find cafes at the lodges in both places (559–335–5500). Moderate.

Take as long as you want to explore Grant Grove, Cedar Grove, or both. At Grant Grove you'll find the **General Grant Tree,** the world's third-largest living tree, and the **Nation's Christmas Tree.** It's also the nation's only living memorial to those who died in war. Along the easy trail to the tree you'll see historic **Gamlin Cabin** and the **Fallen Monarch.** Grant Grove also is the site of **Redwood Canyon,** the world's largest grove of sequoias, and a number of trails, many of which offer spectacular views of the high Sierra. Grant Grove is about a one-hour drive from Giant Forest, which is in turn about a one-hour drive from the Foothills area.

Cedar Grove, another hour beyond Grant Grove, is the site of **Canyon View,** the best vantage point for seeing the glacially formed U-shaped Kings Canyon. Roaring River Falls is a forceful waterfall that pushes its way through a granite chute. And to feel like you're at the end of the world, drive to Road's End, which is just what it says: To cross the Sierra from this point, you'd have to walk.

LUNCH: Anne Lang's Emporium (41651 Sierra Drive, Three Rivers, CA 93271; 559–561–4937) offers more than twenty-five varieties of tea, plus coffee and deli sandwiches to fortify you for the trip home. Inexpensive.

Afternoon

Then it's time to head back through Three Rivers to Visalia and retrace your steps to Las Vegas.

THERE'S MORE

Reedley, California

Mennonite Quilting Center, 1012 G Street; (559) 638–3560. See Mennonite quilters at work; quilts for sale. Gift shop of works by people in developing nations.

Three Rivers, California

Beyond Limits Adventures, 40501 Sierra Drive; (559) 869–6060 or (800) 234–7238. White-water rafting adventures.

Crystal Hill Winery/Bullene Vineyards, Sierra Drive; (559) 561–9463. Winery and gift shop.

Kaweah White Water Adventures, P.O. Box 1050; (559) 561–1000. White-water rafting.

Three Rivers Golf Course, 41117 Sierra Drive; (559) 561–3133. Nine-hole course; mostly flat with several lakes.

Visalia, California

Valley Oaks Golf Course, 1800 South Plaza Drive; (559) 651–1441. Twenty-seven hole flat municipal course with some water.

SPECIAL EVENTS

Three Rivers, California

April. Jazzaffair jazz festival; (559) 561–3105.

Lions Team Roping; (559) 561–2222.

May. Redbud Festival, annual arts and crafts show by the Art Alliance of Three Rivers; (559) 561–3160.

September. Annual Celebrate Sequoias Festival, Sequoia & Kings Canyon National Parks; (559) 565–3341.

December. Annual Trek to the Tree, Sequoia & Kings Canyon National Parks; (559) 565–3341.

Visalia, California

February. Mardi Gras, with parade, bands, street dance, and vendors; (559) 734–5876.

March. Civil War battle reenactment; (559) 734–5876.

May. *Cinco de Mayo* celebration; (550) 734–5876.

OTHER RECOMMENDED RESTAURANTS AND LODGINGS

Lemon Grove, California

Plantation Bed and Breakfast, 33038 Sierra Drive; (559) 597–2555 or (800) 240–1466. Specializing in *Gone with the Wind* theme rooms.

Three Rivers, California

Buckeye Tree Lodge, 46000 Sierra Drive; (559) 561–5900. River views a half mile from the park entrance.

Cort Cottage Bed and Breakfast, P.O. Box 245; (559) 561–4671. Private guest cottage 4 miles from park entrance.

Visalia, California

The Depot Restaurant, 207 East Oak Street; (559) 732–8611. Varied menu; Spanish decor in restored railroad depot.

Double LL Steakhouse, 401 East Center Street; (559) 627–1126. Steak, prime rib, barbecue ribs, and seafood in casual Western atmosphere.

The Vintage Press, 216 North Willis Street; (559) 733–3033. Varied menu and extensive wine list; garden-patio dining available.

FOR MORE INFORMATION

Sequoia and Kings Canyon National Parks, 47050 Generals Highway, Three Rivers, CA 93271-9651; (559) 565–3341; www.nps.gov/seki.

Visalia Chamber of Commerce, 720 West Mineral King, Visalia, CA 93291; (559) 734–5876 or (877) VISALIA; www.visaliachamber.org.

SEASIDE
ESCAPES

Anaheim

WHAT WALT HATH WROUGHT

2 NIGHTS

Amusement parks • Family adventures
Old California attractions

Disneyland is dedicated to the ideals, the dreams and the hard facts
that have created America . . . with the hope that it will be
a source of joy and inspiration to all the world.

—Walt Disney, 1955

Inspiration, indeed. It's hard to say whether Walt Disney had an inkling lo, those many years ago, but his land would change the face of our land for generations to come.

And it all started in Anaheim, California. Whenever a kid—and this designation would cover anybody with a heartbeat—hears the name "Anaheim," he or she is sure to think "Disney," for this is where, in 1955, Walt Disney started the country's theme-park merry mayhem with his beloved Disneyland.

Plenty of people lived in Orange County long before Walt made his magic here, of course. The roots of modern Anaheim date to 1857, when German immigrants established a settlement with farming and wine-making in mind, naming the community Anaheim—"Ana" for the nearby Santa Ana River, and "heim" for the German word for home.

Disease wiped out the grapevines in the 1870s, and the settlers replanted with orange trees—the first commercially grown oranges in what would become Orange County. They also planted chili peppers and walnuts, but it was the production of oranges that would put Anaheim in the spotlight and

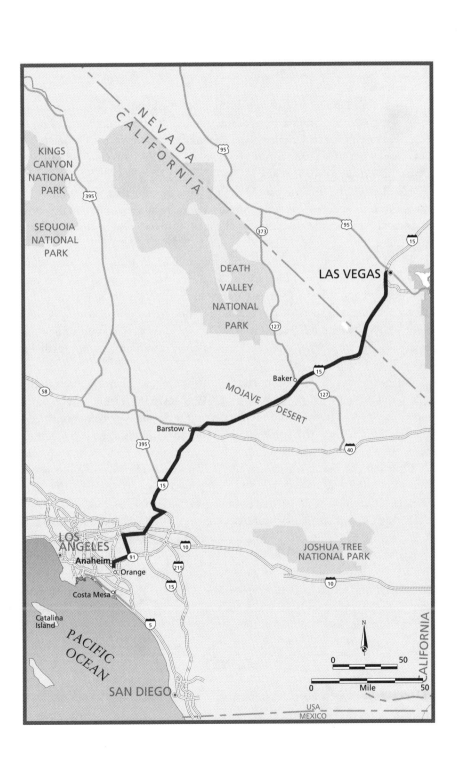

bring prosperity to the community. Orange production would continue to dominate the area until the 1960s.

It was Walt Disney who changed things for Anaheim. Babies had boomed in the post-war era; families were numerous and, thanks to the wave of post-war prosperity, they had plenty of leisure time—but not many leisure activities. Disney felt that need with his own two daughters, and resolved to build a park designed just for families.

He planned to build the park on an eleven-acre parcel across from his film studios in Burbank, but—in what would eventually be seen as one of the most ill-advised bureaucratic decisions of all time—Burbank officials turned down his request.

By that time, Walt's plans were growing, and he decided he needed more than eleven acres anyway. He headed south on the new Santa Ana Freeway and found in agricultural Orange County the sort of wholesome atmosphere he was seeking. He struck a partnership with the American Broadcast Company (ABC), which was then the new kid on the block looking for some credibility. He considered various Orange County communities, but Anaheim seemed the best fit.

Anaheim officials weren't much more visionary than their brethren to the north, and balked at Disney's plans as well. Walt agreed to various concessions, some major, some minor. Among them: After the Anaheim mayor complained that he didn't want a park strewn with peanut shells in his city, Disney agreed never to sell peanuts in the shell.

Opening day was a nightmare; the park just wasn't ready. But just seven weeks later, the one millionth visitor had passed through the gates. Bye-bye oranges; Anaheim was on its way to becoming a top vacation spot.

Today, Disneyland draws more than thirteen million visitors a year and makes a huge footprint on the Anaheim area. But Anaheim isn't all Disney, of course; there are other attractions in and around the city, and revitalization in the 1,100 acres surrounding the newly expanded Anaheim Convention Center and Disneyland Resort has created the Anaheim Resort District. Add to that Anaheim's temperate climate, which is sweet relief from Las Vegas's sweltering summers, and it all makes for a great quick escape.

DAY 1

Afternoon

Anaheim is about 270 miles from Las Vegas for a traveling time of about four hours, which makes a Friday-afternoon departure timely.

Drive south on Interstate 15 for about 230 miles to the California Route 60 West exit, heading toward Los Angeles. Continue west on CA 60 for about 17 miles to California Route 57 South, toward Santa Ana. Follow CA 57 for about 15 miles to the Katella Avenue exit, turning right onto East Katella Avenue, then turn right onto Disneyland Drive.

DINNER: Ralph Brennan's Jazz Kitchen in Downtown Disney (1590 South Disneyland Drive, Anaheim, CA 92802; 714–776–5200; www.rbjazz kitchen.com) is a piece of New Orleans—appropriate enough, since Brennan's family has been involved in New Orleans restaurants since 1947 and owns the legendary Commander's Palace, where famed chef Emeril Lagasse earned his chops. The interior decor is reminiscent of New Orleans—don't miss the hand-beaded piano and the Mardi Gras murals—and so is the food.

For starters, consider some spicy boudin and smoked Andouille sausages steamed in Abita beer, or maybe some crawfish *beignets*. Entrees include New Orleans BBQ shrimp, molasses-roasted chicken, or a French Quarter salad with Louisiana cane vinaigrette. And of course you won't want to miss the New Orleans bread pudding, complete with whiskey *crème anglaise*. There's even an adjoining jazz club, Flambeaux's, if you really want to feel like you're in the Big Easy. Expensive.

LODGING: Disney's Grand Californian Hotel (1600 South Disneyland Drive, Anaheim, CA 92802; 714–956–6425; www.disneyland.com; rates from $225 to $290) is located on the edge of two major attractions, Disney's California Adventure and Downtown Disney, and Disneyland is close by. This is a new hotel with all of the upscale luxuries you'd expect in a Disney resort, including restaurants, lounge, health club, themed pools, wedding services, child care—you name it.

DAY 2

Morning

BREAKFAST: Oh, go ahead; you're at Disneyland. Just off the lobby at the Grand Californian Hotel, go to the **Storytellers Cafe** for a character breakfast hosted by Chip and Dale. Even if you don't have small children in your group, you might want to try this just to see another aspect of the Disney magic. Breakfast is served buffet-style and you can expect all of the usual offerings, including eggs and pancakes and bacon and sausage. A bonus: The walls of the

Storytellers Cafe are lined with paintings depicting California's past and some of its folklore (some of the latter created by Disney, of course) and the servers are storytellers. Ask a few to tell you about some of the paintings. Moderate.

Like all of the company's theme parks, **Disney's California Adventure** (714–781–4565) is divided into separate areas; in this case, each area is designed to represent a different aspect of California.

You enter DCA, as it's known to employees and fans, beneath a scaled-down replica of the Golden Gate Bridge. Then it's time to start exploring the individual areas of Golden State, Paradise Pier, and the Hollywood Pictures Backlot.

In Golden State you'll find Condor Flats, which highlights California aviation and is the home of Soarin' over California, a popular Imax-style hang-gliding–themed attraction; Grizzly Peak Recreation Area, with its Grizzly River Run white-water ride and Redwood Creek Challenge for kids; Bountiful Valley Farm, with its not-to-be-missed "It's Tough to Be a Bug" multimedia attraction and citrus groves you can walk through; The Bay Area, with Golden Dreams, a Whoopi Goldberg–narrated film about Californians' dreams and struggles over the years; Golden Vine Winery, hosted by Robert Mondavi, where visitors can stroll through vineyards and taste new vintages as they learn about California winemaking; and Pacific Wharf, where you can tour two working food factories, sample Mexican and Asian cuisine, and hear live entertainment.

Paradise Pier is themed to the golden age of boardwalk amusements parks and is the place the kids will want to visit for rides like the California Screamin' wooden roller coaster; Sun Wheel, which has both stationary and sliding gondolas; and the Maliboomer's triple 180-foot towers, where riders go up, up, up—and down, down, down.

Hollywood Pictures Backlot is a tribute to Hollywood's golden age, with theaters, shops, cafes—such as the ABC soap opera bistro—and behind-the-scene peeks at moving making.

LUNCH: Food stands and fast-food outlets abound, but another option is the **Vineyard Room** in the Golden Vine Winery (714–781–4565), which specializes in food-and-wine pairings. Expensive.

Afternoon

If you're not Disneyed out yet, consider a visit to the park that started it all, **Disneyland** (714–781–4565), which has many old-favorite attractions you

Anaheim gateway

no doubt remember and a number of newer ones you don't. There's the charm of the *Mark Twain* riverboat and New Orleans Square and its Pirates of the Caribbean, the slight spookiness of the Haunted Mansion, and the thrills of Splash Mountain and Big Thunder Mountain Railroad.

Newly updated is Tomorrowland, with its old favorites Space Mountain and Star Tours, plus newer attractions such as "Honey I Shrunk the Audience." Autopia has been updated with an off-road adventure for all of those little SUV passengers.

If you *are* Disneyed out, **Knott's Theme Park** is not far away in Buena Park (8039 Beach Boulevard; 714–220–5200; www.knotts.com). This park, which used to be called "Knott's Berry Farm" (and still is by most local and many visitors) has 160 acres of attractions. New among them are Perilous Plunge, the world's tallest and steepest water ride, which makes a 115-foot drop at a 75-degree angle. There's also Ghostrider, a wooden roller coaster; the thirty-story up-and-down towers of Supreme Scream; and the six loops of the Boomerang, which also runs backward.

For milder types, there's a steam train and a stagecoach; for the little ones, there's Camp Snoopy.

If being cool is high on your agenda, go next door to **Knott's Soak City U.S.A. Water Park** (8039 Beach Boulevard; 714–220–5200) for slides, a wave pool, and a lazy river.

DINNER: Surely you joust? Surely they do at **Medieval Times Dinner and Tournament** (7662 Beach Boulevard, Buena Park, CA 90622; 888–WEJOUST or 714–521–4740). You'll be eating with your hands, but that's just part of the fun, of course. Besides jousting, you'll see knights embarking in hand-to-hand combat and lots of thundering horses. Moderate.

LODGING: Disney's Grand California Hotel (see above).

DAY 3

Morning

BREAKFAST: Tiffy's Family Restaurant (1060 West Katella Avenue, Anaheim, CA 92802; 714–635–1801) is as homey as the name implies. Breakfast includes Belgian waffles with fresh strawberries, eggs, pancakes, and the like. Inexpensive.

Downtown Disney (714–300–7800) has lots to check out, so if you didn't take your time exploring Friday night, do some shopping and browsing now. Among the shops are a LEGO Imagination Center, Department 56, World of Disney, Sephora, and Something in Silver; restaurants include Rainforest Cafe and La Brea Bakery Cafe; entertainment includes an ESPN Zone and a House of Blues.

The city of Orange is another option for shopping. Its antiques district at Chapman and Glassel Streets (714–997–1370) has fifty antiques and specialty shops representing more than 500 dealers. There's a **Hilo Hattie – The Store of Hawaii** (714–769–3255) and a **Ron Jon Surf Shop** (714–939–9822) at 20 City Boulevard West in The Block at Orange.

For something a little quieter, the **Fullerton Aboretum** (1900 Associated Road; 714–278–3579) comprises twenty-six acres of carefully tended botanical gardens, with a waterfall, lakes, and streams. The gardens are centered on the 1894 Victorian Heritage House, which is open for tours on Sunday afternoons and by appointment on weekdays.

In Garden Grove is the **Crystal Cathedral** (12141 Lewis Street; 714–971–4013), an all-glass church designed by Philip Johnson, with 10,000 mirrored windows.

LUNCH: Alcatraz Brewing Company (20 City Boulevard West, Orange, CA 92868; 714–939–8686) is a microbrewery specializing in beer-friendly bistro food, served in a prison-themed atmosphere.

Afternoon

Then it's time to retrace your route to Las Vegas.

THERE'S MORE

Anaheim, California

Anaheim Angels, Edison International Field; (714) 634–2000. Major League Baseball regular season April through October.

Anaheim Mighty Ducks, Arrowhead Pond; (714) 704–2500. NHL Hockey from October through April.

Joey and Maria's Comedy Italian Wedding, various locations on weekends; (800) 944–5639. Dinner-theater with a twist (of pasta).

Buena Park, California

Movieland Wax Museum, 7711 Beach Boulevard; (714) 522–1154. Wax representations of stars of stage and the large and small screens.

Ripley's Believe It or Not! Museum, 7850 Beach Boulevard; (714) 522–1155. Want to see *The Last Supper* made out of toast? This is your place.

Irvine, California

Wild Rivers Waterpark, 8770 Irving Center Drive; (949) 768–WILD. Water slides, wave pools, and more.

Los Angeles, California

Autry Museum of Western Heritage, 4700 Western Heritage Way; (323) 667–2000. Showcases history and traditions of the American West.

Santa Ana, California

Bowers Museum of Cultural Art, 2002 North Main Street; (714) 567–3600. Celebrates diversity of world cultures.

Yorba Linda, California

Richard Nixon Library and Birthplace, 18001 Yorba Linda Boulevard; (714) 993–5075. Nixon's birthplace, plus museum galleries, movie, video theaters, and memorial sites of Richard and Pat Nixon.

SPECIAL EVENTS

Anaheim, California

February. Chamber Wine and Jazz Festival, celebrating city's music, food, and spirits; (714) 606–2819.

March. St. Patrick's Day Celebration, with dancers, music, and food, Downtown Farmer's Market; (714) 704–2500.

May. *Cinco de Mayo* Festival, with carnival, entertainment, food, and a soccer tournament, La Palma Park; (714) 765–5274.

June. Taste of Anaheim, showcasing local food and wine, plus entertainment, Arrowhead Pond; (714) 758–0222.

August. International Street Fair, with folk dancing, music, food, and more than a hundred craft booths; (714) 532–6260.

October. Oktoberfest, with German food, beer, and music, Phoenix Club; (714) 563–4166.

Costa Mesa, California

July. Orange County Fair, more than a century old, with headline entertainment, carnival, food, and traditional fair offerings, Orange County Fairgrounds; (714) 708–FAIR.

September. Irish Festival, celebrating the wearin' of the green, Orange County Fairgrounds; (714) 284–9558.

Fullerton, California

April. Annual Green Scene Garden Show, with sales, speakers, tours, and children's activities, Fullerton Arboretum; (714) 278–3570.

Garden Grove, California

May. Strawberry Festival, with parade, carnival, and entertainment, Euclid and Main Streets; (714) 638–7950.

November–December. Glory of Christmas, living nativity with more than 200 cast members, Crystal Cathedral; (714) 971–4019.

Westminster, California

January. Tet Festival, annual celebration of the Vietnamese New Year, with ethnic dishes, music, and cultural displays; (626) 576–8338.

OTHER RECOMMENDED RESTAURANTS AND LODGINGS

Anaheim, California

The Anabella Hotel, 1030 West Katella Avenue; (714) 905–1050. Newly renovated hotel with old-Spanish styling, located in the Anaheim Resort.

Disney's Paradise Pier Hotel, 1717 Disneyland Drive; (714) 999–0990. Beach-themed resort in coordination with Paradise Pier section of Disney's California Adventure.

Westcoast Anaheim Hotel, 1855 South Harbor Boulevard; (714) 750–1811. Newly renovated guest rooms; within walking distance of Disneyland.

Garden Grove, California

Pinacle Peak Steakhouse, 9100 Trask Avenue; (714) 892–7311. Steaks cooked over an open mesquite grill.

Irvine, California

Gulliver's Restaurant, 18482 MacArthur Boulevard; (949) 833–8411. Famous for prime rib and English trifle; English tavern specialties.

Orange, California

The Hobbitt, 2932 East Chapman Avenue; (714) 997–1972. Seven-course dinner that begins with champagne and hors d'oeuvres in the wine cellar.

FOR MORE INFORMATION

Anaheim/Orange County Visitor and Convention Bureau, 800 West Katella Avenue, Anaheim, CA 92802; (714) 765–8888; www.anaheimoc.org.

Buena Park Convention and Visitors Office, 6601 Beach Boulevard, no. 200, Buena Park, CA 90621; (714) 562–3560; www.buenapark.com.

Disneyland Resort, Disneyland Drive, Anaheim, CA 92802; (714) 956–MICKEY; www.disneyland.com.

San Diego

CENTURIES OF OLD-WORLD CHARM
BY THE PACIFIC

2 NIGHTS

Missions • Zoos • Beaches • Historic sites • Coronado Island

At about 335 miles from Las Vegas, San Diego may seem like a bit of a hike, but several factors make this a popular destination for Las Vegans planning weekend trips.

One is the availability of bargain airfares; it's not unusual to find a Las Vegas–San Diego fare for $60, round trip. Another is the fact that the drive from Las Vegas to San Diego and back is pleasant and naturally broken up into several very different legs. And third, of course, is San Diego itself: A well-established city filled with history and color, San Diego offers lots of weekend activities that simply can't be found in Las Vegas. Add to that the fact of the San Diego metropolitan area's numerous microclimates, from desert to Pacific shore, and this city in the southernmost part of Southern California makes for a great quick escape.

DAY 1

Afternoon

You'll want to leave by mid-day Friday or even Thursday night; there are motels in various California communities along the way, including Barstow, San Bernardino, Riverside, and in the wine country around Temecula.

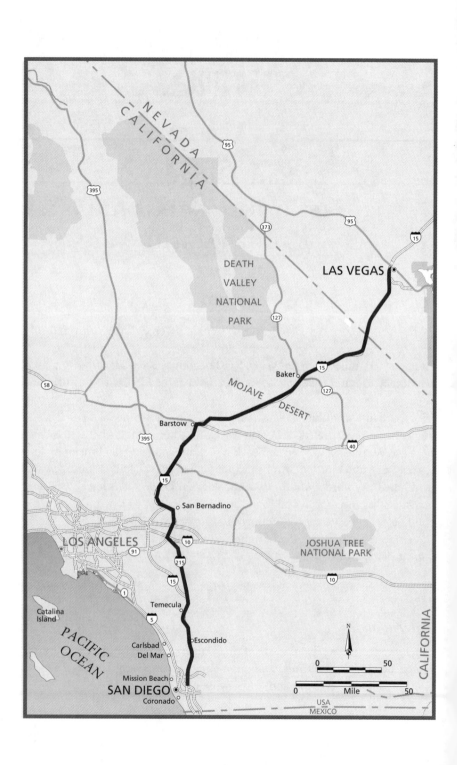

Head south on Interstate 15 for about 210 miles, picking up Interstate 215 South in the San Bernardino area. Continue on I–215 for about 55 miles until it rejoins I–15 near Temecula and continue south to San Diego, about 50 miles.

(An alternative route—and there is some dispute among those who frequently make the trip as to which one is better—is to stay on I–15 through the entire trip. That route may be longer, but may cut off some congestion in the Riverside area.)

In the San Diego metropolitan area, pick up California Route 163 South to the Hotel Circle/Interstate 8 exit, then, in about 3 miles, take the Old Town Avenue exit. Turn left onto Old Town Avenue, then left onto San Diego Avenue, and look for parking for the **Old Town San Diego State Historic Park** (San Diego and Twiggs Streets; 619–220–5422).

Once you park, take some time to explore the buildings in the 6-block state park, which commemorates the first European settlement in what now is California. Among them are La Casa de Estudillo, the home of a retired commander of the San Diego presidio, or fort; construction on his house was begun in 1827. Numerous items of Western memorabilia are displayed in the nearby Seeley Stable Museum.

The state park also has various shops and galleries mixed right in with the historic buildings, which gives it a lively feel at nearly any time of day. One of these establishments is Racine and Laramie of Old Town (2737 San Diego Avenue; 619–291–7833), which is a combination cigar shop and historic museum, tracing its history as San Diego's first cigar store in 1868.

DINNER: Stay in Old Town for dinner at **Casa de Pico** at Bazaar del Mundo within the park (619–296–3267), a thirty-year-old restaurant on the site of the home of the last governor of California under Mexican rule. Casa de Pico offers courtyard dining and specializes in moderately priced Mexican food, plus margaritas and mariachi music. Moderate.

LODGING: Just a few blocks from Old Town State Historic Park is the **Holiday Inn Hotel and Suites Old Town** (2435 Jefferson Street, San Diego, CA 92110; 619–260–8500; rates from $149 to $169), a historic building recently renovated to old-California grandeur, with courtyard restaurant and adjacent pool and spa. It's a far cry from your standard Holiday Inn.

ESCAPE TWO

SEASIDE

DAY 2

Morning

BREAKFAST: Have the eggs Benedict at the Holiday Inn, or enjoy a border breakfast at the **Old Town Mexican Cafe** (2489 San Diego Avenue, San Diego, CA 92110; 619–297–4330), where breakfast specials include a Spanish omelet, *chilaquiles,* New Mexico–style *enchiladas con huevos,* pork carnitas hash—even a Gringo Special of eggs and bacon, ham, or sausage, served with rice and beans. Moderate.

Be sure you're amply fortified for the day ahead, because the **San Diego Zoo** (2920 Zoo Drive; 619–234–3153; www.sandiegozoo.org) is a challenging experience. The zoo is billed in various quarters as "world famous," and that would be true if for no other reason than Joan Embery and the animals she used to bring to *The Tonight Show* when Johnny Carson was host. But this zoo is famous for lots of other reasons, foremost being its endangered-species programs and educational programs.

To get an overview of the zoo, be sure to take the thirty-five-minute bus tour; the Kangaroo Bus is another option, with various stops throughout the park. Whichever mode you use to make your way around, don't miss the polar bears goofing around in their special 55-degree pool, or the tigers of Tiger River, or the meerkats, the giraffes—you get the picture; there are more than 4,000 animals in all.

LUNCH: Albert's Restaurant (619–234–3153) at the zoo is a cafe in a genuine rainforest setting, offering various pasta, chicken, salad, and seafood dishes. Moderate.

Afternoon

If you'd rather pass on the zoo, another polar-bear–viewing option is **SeaWorld Adventure Park** (1720 South Shores Road; 619–226–3901), a 150-acre attraction, on the south shore of Mission Bay, with its Wild Arctic, Penguin Encounter, Dolphin Stadium, and of course Shamu Stadium, plus much, much more.

For more of an indoor adventure, spend an afternoon—or a day, or a week—at the museums of **Balboa Park** (1549 El Prado; www.balboapark. org). Among the park's many offerings are the **Museum of Photographic Arts** (619–238–7559), the **San Diego Automotive Museum** (619–231–2886), the **San Diego Museum of Art** (619–232–7931), and the **San**

San Diego Zoo

Diego Natural History Museum (619–232–3821); a one-week passport available at the Balboa Park Visitors Center in the House of Hospitality Building in the Plaza de Panama parking lot (619–239–0512) will get you into twelve museums at a reduced rate.

Are you a sports fan? Check the schedule to see if the **San Diego Chargers** football team or **San Diego Padres** baseball team is playing at Qualcomm Stadium (9449 Friars Road; Mission Valley; 619–525–8266 for Padres or 619–280–2121 for Chargers).

DINNER: The Prado (House of Hospitality, Balboa Park, 1549 El Prado, San Diego, CA 92101; 619–557–9441) offers Latin and Italian cuisine—with a touch of California flavor—in a historic setting. An example is an entree of achiote-marinated seabass steamed in a banana leaf with chayote squash, red onions, and seasoned jicama. Expensive.

LODGING: Holiday Inn Hotel and Suites Old Town (see above).

DAY 3

Morning

BREAKFAST: Have coffee in your room, but check out before breakfast. Take Interstate 5 South to the exit for California Route 75, Coronado Island. Proceed straight ahead along Fourth Street to Orange Avenue; turn left onto Orange and follow it until you see a Victorian behemoth on your right. That'll be the **Hotel del Coronado** (1500 Orange Avenue, Coronado, CA 92118; 800–HOTELDEL or 619–435–6611).

The "Del," as it's affectionately known to San Diegans, was the site of the filming of the classic *Some Like It Hot,* the 1959 Billy Wilder comedy starring Marilyn Monroe, Tony Curtis, and Jack Lemmon—and set in Florida (so much for geographic accuracy).

The hotel revels in its "Hot" glory—its Web site at www.hoteldel.com occasionally announces showings of the film on Turner Classic Movies—but its allure is so much more. Opened in 1888, this is the type of grand old hotel, with white-painted siding and red-shingled peaked roofs, that just isn't built anymore—although it's obvious that the Grand Floridian Resort at Walt Disney World in Florida was inspired at least in part by the Del.

At any rate, take some time to stroll through the Del, and stop for **brunch** at the **Prince of Wales,** which has been voted "San Diego's most romantic restaurant." Expensive.

After brunch, stretch your legs with a stroll around Coronado Island. Orange Avenue is lined with shops and the city also offers an eighteen-hole golf course, tennis courts, and 15 miles of bicycle and skating paths.

As you're heading back across San Diego–Coronado Bridge, check out the ships in the harbor; there are naval installations on and around Coronado Island, including the U.S. Naval Amphibious Base.

After you cross the bridge, exit at Nineteenth Street. Turn left onto Market Street, right onto Eleventh Avenue, and left onto Broadway and you'll find yourself in the **Gaslamp District** of San Diego.

The 16-block downtown Gaslamp District had its heyday in the mid- to late 1800s and had fallen into decay a hundred years later, when urban renewal came calling. In 1980, the entire district was placed on the National Register of Historic Places and redevelopment began.

Today, it's a district of fascinating old buildings restored to reflect the grandeur of their times, housing restaurants, shops, and clubs; the Gaslamp District boasts a lively and entertaining nightlife.

Spend some time shopping; stores include clothing shops, jewelry shops, a cigar factory, florists, a Wyatt Earp museum, hat sales and repairs—almost anything you could imagine.

LUNCH: Hard Rock Cafe, 801 Fourth Avenue, San Diego, CA 92101; (619–615–7625), offers salads, sandwiches, and entrees in an atmosphere laden with rock memorabilia. This may be a chain, but each one is different and has different furnishings; the San Diego Hard Rock is in the 1900s-era Golden Lion Tavern, carefully restored. Moderate.

Afternoon

After lunch, it's back up I–5, then north on CA 163 to I–15 and on to Las Vegas.

THERE'S MORE

Carlsbad, California

Legoland, 1 Legoland Drive; (760) 720–LEGO. This 128-acre family theme park is dedicated to all things Lego.

Escondido, California

San Diego Wild Animal Park, 15500 San Pasqual Valley Road; (760) 747–8702. This 1,800-acre sister to the San Diego Zoo was started as a breeding facility for the zoo and now is home to more than 3,200 animals, with most roaming freely.

San Diego, California

Belmont Park, Mission Beach; (619) 491–2988. Oceanside park with renovated 1925 roller coaster, carousel, indoor pool, and indoor family playland.

Birch Aquarium, Scripps Institute of Oceanography, University of California, San Diego, 2300 Expedition Way, La Jolla; (858) 534–FISH. Largest oceanography museum in the country.

Children's Museum/Museo de los Niños, 200 West Island Avenue; (619) 233–5437 or (619) 233–8792. Hands-on introduction to various cultures, plus design and health exhibits.

Old Town Trolley Tours, boarding at several locations; (619) 298–8687. Tours of Old Town, Gaslamp Quarter, Coronado Island, and more, plus Ghosts and Gravestones tour.

San Diego Harbor Excursions, 1050 North Harbor Drive; (619) 234–4111 or (800) 442–7847. Harbor tours (including dinner cruises) and Coronado ferry.

San Diego Maritime Museum, 1306 North Harbor Drive; (619) 234–9153. Ships, artifacts, and models.

SPECIAL EVENTS

Del Mar, California

June. San Diego County Fair, three-week event with usual stuff plus top rock and country performers, Del Mar Fairgrounds, 2200 Jimmy Durante Boulevard; (858) 792–4252 or (858) 793–5555 (twenty-four-hour event hotline).

El Cajon, California

November. Mother Goose Parade, old-fashioned children's parade, West Main and Chambers Streets; (619) 444–8712.

December. Old Town Holiday in the Park and Candlelight Tours, Old Town State Historical Park; (619) 220–5422.

Whale-watching, annual migration of California gray whales, which continues through February. View from beaches or cliffs along the coast or from a boat; (619) 557–5450 or (619) 236–1212.

Imperial Beach, California

July. U.S. Open Sand Castle Competition, with various competitions plus a parade, Imperial Beach Pier; (619) 424–6663.

San Diego, California

January or February. Chinese New Year Celebration, Third Avenue and J Street; (619) 234–4447.

February. Annual Folk Fair, Balboa Park Club Building; (619) 479–8015.

Buick Invitational of California, PGA event that annually draws 100,000 spectators, Torrey Pines Municipal Golf Course, 11480 North Torrey Pines Road; (619) 281–4653.

Mardi Gras in the Gaslamp, parade and festival with food, music, and other entertainment, Gaslamp Quarter; (619) 233–5227.

March. Ocean Beach Kite Festival, make-it-yourself event with prizes, parade, food, and demonstrations, 4741 Santa Monica Avenue; (619) 224–0189.

St. Patrick's Day Parade (followed by Irish Festival in Balboa Park), Sixth Avenue; (619) 299–7812.

April. Schooner Cup Regatta, largest schooner regatta on the West Coast and largest charity regatta in the country, Harbor Island and Shelter Island, San Diego Bay; (619) 233–3138.

June. Greek Festival, with food, dancing, Greek imports, and crafts, 3655 Park Boulevard; (619) 297–4165.

September. *Día de la Independencia* (Mexican Independence Day), Old Town State Historical Park, Old Town; (619) 291–4903.

Rosarito-Ensenada 50-Mile Fun Bicycle Ride, which attracts more than 8,000 riders for ride to Ensenada, Baja California. Call for starting point: (619) 583–3001.

San Marcos, California
July. Scottish Highland Games. Rancho Santa Fe Park at La Costa Meadows Drive; (619) 645–8080.

OTHER RECOMMENDED RESTAURANTS AND LODGINGS
Coronado, California
The Chart House, 1701 Strand Way; (619) 435–0155. Seafood and steaks in an 1887 Coronado boathouse filled with antiques, and with a view of Glorietta Bay.

Coronado Island Marriott Resort, 2000 Second Street; (619) 435–3000. Three hundred–room resort on sixteen acres on San Diego Bay.

La Jolla, California

Crabcatcher Restaurant and Seaside Grill, 1298 Prospect Street; (858) 454–9587. Seafood and oyster bar; brunch, lunch, and dinner.

San Diego, California

The Brigantine, 2444 San Diego Avenue; (619) 298–9840. Old Town restaurant serving seafood and steaks.

Croce's Restaurant and Jazz Bar, 802 Fifth Avenue; (619) 233–4355. Gaslamp Quarter club owned by Ingrid Croce, widow of musician Jim Croce. Serving meats, poultry, pastas, and seafood.

Dakota Grill and Spirits, 901 Fifth Avenue; (619) 234–5554. In the Gaslamp Quarter, offering Southwestern cuisine in a casual atmosphere with entertainment.

Gaslamp Plaza Suites, 520 E Street; (619) 232–9500 or (800) 874–8770. European-style hotel built in 1913; on National Register of Historic Places. Rooftop hot tub.

Sheraton San Diego Hotel and Marina, 1380 Harbor Island Drive; (619) 291–2900. Most rooms overlook bay or yacht harbor.

U.S. Grant, 326 Broadway; (619) 232–3121 or (800) 237–5029. Historic hotel, built in 1910 and now registered as a National Historic Site, in the Gaslamp Quarter.

Wyndham Emerald Plaza, 400 West Broadway; (619) 239–4500. High-rise tower downtown on edge of Gaslamp District.

FOR MORE INFORMATION

Coronado Visitors Bureau, 1047 B Avenue, Coronado, CA 92118-3418; (619) 437–8788; www.coronadovisitors.com.

San Diego Convention and Visitors Bureau, 401 B Street, Suite 1400, San Diego, CA 92101-4237; (619) 236–1212; www.sandiego.org.

Long Beach

AN ESCAPE FIT FOR A QUEEN

2 NIGHTS

The Queen Mary • *Aquarium* • *Tall ships*
Catalina Island • *Pacific beaches*

The desert has its own particular (and at times peculiar) beauty; no doubt about that, but occasionally, most us get a longing for the water. And while Lakes Mead and Mohave are broad and deep, they're no match for the rolling Pacific breakers that can be found just a few hours away in Long Beach, California.

Long Beach was "discovered" by Spanish explorers just fifty years after Columbus came to what he called America, but the first European settlements in the area didn't appear until more than 200 years later when, in 1784, Spanish soldier Manuel Nieto received a sprawling land grant that encompassed the 28,000-acre Rancho Los Alamitos and 27,000-acre Rancho Los Cerritos, which were used for cattle and sheep operations.

Cut to nearly one hundred years later, when developer William Willmore, an Englishman, subdivided part of Los Cerritos in 1880 and grandly named the new city for himself. Ah, but Willmore City was not to be; with only twelve houses in the town four years later, Willmore gave up and left for Arizona.

Others showed more perseverance. Visitors and settlers drawn by the Santa Fe Railroad and Pacific Railroad in the area created a boom of sorts, and by 1888, the city of Long Beach—named for its long, wide Pacific beaches—was incorporated.

Back off; the city was disincorporated nine years later because of dissatisfaction with prohibition and high taxes. Back on; before the year was over, the

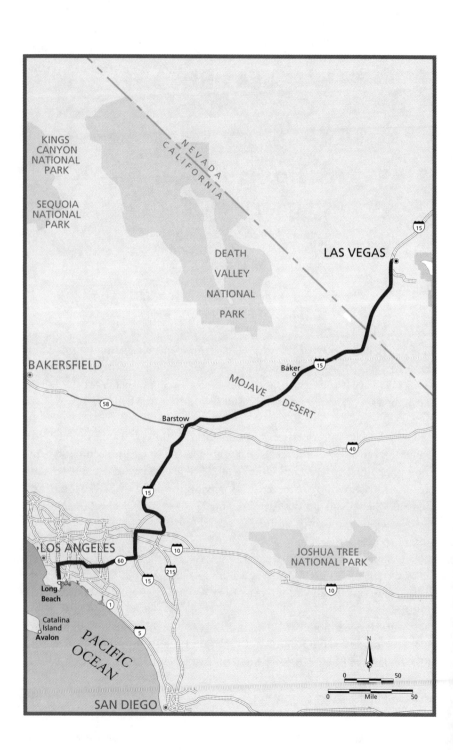

city was reincorporated. The new Pacific Electric trolley in 1902 brought more visitors and commercial growth, and between 1902 and 1910, Long Beach was the fastest-growing city in the United States.

Growth and fame continued to come to Long Beach. A U.S. naval base was built in 1941; California State University Long Beach was founded in 1949. And Howard Hughes's *Spruce Goose,* then the world's largest airplane (which was displayed in Long Beach for a time during the late 1980s), took off over Long Beach Harbor for its first—and only—flight in 1947.

Today, this fifth-largest city in California (with 440,000 residents within its 50 square miles) is a great choice for a quick escape to the seashore. It's close enough to the major attractions of Southern California to give you a whole cornucopia of choices, but recent urban renewal efforts also have created a range of choices within Long Beach itself, including the *Queen Mary* and the Aquarium of the Pacific. So escape the desert for a few days by the sea.

DAY 1

Afternoon

Long Beach is about 280 miles from Las Vegas, for a drive of about four hours—perfect for a late-afternoon departure. Drive south on Interstate 15 for about 220 miles to California Route 60 West. Follow CA 60 for about 28 miles to Interstate 605 South for 10 miles to Interstate 105 West. Take this for 3 miles to Interstate 710 South to the Queen Mary/Piers F-J exit to South Harbor Scenic Drive to Harbor Place to Queens Highway.

You'll see the *Queen Mary*—now officially the **Hotel Queen Mary**— (1126 Queens Highway; 562–435–3511) long before you arrive; it's hard to miss this majestic ship with its three funnels moored in Long Beach Harbor.

The *Queen Mary* made her maiden voyage in 1936 for the first of what would be 1,001 trans-Atlantic crossings. By 1967, however, she was for sale, and the city of Long Beach purchased her to serve as a tourism attraction and hotel for the city. Today, the grand old lady draws local residents in search of romantic getaways, visitors, and those attending conferences and conventions.

She's also great fun to tour. The ship has been carefully restored and today's visitors get a mini-education on her years as a troop ship as well as a luxury liner. During World War II, the *Queen Mary* was handling the trans-Atlantic crossings of soldiers instead of the moneyed rich, and the ever-increasing need for troops meant she once carried 16,000 in one crossing, which still stands as a world record.

The *Queen Mary* reportedly is home to another type of passenger as well, and that's the focus of one of the ship's newest attractions, the **Ghosts and Legends Tour.** Ghost sightings aren't a certainty on the multimedia interactive tour but lots of fun is, as visitors are guided through parts of the ship until recently off-limits, including a spot well below the waterline in the bowels of the ship.

A self-guided tour also is part of the Queen Mary experience. Map in hand, you'll journey through the engine room, past the wedding chapel and isolation ward, through the **Treasures of the *Queen Mary*** archive exhibit, and along each of the ship's decks. Along the way you'll note plaques pointing out spots where ghosts reportedly were sighted or other-worldly experiences occurred.

DINNER: Stay on the *Queen Mary* for dinner at **Sir Winston's** (reservations required; 562– 499–1657), where the California/continental cuisine includes such offerings as warm goat cheese in a crispy potato basket with grilled vegetables and pistachios, beef tenderloin and *foie gras* wrapped in phyllo dough, or venison *en croute*. Expensive.

LODGING: The **Hotel Queen Mary** has 365 original Art Deco staterooms, including eight suites (562–432–6964 or 800–437–2934; www.queenmary. com; rates from $109 to $500).

DAY 2

Morning

BREAKFAST: Grab an old-fashioned cream scone and a cup of tea (or coffee) from **The Starboard Bakery** on the *Queen Mary*. Or, for something more substantial, go ashore to the **Colonial Buffet** (355 East First Street, Long Beach, CA 90802; 562–471–5465) and load up on bacon and eggs, with fresh home-baked breads, rolls, and pastries. Inexpensive.

Want to have even more of a getaway? Board the *Catalina Express* ferry (310–519–1212 or 800–481–3470; www.catalinaexpress.com) at its port adjacent to the *Queen Mary* and take off on the one-hour trip to Avalon on Catalina Island. Located 22 miles from the mainland, the island is 21 miles long and 8 miles wide and was a base for smugglers and pirates before it was discovered by tourists and sport fisherman.

Stay as long as you like; depending on the season, the ferry company may have as many as thirty trips per day. The island's environment is a fragile one

View of Long Beach Harbor from the Queen Mary

so you can't take cars, but bicycles and motorized carts are available for rent. Tours of the island and surrounding waterways—including glass-bottom boat trips and trips to the home of a seal colony—also are available from several companies, including **Catalina Island Company's Discovery Tours Center** (310–510–2500 or 800–428–2566).

The **Wrigley Memorial and Botanical Gardens** (Avalon Canyon Road; 310–510–2288) is maintained in memory of William Wrigley Jr. of chewing-gum fame, who is generally credited with developing the island into a resort.

LUNCH: Rick's Cafe Catalina (417 Crescent Avenue, Avalon, CA 90704; 310–510–0333) offers sandwiches, salads, seafood, and pasta amid decor featuring photos from *Casablanca.* An open-air patio also is available. Moderate.

Afternoon

To get another perspective of the water and the crafts that ply it, visit one of the tallships that make their homes at Long Beach Harbor. But first: If you're going to be moving around the harbor, make the trip a fun one by boarding the *AquaLink* (562–591–2301) that stops at the *Queen Mary* and at the Aquarium of the Pacific and Alamitos Bay Landing on the mainland. The 60-foot water-taxi catamaran runs every ninety minutes and saves you the hassle of having to find your way between stops and of parking your vehicle.

At Rainbow Harbor, between the aquarium and Shoreline Village, you'll find the American Heritage Marine Institute's **American Pride** (714–970–8800; www.americanpride.org), the **Pilgrim of Newport** **Historic Sailing Ship** (714–966–0686; www.sailpilgrim.com), and the Nautical Heritage Society's **Tallship Californian** (800–432–2201; www.californian.org), tallships all. The three-master *American Pride,* which dates to 1941, offers whale-watching cruises, sea camps, and charters. The *Pilgrim of Newport,* a replica of a 1700s topsail schooner, offers educational marine programs, weddings at sea, and whale-watching, and the *Californian,* a replica of an 1848 Revenue Service cutter, schedules day sails, weddings, and educational cruises.

Or, head to the nearby **Aquarium of the Pacific** (100 Aquarium Way; 562–590–3100; www.aquariumofpacific.org) for an up-close-and-personal look at marine life. The aquarium is home to 12,000 inhabitants; you'll see jellyfish, seals, sea lions, skates, rays, sea turtles, and fish of every possible description.

DINNER: Parkers' Lighthouse (435 Shoreline Village Drive, Long Beach, CA 90802; 562–432–6500), on a promontory near the aquarium and Rainbow Harbor and overlooking the *Queen Mary,* has a commanding view of Long Beach harbor and the Pacific coastline. The menu focuses on seafood, beef, and chicken, with dishes such as spicy seared ahi tuna, fresh crab cakes with aioli sauce, penne with rock shrimp and Romano rossa sauce, or a mesquite-grilled shrimp and tortilla salad. Expensive.

LODGING: The Queen Mary Hotel (see above).

DAY 3

Morning

BREAKFAST: The **Queen Mary Hotel** (562–499–1606) is known far and wide for its champagne Sunday brunch in the Grand Salon, the ship's original first-class dining room, which is a grand way to cap your weekend. The buffet features more than fifty entrees, including carving, Asian, pasta, seafood, and Mexican stations, a salad bar, and an extensive dessert station where selections include chocolate-covered strawberries. Expensive.

If the weather's warm and you're itching to get into that water you've been seeing all weekend, rest assured that Long Beach has 5½ miles of beach. To get to the water, drive to **Marina Green Park** off Shoreline Drive, or to **Bluff Park** at the corner of Ocean Boulevard and Juniper Avenue.

If shopping's more your thing, check out the **Queen's Marketplace** near the *Queen Mary,* which is an open-air center in an Old English style; **Shoreline Village**, near Rainbow Harbor; or **Downtown Long Beach**, with its trendy outdoor dining and shopping alone Pine Avenue.

LUNCH: For a last lingering look at that gorgeous waterfront, go to **Buster's Beach House Grill and Longboard Bar** (168 Marina Drive at Alamitos Bay Landing, Long Beach, CA 90803; 562–598–9431) for selections such as fish and chips, coconut shrimp tempura, macadamia-crusted chicken, "unfashionable steak," or pork cooked in banana leaves. Moderate.

Afternoon

Time to go home; it's back in the car to retrace your route and return to Las Vegas.

THERE'S MORE

Catalina Island, California

Catalina Island Museum, casino building at west end of Avalon Bay, Avalon; (310) 510–2414. Historical items from the island's past.

Long Beach, California

Biplane Rides, 3355 East Spring Street; (562) 427–9433 or (866) 331–3333. Scenic rides in open-cockpit biplane over *Queen Mary,* Pacific Ocean, Los Angeles, and Hollywood Hills. Aerobatic rides for thrill-seekers.

Earl Burns Miller Japanese Garden, 1250 Bellflower Boulevard; (562) 985–8885. Gardens with koi pond, waterfalls, tea house, and bonsai collection.

El Dorado Nature Center, 7550 East Spring Street; (562) 570–1745. Wildlife sanctuary of more than a hundred acres with nature trails, displays, and programs.

Gondola Getaway, 5437 East Ocean Boulevard; (562) 433–9595. One-hour cruises through the canals of Naples Island.

Long Beach Heritage, P.O. Box 92521; (562) 493–7019. Scheduled and customized walking tours of historic and architectural downtown.

Long Beach Museum of Art, 2300 East Ocean Boulevard; (562) 439–2119. Collection of more than 2,500 works.

Rancho Los Alamitos, 6400 East Bixby Hill Road; (562) 431–3541. Seven-acre historic ranch with circa-1800 adobe ranch house.

Rancho Los Cerritos, 460 Virginia Road; (562) 570–1755. Historic ranch in rare Monterey-style adobe with gardens and visitor center.

SPECIAL EVENTS

January through April. Whale-watching, the annual migration of the Pacific gray whale; (562) 436–3645 or (800) 452–7829.

February. *Queen Mary* Scottish Festival, with pipe bands, highland dancing, parades, competitions, exhibits, performances, and food and drink; (562) 436–3645 or (800) 452–7829.

April. Kaleidoscope Festival, with Renaissance Faire, live entertainment and vendor booths; (562) 436–3645 or (800) 452–7829.

Toyota Grand Prix of Long Beach, with an international field of drivers; (562) 436–9953.

May. Lesbian and Gay Pride Parade, one of the largest in the nation; (562) 436–3645 or (800) 452–7829.

June. Beach Fest, with fifty bands and the world's largest chili cook-off; (562) 436–3645 or (800) 452–7829.

July. Chinese Dragon Boat Races, Marine Stadium; (562) 436–3645 or (800) 452–7829.

August. Long Beach Jazz Festival; (562) 436–3645 or (800) 452–7829.

September. Long Beach International Film Festival, bringing together films and filmmakers from around the world, the *Queen Mary;* (562) 436–3645 or (800) 452–7829.

December. Daisy Avenue Christmas Tree Lane, featuring creative displays and thousands of twinkling lights along Daisy between Hill Street and the Pacific Coast Highway, plus holiday entertainment; (562) 436–3645 or (800) 452–7829.

OTHER SUGGESTED RESTAURANTS AND LODGINGS

Catalina Island, California

The Channel House, 205 Crescent Avenue, Avalon; (310) 510–1617. Beef, poultry, fish, and pasta entrees. Patio seating available.

Hotel Metropole, 208 Crescent Avenue, Avalon; (310) 510–1884. Forty-eight rooms with ocean views, fireplaces, and private balconies.

Hotel St. Lauren–Catalina, 231 Beacon Street, Avalon; (310) 510–2299. Victorian oceanview hotel.

Long Beach, California

Belmont Brewing Company, 25 36th Place; (562) 433–3891. California cuisine and freshly brewed beer; ocean view.

The Crab Pot Restaurant and Bar, 2165 Marina Drive; (562) 430–0272. Local seafood and seafood native to the Northwest.

Dockside Boat and Bed, Rainbow Harbor; (562) 436–3111. Spend the night on a private sailing or motor yacht.

Lord Mayor's Bed and Breakfast Inn, 435 Cedar Avenue; (562) 436–0324. Home and cottages near the heart of the city.

The Reef, 880 Harbor Scenic Drive; (562) 435–8013. Victorian decor and waterfront verandas overlooking downtown skyline; specializing in steaks and seafood.

The Sky Room, 40 South Locust Avenue; (562) 983–2703. Panoramic views of skyline and ocean.

The Turret House Bed and Breakfast, 556 Chestnut Avenue; (562) 983–9812. Turn-of-the-century Victorian home with five bedrooms.

FOR MORE INFORMATION

Catalina Island Visitors Bureau and Chamber of Commerce, No. 1 Green Pier, P.O. Box 217, Avalon, CA 90704; (310) 510–1520; www.catalina.com.

Long Beach Area Convention and Visitors Bureau, One World Trade Center, 3rd floor, Long Beach, CA 90831-0300; (562) 436–3645 or (800) 4–LB-STAY; www.golongbeach.org.

California Beaches

SURF'S UP

---

2 NIGHTS

Beaches • Surfing • Oceanfront fun • Pacific Coast Highway

When most people think of California, what immediately comes to mind is beaches—miles and miles of beaches, especially those in the sunny southern part of the state. That's especially true with baby boomers, who grew up with the beach-blanket movies, Jan and Dean, and the Beach Boys.

The allure of the beach started long before that, of course, and by the turn of the twentieth century, the California beach communities had more than their share of seasonal residents. But while the state has grown up around them in just about every way imaginable, it's managed to preserve most of its beaches, a large portion of them for recreational use.

And beaches are among the things that, try as it might, Las Vegas definitely doesn't have—the beach area at the Mandalay Bay Casino-Resort on the Strip notwithstanding. OK, so Lake Mead does technically have a beach, but when you take into account that this "shoreline" was until about seventy years ago actually a mountain slope, you can understand just how rocky and uncomfortable that beach can be.

Luckily, the beaches of Southern California are just a few hours away; that fabled Los Angeles–to–Las Vegas traffic jam is going in the other direction as Southern Californians come east for the weekend to do a little gambling in the desert. So grab a board and your guy or girl and get away to the Southern California beaches for a quick escape.

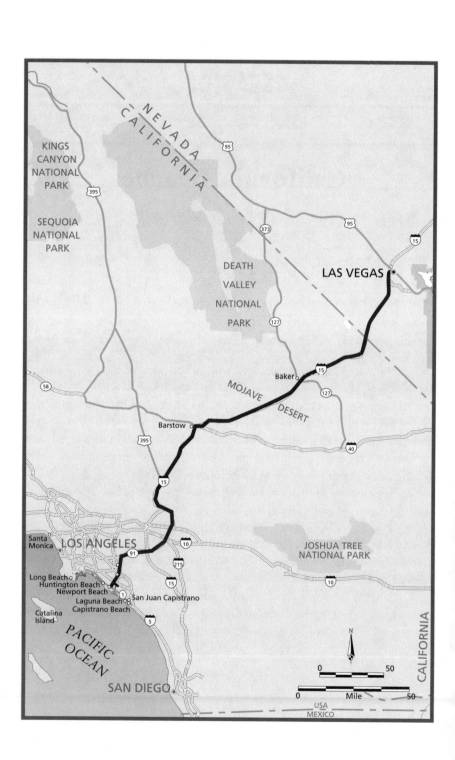

DAY 1

Afternoon

A good place to stay is **Newport Beach,** which is sort of centralized along the Santa Monica–to–San Clemente stretch of the oceanfront. Newport Beach is about 278 miles from Las Vegas; a late-morning or early-afternoon departure should give you a good start on the weekend. Start by taking Interstate 15 South for about 240 miles to California Route 91 West toward Beach Cities (you'll know you're going in the right direction!). Follow CA 91 West to California Route 55 South/Costa Mesa Freeway toward Newport Beach, then follow CA 55 South. After about 12 miles take California Route 73 South for a few miles to the University Drive exit, turn right onto University Drive, left onto Jamboree Road, left onto San Joaquin Hills Road, right onto Santa Rosa Drive, and left onto Newport Center Drive.

DINNER: Roy's Newport Beach (453 Newport Center Drive, Newport Beach, CA 92660; 949–640–7697) is another from Hawaiian restaurant genius Roy Yamaguchi. It's Pacific Rim with French inspiration, with an emphasis on fresh seafood and Asian seasonings. And don't forget Roy's signature chocolate soufflé for dessert. Expensive.

LODGING: Head back to CA 55 South and follow it until it becomes Newport Boulevard; follow Newport Boulevard to Balboa Boulevard out onto the Balboa Peninsula and Palm Street. Turn right onto Palm and follow it to Main Street. The **Balboa Inn** (105 Main Street, Balboa Peninsula, Newport Beach, CA 92661; 714–675–3412 or 877–BALBOA–9; www.balboainn.com; rates from $169 to $249) is a recently renovated 1929 landmark that advertises itself as "on the sand at Newport." It's got an outdoor pool and Jacuzzi, but there's plenty of beach; erstwhile guest Johnny Weismuller was reputed to like the 2½-mile swim between the Balboa and Newport piers. And the oceanview terrace is a great place to catch the sunset over the Pacific.

DAY 2

Morning

BREAKFAST: Wilma's Patio on Balboa Island (203 Marine Avenue, Newport Beach, CA 92662; 949–675–5542)—you'll need to take a ferry from the peninsula—prides itself on its friendliness and on its breakfasts, and rightfully so. Breakfast selections include the Balboa Belly Bomber (a warm French roll stuffed with eggs) as well as homemade pancakes, all sorts of egg dishes (including three Mexican variations and five variations on eggs Benedict), waffles, and French toast. Moderate.

Back on the Balboa Peninsula, consider a stop at the **Balboa Fun Zone** (600 East Bay Avenue, 949–673–0408), a historic spot whose old-fashioned attractions such as a carousel, merry-go-round, and bumper cars still retain their charm.

Now it's time to start your tour of the beaches, by heading up CA 55 to Interstate 405 North to Interstate 10 West to **Santa Monica.** Santa Monica is known for its beaches, of course, and its shops, restaurants and boutiques, but it's also home to more than sixty-five museums and art galleries.

Also among the attractions is **Pacific Park** at Santa Monica Pier (310–260–8744), a "park on a pier" that has a dozen rides including a roller coaster that seems to swoop out over the ocean.

Speaking of swooping: In Santa Monica you'll find the **Museum of Flying** (2772 Donald Douglas Loop North; 310–392–8822), on the site where the first DC-3 was built, which showcases more than forty aircraft—including a Grumman Bearcat and a Hawker Hurricane—in various spots on the grounds.

Head south on the Pacific Coast Highway (California Route 1) to **Venice,** home of the celebrated Muscle Beach. The **Venice Pier** (310–392–4687) is the site of all of the action; there you'll see—in addition to weightlifters actually doing their thing—sidewalk performers on the boardwalk and visitors and locals rollerblading and biking (rentals available in nearby shops), playing pickup basketball, sunbathing, swimming, and surfing. There also are restaurants and shops if you're so inclined.

Next along down the highway is Marina del Rey, known as the site of the biggest manmade small-craft harbor in the world, with more than 6,000 boats. In Marina del Rey you'll find **Fisherman's Village** overlooking the harbor (13755 Fiji Way; 310–823–5411), with restaurants, shops, boat and personal watercraft rentals, and whale-watching and deep-sea sportfishing charters.

LUNCH: Grab a fish sandwich or a burger at **Tony P's Dockside Grill** (4445 Admiralty Way, Marina del Rey, CA 90292; 310–823–4534). Tony P's advertises that it has a million-dollar view and no kidding; the view is of the marina and all of those boats. Moderate.

Afternoon

Driving south, you'll pass state beaches at Manhattan Beach and Redondo Beach; stop for a swim, sunbathing or to watch the surfers in their wetsuits, trying to catch that next big wave. Redondo Beach Pier has seafood restaurants and souvenir shops, and if the weather's clear, you may catch a glimpse of Catalina Island from the beach.

Follow along on the Pacific Coast Highway (PCH) as it winds inland for a bit past Long Beach and back to the coast at Seal Beach. A little farther south, you'll come to Beachgoers' Mecca: **Huntington Beach.** Huntington Beach is blessed with 8½ miles of uninterrupted shoreline, and as you drive along, you'll see that it's all connected by a paved walkway. You'll also see numerous birthday parties, anniversary parties, graduation parties—just about any celebratory event you can imagine—announced with banners strung on the beach. You'll also see lots of people walking their dogs in a beach area designated for that, beach volleyball being played with fervor, closely-spaced lifeguard stations that are fully enclosed, a farmer's market on certain days, and even an electric-vehicle recharging station.

This is surfers' paradise, maybe what the Beach Boys were referring to when they sang about "Surf City USA." It's been called the most heavily surfed beach on the U.S. west coast and there's a **surfers' walk of fame** near the Huntington Beach Pier. Further testimony is the **Huntington Beach International Surfing Museum** (411 Olive Avenue; 714–960–3483), which has a collection of surfboards and related ephemera. These people are serious surfers; a visit to their Web site found an announcement for a campaign to "help make the Duke Kahanamoku postage stamp a reality."

As you cruise down the PCH, you'll also smell charcoal on the air, especially if it's evening; beach barbecues are a popular tradition.

DINNER: And the smell of charcoal no doubt got those tastebuds going, so drive just a little bit farther south to the **Five Crowns** (3801 East Coast Highway, Corona del Mar, CA 92625; 949–760–0331). The Five Crowns is a replica of Ye Olde Bell, considered the oldest country inn in England. It has a cozy English-parlor atmosphere and serves appetizers such as Maryland crab cakes and porcini ravioli, entrees such as potato-crusted salmon, roast rack of Colorado lamb, and of course its signature prime rib, which is available in four cuts and served with Yorkshire pudding and horseradish crème. Save room for some English trifle. Moderate.

LODGING: It's just a short jog back to the Balboa Peninsula and the Balboa Inn (see above).

DAY 3

Morning

BREAKFAST: Start the day off with brunch at **The Yankee Tavern** (333 Bayside Drive, Newport Beach, CA 92660; 949–675–5333), a waterfront restaurant overlooking the serene beauty of Newport Harbor. Brunch selections include a traditional egg breakfast, three different types of eggs Benedict, omelets, quiches, crepes—even Hawaiian Portuguese sausage and eggs. Moderate.

Then it's back to the Pacific Coast Highway, heading south through **Laguna Beach** with its many art galleries, through **Dana Point** with its natural cove to **Capistrano Beach,** where you'll turn north on Interstate 5 to **San Juan Capistrano.** The main attraction at San Juan Capistrano is of course the **Mission de San Juan Capistrano** (Ortega Highway and Camino Capistrano; 949–234–1360), famous for the swallows that for more than 200 years returned each spring (although those storied swallows have been disturbed by recent restoration and have fled to the suburbs, nesting on the roof of a nearby shopping mall).

At any rate, swallows or no swallows, the mission truly is worth seeing. It was founded in 1776 by Father Junipero Serra, who established a string of missions throughout coastal California. The original building was partially toppled in an earthquake in 1812 and is now being restored. Padre Serra's Church, which dates to 1778, still is in use; you might even see a wedding taking place within its hallowed walls.

The complex also has a number of museum rooms and outdoor displays that depict life in the mission in the eighteenth century and extensive gardens that provide a serene spot to simply sit and reflect.

A walking tour of the historic city of San Juan Capistrano also is available; look for a map in the information booth near the mission.

LUNCH: Cedar Creek Inn (26860 Ortega Highway, San Juan Capistrano, CA 92675; 949–240–2229) has an outdoor patio overlooking the mission, which is perfect on days when the weather is pleasant—and even when it's not, thanks to an outdoor fireplace. The menu includes such dishes as a Margarita shrimp salad, crab-scallop cakes, fish tacos, or an ahi salad. Moderate.

Mission de San Juan Capistrano

Afternoon

Then it's time to head back to Las Vegas. Take I–5 north to California Route
133 North to California Route 241 North to CA 91 East to I–15, and follow
I–15 home.

THERE'S MORE

Corona del Mar, California

Sherman Library and Gardens, 2647 East Pacific Coast Highway; (949)
673–2261. Botanical collection ranging from desert to tropical vegetation
amid fountains, plus sculptures and seasonal flowers.

Dana Point, California

Ocean Institute, 24200 Dana Point Harbor Drive; (949) 496–2274. Sea-life exhibits and full-size replica of Richard Henry Dana's *Pilgrim,* which he described in the novel *Two Years before the Mast.*

Newport Beach, California

Adventures at Sea, 3101 West Coast Highway, Suite 209; (949) 650–2412. Dining cruises, sailing, sportfishing, harbor tours, and gondola cruises.

Hornblower Cruises and Events, 2431 West Pacific Coast Highway, Suite 101; (949) 646–0155. Weekend dinner-dance cruises and Sunday champagne brunch cruises.

Newport Beach Whale Watching; (949) 673–0240. Daily departures late December through late April.

Newport Harbor Nautical Museum, 151 East Pacific Coast Highway; (949) 675–7863. Model ship gallery, Newport Harbor gallery, changing exhibits.

Orange County Museum of Art, 850 San Clemente Drive; (949) 759–1122. Collection showcasing California's art history from mid-1800s to the present.

Santa Monica, California

California Heritage Museum, 2612 Main Street; (310) 392–8537. Restored period rooms from before the turn of the twentieth century through the 1930s.

SPECIAL EVENTS

Corona del Mar, California

September. Annual Sand Castle and Sand Sculpture Contest, drawing adults and children, amateurs and professionals, Corona Del Mar State Beach; (949) 729–4400.

Costa Mesa, California

December. *La Posada Mágica,* candlelight procession depicting Mary and Joseph's journey for shelter, South Coast Repertory; (714) 708–5555.

Dana Point, California

March. Taste of Dana Point Harbor, showcasing local restaurants; (949) 496–1094.

May. Dana Point Harbor Boat Show, with old and new boats; (949) 496–1094.

Huntington Beach, California

July. Annual Independence Day Celebration, with largest parade west of the Mississippi, plus 5K run/walk, bands, and fireworks; (714) 536–5486.

December. Cruise of Lights, narrated cruise to see holiday displays, Huntington Harbor; (714) 840–7542.

Laguna Beach, California

Mid-November through mid-December. Sawdust Winter Fantasy, arts and crafts festival with holiday entertainment, Laguna Beach Sawdust Festival Grounds; (949) 494–3030.

Newport Beach, California

January–April. Whale-watching excursions, migration of hundreds of California gray whales; Newport Beach (949–673–1434) and Dana Point (949–496–1094).

February. Newport Beach Jazz Party, with local and regional jazz artists, Newport Beach Marriot Hotel and Tennis Club; (949) 759–5003.

April. Newport-Ensenada Yacht Race, with more than 500 yachts in various sizes and classes; (949) 771–0691.

September. Taste of Newport, showcasing local restaurants, plus entertainment; (949) 729–4400.

December. Menorah Lighting Ceremony, plus music and dancing, Fashion Island; (949) 786–5000.

OTHER RECOMMENDED RESTAURANTS AND LODGINGS

Costa Mesa, California

Yard House Restaurant, 1875 Newport Boulevard; (949) 642–0090. American fusion cuisine served from exhibition kitchen.

Huntington Beach, California

Hilton Waterfront Beach Resort, 21100 Pacific Coast Highway; (714) 845–8000. Mediterranean-style resort.

Laguna Beach, California

Aliso Creek Inn, 31106 South Coast Highway; (949) 499–2271. Suites with kitchens, in the Aliso Creek canyon.

Bistro 201, 3333 West Pacific Coast Highway, Suite 200; (949) 631–2487. Contemporary American cuisine.

Capri Laguna Inn on the Beach, 1441 South Coast Highway; (949) 494–6533. On the beach; private decks.

La Casa del Camino, 1289 South Coast Highway; (949) 497–2446. Historic 1927 hotel on bluff above the Pacific, with rooftop deck.

Newport Beach, California

Aysia 101 Restaurant, 2901 West Pacific Coast Highway, Suite 310; (949) 722–4128. Pan-Asian cuisine in waterfront dining room.

Bayside Restaurant, 900 Bayside Drive; (949) 721–1222. American contemporary cuisine specializing in seafood, steaks, and chops.

FOR MORE INFORMATION

Huntington Beach Conference and Visitors Bureau, 417 Main Street, Huntington Beach, CA 92648-5131; (800) 729–6232 or (714) 969–3492; www.hbvisit.com.

Laguna Beach Visitors Bureau, P.O. Box 221, 252 Broadway, Laguna Beach, CA 92652; (800) 877–1115; www.lagunabeachinfo.org.

Newport Beach Conference and Visitors Bureau, 3300 West Pacific Coast Highway, Newport Beach, CA 92663; (949) 722–1611 or (800) 94–COAST (942–6278); www.newportbeach-cvb.com.

San Juan Capistrano Chamber of Commerce, 31871 Camino Capistrano, Suite 306, San Juan Capistrano, CA 92675; (949) 493–4700; www.sanjuanchamber.com.

OLD WEST
ESCAPES

OLD WEST

Virginia City and Carson City

NEVADA HISTORY LIVES ON

2 NIGHTS

*Authentic nineteenth-century towns • "Talking" houses
Sites of gold-mining history • Old-West town
Unique cemeteries • Historic lodgings*

> *To find a petrified man, or break a stranger's leg, or cave an imaginary
> mine, or discover some dead Indians in a Gold Hill tunnel, or massacre a
> family at Dutch Nick's, were feats and calamities that we never hesitated
> about devising when the public needed matters of thrilling interest for break-
> fast. The seemingly tranquil Enterprise office was a ghastly factory of
> slaughter, mutilation and general destruction in those days.*
> — Mark Twain, about the Virginia City *Territorial Enterprise*, 1868

It's true that even during its heyday as a mining capital in the late nineteenth century, Virginia City, Nevada, wasn't quite as colorful as Mark Twain
and his cohorts might have made it sound when he wrote for the town's
newspaper, the *Territorial Enterprise*. But the reality was colorful enough, especially by today's standards.

The Comstock Lode, which held more than $400 million worth of gold
mixed with high-quality silver, made Virginia City (once known as "the rich-
est town on earth") the first industrial town in the West and the most impor-
tant between Denver and San Francisco; it also gave birth to a raucous mining
economy that had more than its share of bars and bordellos—in addition to a
variety of churches for the good citizens of Virginia City.

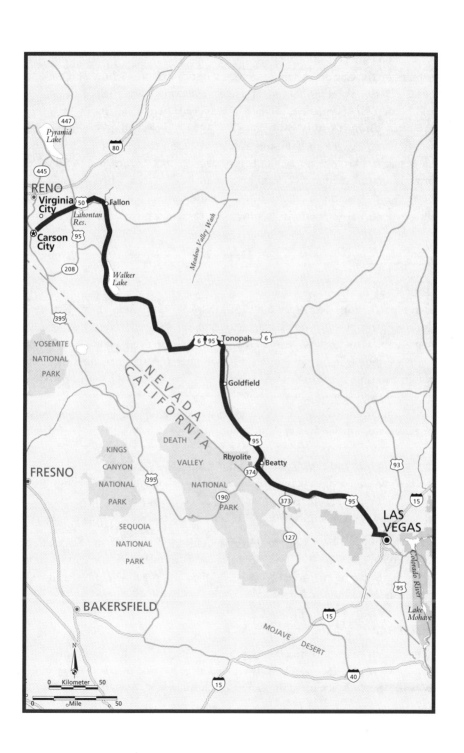

Carson City, Nevada, its somewhat more genteel neighbor to the south, was named for Kit Carson, the most famous scout of explorer John C. Fremont. It became Nevada's territorial capital when the territory was established in 1861 and became the permanent capital when Nevada became a state in 1864.

Today, Virginia City and Carson City provide a clear (if a little rosy-hued) window into Nevada's past. History is revered there, unlike in live-for-tomorrow Las Vegas. Various historic sites and even the ambience of the towns themselves provide complementary contrasting pictures of the era when Nevada first burst into the frontier spotlight. To wander their streets is to get an idea of how the pioneers who settled this frontier state lived and played.

DAY 1

Morning

Drive north from Las Vegas on U.S. Highway 95, passing through Beatty, Tonopah, and Hawthorne. Carson City is about 450 miles from Las Vegas, so you might want to leave early Friday morning or even Thursday evening; there are motels in all three towns. (Remember, too, that bargain airfares are readily available between Las Vegas and Reno, the airport that serves both Virginia City and Carson City.)

If you choose to make it a leisurely drive, take a side jog to the ghost town of **Rhyolite,** outside Beatty. And be sure to drive slowly through **Goldfield,** just south of Tonopah, and check out the vintage buildings such as the gracious old hotel and the abandoned high school.

Follow US 95 until you reach the town of Fallon, about 385 miles northeast of Las Vegas, and then head west on U.S. Highway 50 for about 61 miles to Carson City. Once in town, US 50 also is named William Street.

LUNCH: Stop at **The Cracker Box** restaurant (402 East William Street, Carson City, NV 89701; 775–882–4556), a local landmark of more than thirty years that serves up the usual burgers and fries and tuna melts, plus salads and fresh fish. Moderate.

Afternoon

Then spend the rest of the day exploring the sights of this state capital that has more of the feel of small-town America. A good place to start is the **Nevada State Museum.** To get there, continue west on William to Carson

Street and turn left; the stately museum is on the northeast corner of Carson and Robinson Streets (600 North Carson Street; 775–687–4810).

The gold and silver produced from the Comstock necessitated the construction of a U.S. Mint in Carson City in 1866. Today, it's the Nevada State Museum. Exhibits inside include old coin stamps, a replica of a silver mine, a life-sized vignette of Paiute Indian life, minerals, exceptional-quality baskets, guns, and the usual taxidermy.

Want to learn more Nevada history? To fully appreciate the rich past of Carson City in a new, high-tech way, visit with the city's "talking houses," which are along the 20-mile **Kit Carson Trail** (pick up a map of the trail while you're at the Nevada State Museum). The trail can be accessed from various points, including off Carson Street just across the street from the museum. The houses' "voices" are broadcast on four AM frequencies. The ninety-second segments include the secrets of each home—and accompanying anecdotes—complete with sound effects from the house's era. A special bonus is the voice of John Wayne, who filmed *The Shootist,* his last movie, at the Krebs-Petersen house.

While the proximity of a car radio makes it tempting to hear the houses from a vehicle, bring along a portable radio and take to the sidewalks, or return for a second trip on foot following the thin blue line; the map gives separate routes for driving and walking tours. The combined trails encompass more than sixty landmarks, including the **Governor's Mansion,** the former Nevada Supreme Court, and the home of Orion Clemens, brother of Mark Twain.

The **Nevada State Capitol** is nearby, at 101 North Carson Street. Its halls of Alaska marble are decorated with detailed friezes and portraits of former governors. Also check out the area between the Capitol and the Legislative Building, where you'll find statues of prominent early Nevadans.

DINNER: Adele's (1112 North Carson Street, Carson City, NV 89701; 775–882–3353) is a local landmark that's been drawing movers and shakers for more than twenty years with its menu of steaks and chops, fresh seafood and pasta, award-winning wine list, and setting in a historic building. Moderate.

LODGING: Bliss Mansion (710 West Robinson Street, Carson City, NV 89703; 775–887–8988; rates from $195 to $215). Across from the governor's mansion, this bed and breakfast was built in 1879, when it was the largest private residence in the state. Room rates include coffee served in your room before the gourmet breakfast, plus afternoon wine and cheese.

Capitol Building, Carson City

DAY 2

Morning

BREAKFAST: Enjoy the offerings at the Bliss Mansion, or wait to eat until after the short drive to Virginia City.

To get to **Virginia City,** head northeast on US 50 about 10 miles to Nevada Route 341 and then north into town. NV 341 will lead you directly to C Street, the town's main drag. Parking is never easy in a town that was built for horses and stage coaches, but look for a spot along the street or in one of the many public lots that can be accessed right off of C Street. Most of Virginia City can easily be seen on foot.

If you didn't have breakfast at the Bliss Mansion, try one of the omelets at **Solid Muldoons** (65 North C Street, Virginia City, NV 89440; 775–847–9181). Inexpensive. Then spend the morning on **C Street** for a leisurely stroll that will enable you to fully appreciate the late 1800s-era buildings that house shops selling everything from antiques and collectibles to T-shirts and pizza.

Remember those Western towns you saw in the movies and thought didn't actually exist? Here's one right before your eyes—complete with plank sidewalks. If you'd prefer not to walk, take a tour with **A & M Horse Drawn Carriage Rides** (775–246–0322) or **Virginia City Tram Tours** (916–587–5742).

LUNCH: As you're wandering the handful of blocks that make up the main commercial area, keep an eye peeled for the **Brass Rail** (55 North C Street, Virginia City, NV 89440; 775–847–0304). If the weather's chilly, you'll appreciate the warmth of the Brass Rail's homemade cobblers and pot pies; a piece of warm peach cobbler a la mode is guaranteed to prepare you for an afternoon of adventure. If the weather is pleasant, plan on sitting on the porch and taking in the mountain views. Oh, and don't be alarmed by the sagging second-story porch across the front of the Brass Rail; the dining porch is in the back. Inexpensive.

Afternoon

After lunch, make your way along C Street to the north end of town and Virginia City's **cemeteries.** The town's contiguous cemeteries number anywhere from seven to sixteen, depending on how you separate (and count) them, and include the Masonic and Catholic cemeteries, the Exempt Firemen Cemetery, and the Odd Fellows Cemetery.

These are not your basic burial grounds. Oh, the cemeteries still are in use, but the most interesting of them date to the heyday of the Comstock Lode. The cemeteries are hilly, the ground uneven in most places, so step carefully. Depending on which season you visit, you may find the cemeteries fragrant with the blossoms of the dozens of lilac bushes that have gone wild over the decades and overtaken many of the plots they were planted to mark.

The older graves are commemorated by wooden markers, sometimes wooden fences and rails. It's easy to see which families could afford to do more; some graves have ornate iron fences, most of which have, like the wooden ones, begun the dust-to-dust process of the mortal souls over which they stand guard. The markers that still can be read tend to be poignant. Peter Eddy's stone reads, KILLED IN THE GOULD & CURRY MINE JUNE 24, 1887. 39 YEARS. ERECTED BY HIS BELOVED WIFE EMMA.

Near the parking-area entrance to the cemeteries—where few visitors could miss it—is a memorial to Mary Jane Simpson, who was killed in the fire of 1875. SACRED TO THE MEMORY OF MARY JANE SIMPSON, it reads. THE WITHIN WAS ONLY A MULE. STILL SHE WAS NOBODY'S FULE. STRANGER TREAD LIGHTLY.

After exploring the cemeteries, head back to C Street and the ticket office for the **Virginia & Truckee Railroad** (775–847–0380). The train line offers a narrated, thirty-five-minute round-trip ride to the hamlet of Gold Hill. Along the way you might see deer as well as old train tunnels and a view of the area the way passengers saw it more than 125 years ago. The train runs daily from the end of May to October 1, weekends during October and November.

You can't leave Virginia City without seeing a mine, so tour the **Chollar Mine** and see equipment from the Comstock's fifth-largest producer (775–847–0155; open May through September). Then stop by the **1876 Territorial Enterprise Building** for a look at the Mark Twain exhibit before heading over to the nearby **Bucket of Blood Saloon** for a cold one.

DINNER: Crown Point Restaurant 1 mile south of Virginia City, in the historic **Gold Hill Hotel** (1540 South Main Street, Virginia City, NV 89440; 775–847–0111; www.goldhillhotel.net). Specialties include various types of game, such as smoked wild boar-and-venison sausages, elk, buffalo, and venison, and Louisiana pan roast. Moderate.

LODGING: The Gold Hill is a good spot to bunk for the night. Nevada's oldest hotel, the Gold Hill opened in 1859. The older part of the hotel has four rooms (one of which is home to William, the ghost) and the newer section has eight rooms, including a number with fireplaces. Weekend room rates range from $45 to $145; suites and lodge accommodations also are available.

DAY 3

Morning

BREAKFAST: Fortify yourself with breakfast at the Gold Hill (moderate), and then it's time to head back to Las Vegas. If you didn't stop at Rhyolite on the way up, it'll be a good break on the way back.

THERE'S MORE

Carson City, Nevada

Carson Hot Springs Resort, 1500 Hot Springs Road; (888) 917–3711 or (775) 885–8844. Historic natural hot-water pool complex with large mineral pool and private baths.

The Children's Museum, 813 North Carson Street; (775) 884–2226. Hands-on learning and entertainment for toddlers through pre-teens.

Nevada State Railroad Museum, 2180 South Carson Street; (775) 687–6953. More than sixty train engines and other cars, most from the Virginia & Truckee Railroad, plus a great gift shop.

Warren Engine Company Museum, 777 South Stewart Street; (775) 887–2210. Museum dedicated to the oldest established volunteer fire company in the country.

Virginia City, Nevada

The Castle, 70 South B Street; (775) 847–0275. Once one of the finest homes in the West, The Castle was constructed between 1863 and 1868.

Comstock Firemen's Museum, 125 South C Street; (775–847–0717). 1876 building housing a collection of antique firefighting equipment.

Detours Historical Walking Tours, call for meeting place; (775) 847–9255. Historical walking or driving tours.

Fourth Ward School Museum, 537 South C Street; (775) 847–0975. Four-story Victorian school completed in 1876 and in operation until 1936 has museum and classroom displays.

Julia C. Bulette Red Light Museum, 110 C Street; (775) 847–9991. In the cellar of a saloon named for Virginia City's most renowned prostitute.

MacKay Mansion, 129 South D Street; (775) 847–0173. Ten-room building that was the original headquarters of the Gould & Curry Mine Company. Some original furnishings remain.

SPECIAL EVENTS

Carson City, Nevada

June. Kit Carson Rendezvous and Wagon Train; (775) 885–7491.

July. Carson City Fair; (775) 882–4460.

October. Nevada Day Parade and Contests; (775) 882–1565.

December. Silver and Snowflake Tree Lighting; (775) 885–0411.

Virginia City, Nevada

May. Comstock Historic Preservation Week; (775) 847–0311.

June. Commemoration of Gold Discovered; (775) 847–0311.

June–August. Nevada Shakespeare Festival at The Knights of Pythias Hall; (775) 847–0311.

August. Virginia City Rodeo; (775) 847–0311.

August–September. Theater at historic Piper's Opera House; (775) 847–0311.

September. Annual Camel Races; (775) 847–0311.

October. Annual Outhouse Races; (775) 847–0311.

Commemoration of the Great Fire of 1875; (775) 847–0311.

December. Christmas on the Comstock Parade of Lights; (775) 847–0311.

OTHER RECOMMENDED RESTAURANTS AND LODGINGS

Carson City, Nevada

Garibaldi's, 301 North Carson Street. Italian food and more in a turn-of-the-century storefront.

Grandma Hatties, 2811 South Carson Street; (775) 882–4900. American cuisine with friendly atmosphere.

Hardman House, 917 North Carson Street; (775) 882–7744. Clean motor lodge with a friendly atmosphere and basic but neat rooms.

Heidi's Dutch Mill Restaurant, 1020 North Carson Street; (775) 882–0486. Serving Carson City families since 1935.

Pinon Plaza Resort Hotel—Best Western, 2171 Highway 50 East; (775) 885–9000 or (877) 519–5567. Non-smoking rooms, suites, restaurant, exercise room.

Steakhouse at the Carson Nugget, 507 North Carson Street; (775) 882–1626 or (800) 426–5239. Steaks and chops in a wood-paneled room.

Virginia City, Nevada

Crooked House Bed and Breakfast, 8 F Street; (775) 847–4447; www.ibbp. com/obb/nevada/virginiacity.html. Original nineteenth-century building restored in the early 1990s. Bed-and-breakfast with just four rooms but lots of charm.

Delta Saloon and Casino, Sawdust Corner Restaurant, 18 C Street; (775) 847–0788. Varied menu in an Old West building that opened in 1862.

J&L Miner Diner, 465 South C Street; (775) 847–4739. A down-homey spot with old-fashioned breakfasts.

Sugarloaf Mountain Lodge, 430 South C Street; (775) 847–0505. A 2-block stroll from the center of town, with views of Six Mile Canyon and Sugarloaf Mountain.

FOR MORE INFORMATION

Carson City Convention and Visitors Bureau, 1900 South Carson Street, Suite 200, Carson City, NV 89701; (775) 687–7410 or (800) 638–2321; www.carson-city.org.

Virginia City Chamber of Commerce, 131 South C Street, Virginia City, NV 89440; (775) 847–0311; www.virginiacity-nv.com.

Grand Canyon

GET ACQUAINTED
WITH A WESTERN LEGEND

2 NIGHTS

Touring • Hiking • Mule-riding • Rafting • Art
Indian Artifacts

If you live in the West, there's an incontrovertible truth: You have to see Grand Canyon at least once—and not just from the air. When you do, the reality gives new definition to the term "awe-inspiring." At 277 miles long and an average of 10 miles wide, this is one canyon that certainly earns its name.

The Grand Canyon in Arizona ranks as the country's second most popular national park, drawing more than five million people during 2000. For that reason it's best to visit during spring, fall, or winter, when fewer people are there (and you'll avoid the sometimes oppressive heat of the summertime).

There are two main vantage points for viewing Grand Canyon—the North Rim and the South Rim. While the average distance across the canyon is only about 10 miles—"as the raven flies," the rangers say—it'll take you about five hours to drive the 215 miles between rims, so choose carefully.

The North Rim is higher, at an average of 5,700 feet above the base of the canyon—about 1,200 feet higher than most points on the South Rim. But the area along the South Rim is more developed because it's generally more accessible; the snowier weather at the North Rim mandates its closure during the winter months, which in this case are usually from mid-October to mid-May. The South Rim also is closer to Las Vegas, making it a great spot for a quick escape.

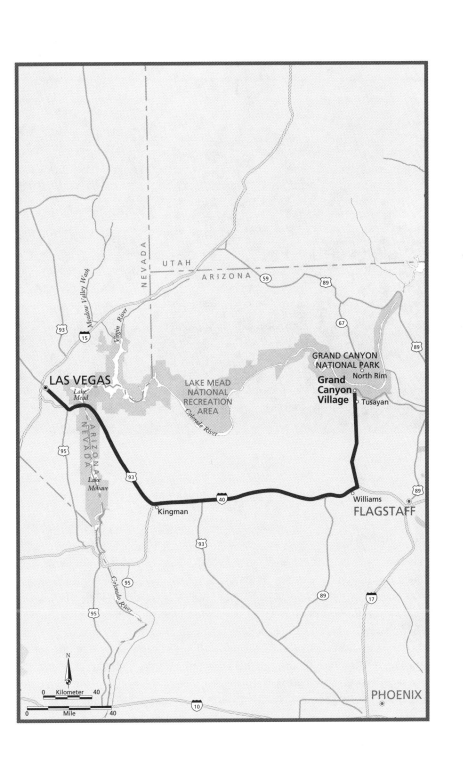

Grand Canyon from the South Rim

DAY 1

Afternoon

The South Rim is about 277 miles from Las Vegas, for a drive of about four
and a half hours. To get there, follow U.S. Highway 93 South to the Kingman
area, then pick up Interstate 40 East and follow it for about 115 miles. At exit
165, switch to Arizona Route 64 and follow it north right into the gates of
Grand Canyon National Park.

There are a couple of ways to approach your visit. If you're a train buff or
just figure that getting there is half the fun, stop in Williams, Arizona, the
home of the **Grand Canyon Railway** (235 North Grand Canyon Boulevard; 800–843–8724 or 928–773–1976), which makes daily runs to the park.

If you leave the night before, you can take the train from Williams in the morning and arrive at the park around noon; packages are available that include one night in Williams and one in the park. Another option is to take the train for a day trip from Williams, spending just a few hours in the park before turning around and heading back. If you do make the trip by train, you'll be continuing a tradition of rail travel to the canyon that began more than one hundred years ago.

Most Las Vegans, however, seem to prefer to drive right to the park. There are a number of hotels and motels in Tusayan and just before the park entrance. In the park itself, accommodations in one hotel, six lodges, and a ranch (Phantom Ranch, which is in the canyon for use by hikers) range from historic to modern, luxurious to rustic.

DINNER: If you stay in the park you'll feel a little like a captive audience, but don't worry, because options are many. One of the most elegant places to dine—and to really feel as though you've arrived at Grand Canyon—is the venerable **El Tovar Dining Room** at the El Tovar Hotel (303–297–2757). The dining room, with its cozy fireplace, features such dishes as Navajo tacos, smoked corn chowder, pan-seared salmon tostadas, and Native American blue corn tamales, in addition to more classic dishes. Expensive.

LODGING: "We're not just close; we're there" is the slogan of the Grand Canyon Lodges, and it's true that staying within the park is a logical choice. One of the best spots is the grand-daddy of 'em all, the **El Tovar Hotel** (303–297–2757; www.grandcanyonlodges.com; rates from $118 to $286). The El Tovar, which dates to 1905, was one of the originators of the style that has come to characterize the country's most historic national park lodges—not quite craftsman, but definitely not rustic. We figure if it was good enough for Theodore Roosevelt, Albert Einstein, and Zane Grey, it's good enough for us.

DAY 2

Morning

BREAKFAST: The **El Tovar Dining Room** breakfast menu includes omelets and such dishes as Sonoran-style eggs with tomatillo salsa, or lighter choices such as pastry and coffee. Another option is the **Bright Angel Restaurant** at Bright Angel Lodge (303–297–2757), which is a couple of lodges west of the El Tovar—easy walking distance, especially if the weather is good. Moderate.

Because of the crowds that flock to Grand Canyon National Park—and because of concerns about the effects pollution is having on the canyon—park managers have instituted a trio of shuttle-bus routes (except during winter months) to limit the number of vehicles that travel its roads.

When you entered from the south entrance road that extends from AZ 64, you were directed to a parking area near the lodges. Leave your vehicle there and pick up a shuttle at one of the nearby stops. The three routes are the Village Route, the Hermits Rest Route, and the Kaibab Trail Route.

The Village Route is the most utilitarian one, serving the parking areas, train depot, and lodges and connecting to the Hermits Rest and Canyon View Routes. Take the Village Route to the **Canyon View Information Plaza,** a great place to get oriented to the park.

The information plaza is home to the new **Canyon View Visitor Center,** which has exhibits on the park and what you can do there. The center also is the site of informational programs, such as "Lure of the Canyon," which explores why we all feel so compelled to visit. Then leave the center and make the short walk to Mather Point and your first clear view of the canyon.

After taking in the view from Mather Point, board the Kaibab Trail Route shuttle, which proceeds out to Yavapai Point and the **Yavapai Observation Station**.

The Yavapai Observation Station is another must-see for visitors to the park. It's constructed far out on the point, and its glass windows afford a sweeping panoramic view of the canyon. Far below, you'll be able to spot the Colorado River, looking like an innocent little trickle that couldn't possibly have had much to do with the formation of the huge canyon around it, and Phantom Ranch, which hosts hikers. The station also has fossil exhibits and a bookstore.

At the opposite end of the Kaibab Trail Route from Yavapai Point, you'll find the trailhead for the South Kaibab Trail, which offers incredible views, especially considering it's not a terribly long trail (if fairly steep). A round-trip hike of 1.5 miles will get you to the aptly named Ooh Aah Point. If you're more ambitious, a 6-mile round trip of four to six hours will take you to Skeleton Point. Be aware that the South Kaibab Trail has no water sources and not much in the way of shade. In view of that, we have to wonder if Skeleton Point is aptly named as well!

Another option for the morning is to go back to the parking area, pick up your car and make the 50-mile round trip **Desert View Drive,** which winds through the eastern section of the park. The Desert View Drive has a number of overlooks with views of the Colorado River, and 7,438-foot Desert View overlook near the east entrance to the park is the highest point on the South Rim; if the clouds cooperate, you'll have a clear view of the river flowing out of Marble Canyon and can see the colors of the Painted Desert. Also at the overlook is the **Desert View Watchtower,** a 70-foot structure designed by Mary Colter, architect of many park buildings, plus an information center, bookstore, snack bar, and gift shops.

Equestrian types can find horseback riding in this part of the park as well; one of the most popular routes is a four-hour ride offered by **Apache Stables** (1 mile north of Tusayan; 520–638–2891) that follows Long Jim Canyon to the East Rim. One- and two-hour rides through the Kaibab Forest, twilight campfire rides, and wagon rides also are available.

LUNCH: Stop at the snack bar in the **Trading Post** at the Desert View overlook or head back to the Canyon View Information Plaza, transfer to the Village Route, and take the shuttle to Market Plaza's Canyon Village Marketplace, where you'll find the **Delicatessen at Marketplace.** There you'll find all manner of sandwiches and snacks; eat in or pack a picnic for an afternoon excursion. Inexpensive.

Afternoon

Time to see a different side of the canyon. Take the Village Route to the Hermits Rest Route transfer stop at the west end of the village area, near the Kolb studios.

The Hermits Rest Route stops at eight canyon overlooks as it heads out from the village, with the Hermits Rest stop the farthest point. This route also pretty much follows the western part of the **Rim Trail,** which provides great views of the canyon yet is easy enough even for the most inexperienced hiker. Another nice thing about the Rim Trail along the Hermits Rest Route: You can use it to walk between shuttle-bus stops, thereby tailoring your hike to your energy level.

Another way to explore the Grand Canyon is to do it by mule. Park concessionaire AmFac (South Rim, Grand Canyon; 520–638–2631) offers one-day, overnight, and two-night **mule trips** into the canyon.

DINNER: The **Arizona Room** at the Bright Angel Lodge, near the El Tovar Hotel (303–297–2757), is known for "Western-style dining," including such dishes as prime rib, grilled salmon with cilantro-lime butter, chicken with zucchini salsa, and barbecue. Some seats in the restaurant have views of the canyon. Moderate.

LODGING: El Tovar Hotel (see above).

DAY 3

Morning

BREAKFAST: To make the most of your last day at the canyon, rise early and head east on the Rim Trail and along a turn-off to Yavapai Lodge (303–297–2757), about a 1.25-mile walk from the El Tovar Hotel. There you'll find the **Yavapai Cafeteria**, which offers most of the standard breakfast favorites. Inexpensive.

Right in Grand Canyon Village are a trio of must-see stops—Hopi House, Lookout Studio, and the Kolb Studio (928–638–7888 for all).

Hopi House, a 1905 structure by Mary Coulter, is designed to look like an adobe building. Inside you'll find a wide variety of merchandise designed and produced by various local Indian tribes, such as Hopi burden baskets in various sizes. There's a gallery upstairs.

The **Kolb Studio** was the studio of Grand Canyon pioneering photographers Ellsworth and Emery Kolb between 1904 and 1926. Today, the studio—which is on the National Register of Historic Places—is home to changing exhibits.

Lookout Studio is one of several bookstores in Grand Canyon National Park and also carries photography materials.

Also worthy of a stop is the **Tusayan Museum** (3 miles west of Desert View on Desert View Drive; 928–638–7888), which provides a glimpse of Indian life in the pueblo nearly 800 years ago. Visitors also have the option of wandering through the 800-year-old ruins on a self-guiding trail.

If you want to get more up-close-and-personal views of the canyon, take in the thirty-four-minute film at the **Grand Canyon Imax Theater** (AZ 64/U.S. Highway 180, south of the park entrance; 928–638–2468). The film *Grand Canyon: The Hidden Secrets* will have you swooping through the air and zooming through the water in the canyon—all from the comfort of your seat as you gaze at the six-story screen.

LUNCH: The **Bright Angel Coffee Shop** at the Bright Angel Lodge (303–297–2757) offers a reasonably broad menu of lunchtime favorites, plus such featured dishes as blackened avocado and salsa burgers and smoked turkey reubens. Inexpensive.

Then it's back down AZ 64 to I–40 and US 93 to return to Las Vegas.

THERE'S MORE

Grand Canyon National Park

Grand Canyon Excursions by Fred Harvey, (928) 638–2631. Tours of various lengths in various parts of the canyon.

Gray Line of Flagstaff, Nava-Hopi Tours Inc., (928) 774–5003 or (877) GO–SEE–AZ. Bus tours of Grand Canyon National Park and surrounding areas.

Rivers and Oceans, (928) 526–4575 or (800) 473–4576. Partial and full-length raft trips on the Colorado River through Grand Canyon.

Southwest Safari, P.O. Box 20362, Sedona, Arizona; (928) 284–1175. Offers a six-day trip that leaves from Sedona and travels through Bryce and Grand Canyons, on foot and by horseback, 4 x 4, river raft, and rappelling.

Williams, Arizona

Elephant Rock Golf Course, 2200 Country Club Drive; (928) 635–4935. Eighteen holes in the pines.

Williams Ski Area, P.O. Box 953; (928) 635–9330. Ski area about 5 miles south of Williams that's geared to novices and families.

SPECIAL EVENTS

Grand Canyon National Park

April. Easter Sunrise Services at Mather Point, Nondenominational. (928) 638–2901.

September. Grand Canyon Chamber Music Festival, Chamber-music concert series, south rim; (800) 997–8285.

Williams, Arizona

May. Annual Fun Run, Two-day car rally across several communities, cruising longest remaining stretch of Route 66. Several downtown activities. (928) 635–1418.

Rendezvous Days, celebrating Williams' Western heritage with buckskinner events, parade, dances, carnival and arts and crafts fair; (928) 635–1418.

June. Hog Rally, official rally of the Harley Owner's Group of Arizona, with more than 1,500 participating motorcycles, parade and street dances; (928) 635–1418.

August. Cowpuncher's Reunion Rodeo. Gathering of actual working cowboys and first rodeo of the season. Arts and crafts fair and other activities downtown; (928) 635–1418.

September. PRCA Rodeo. Parade, dance, arts and crafts fair, and other downtown activities; (928) 635–1418.

OTHER RECOMMENDED RESTAURANTS AND LODGINGS

Grand Canyon National Park

Bright Angel Lodge, South Rim; (303) 297–2757. Rustic 1936 National Historic Landmark a few feet from the canyon rim. Lodge rooms and cabins.

Canyon Star, Grand Hotel, Arizona Route 64, about 9 miles south of the Grand Canyon; (928) 638–3333. Steaks and seafood, salad bar, children's menu.

Coronado Room, Best Western Grand Canyon Squire Inn, Tusayan, (928) 638–2681. Steaks, seafood, pastas, and Mexican dishes.

Williams, Arizona

Canyon Country Inn Bed and Breakfast, 442 West Route 66; (928) 635–2349. Cozy inn with country and teddy bear motif.

Cruisers Cafe 66, 233 West Route 66; (928) 635–2445. Family dining "in the spirit of Route 66"; children's menu; patio dining in summer.

Mountain Country Lodge Bed and Breakfast, 437 Route 66; (928) 635–4341. Eight smoke-free units in downtown Williams.

Pancho McGillicuddy's, 141 Railroad Avenue; (928) 635–4150. Mexican food, children's menu, seasonal patio dining.

Terry Ranch Bed and Breakfast, 701 Quarterhorse Road; (928) 635–4171. Four units in log cabin–style residence.

FOR MORE INFORMATION

Grand Canyon National Park, P.O. Box 129, Grand Canyon, AZ 86023; (928) 638–7888; www.nps.gov/grca.

Grand Canyon Chamber of Commerce, P.O. Box 3007, Grand Canyon, AZ 86023; (928) 638–2901; www.grandcanyonchamber.org.

OLD WEST

Phoenix

GO WEST INTO HISTORY

2 NIGHTS

Old West history • Mystery Castle
Bed-and-breakfasts • Desert beauty

"Go west, young man, and grow up with the country," Horace Greeley wrote in 1850, and he might well have been advising the young'uns to head to Phoenix, Arizona.

This former territorial capital on the edge of the Sonoran Desert has indeed grown up, to become a sprawling, cosmopolitan city with 1.3 million residents, with 3 million residents in its metropolitan area. Another 12 million visit each year.

But it was not, of course, ever thus. Phoenix's roots have been traced to the ancient Hohokam who lived in the Salt River Valley region between about 300 and 1450, when they quietly disappeared. Modern-day Phoenicians pride themselves on the stories of these resourceful ancestors, exhibiting their pottery in museums and noting that the Hohokam built a canal system to irrigate their crops; a modern canal follows much the same route of one constructed more than 600 years ago.

Along came the Spaniards, with the conquistadors arriving by about the middle of the sixteenth century in their search for the Seven Cities of Gold. Things remained fairly quiet until 1821, when the Spanish returned to stake their claim on what now is Arizona; the Arizona–New Mexico Territory became part of the United States by 1850.

True to its name, the area where Phoenix now stands experienced a rebirth in about 1860 in the form of a small settlement on the Salt River. One

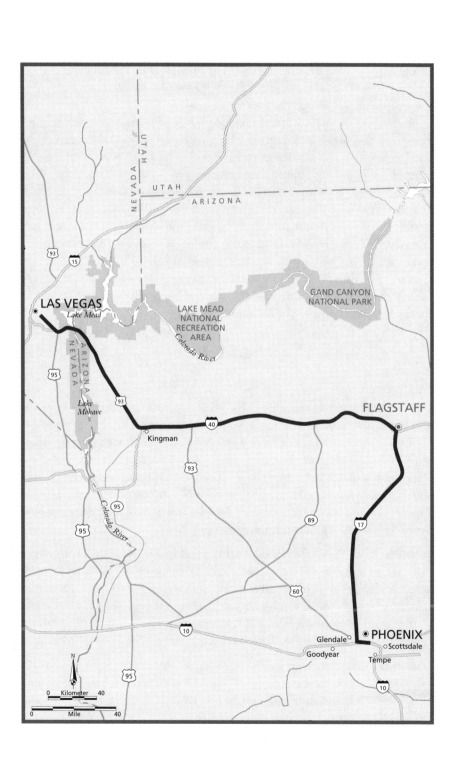

of the early settlers, hearing stories about the earlier civilization and perhaps coming across shards of pottery as he went about his farming, was inspired to come up with the name.

But it was the arrival of the railroad in 1887 that really got things going again, and they were sped along by the completion of the Roosevelt Dam in 1911, harnessing the Salt River to irrigate farmland and produce the power needed for a growing industrial community.

Oh, and don't forget the invention of air-conditioning in the mid-twentieth century. Phoenix residents might like to brag about their "wonderful climate," but tell that to a guy working on a road in the summer sun; the average high temperature in July is 105 degrees, and the heat commonly spikes above that.

But Las Vegans don't go to Phoenix to escape the heat; they go for the vast variety of social, recreational, cultural, and historical offerings there. And that makes Phoenix a prime spot for a quick escape.

DAY 1

Afternoon

Phoenix is about 385 miles from Las Vegas, for a trip of about six hours, so you'll probably want to consider a mid-day departure.

Drive south on U.S. Highway 93 to the Kingman area, picking up Interstate 40 East to Flagstaff, then Interstate 17 into Phoenix. Take exit 232/New River and turn left onto New River Road, which becomes Seventh Street. Turn left onto Carefree Highway, right onto North Scottsdale Road, left onto East Dynamite Boulevard, right onto North Alma School Parkway, right onto Pinnacle Peak Parkway, and right again onto East Jomax Road.

DINNER: The Pinnacle Peak Patio Steakhouse and Microbrewery (10426 East Jomax Road, Scottsdale, AZ 85255; 480–585–1599) dates to 1957, when it was a general store and rest stop whose owner decided to serve dinner on weekends. Today, you'll find anything from the Cowboy (a two-pound Porterhouse) to Pinnacle Pete's Steak Burger, a half-pound grilled over a mesquite fire, plus barbecued baby-back ribs, chicken, and combos. Moderate.

LODGING: After dinner, go west on East Jomax Road to Pinnacle Peak Parkway and turn left, then right onto North Alma School Parkway, right onto East Happy Valley Road, left onto North Pima Road, and right onto East Princess Drive, which becomes North Hayden Road. Drive straight ahead to

North Greenway Hayden Loop and turn left onto North Scottsdale Road and right onto East Greenway Parkway to the ramp for Arizona Route 51. Follow AZ 51 for about 8 miles and take the Colter Street exit, turning right onto East Colter Street, left onto North Sixteenth Street, right onto East Camelback Road, right onto North Central Avenue, and left onto West Pasadena Avenue (still with us?), to **Maricopa Manor Bed and Breakfast Inn** (15 West Pasadena Avenue, Phoenix, AZ 85013; 800–292–6403 or 602–274–6302; www.maricopamanor.com; rates from $99 to $249). The Maricopa Manor is a 1928-era house and adjoining guesthouses that in 1989 was the first bed-and-breakfast licensed by the city of Phoenix. Set on an acre site, the inn has a pool with waterfalls, patios with fountains and lush gardens; four suites have gas fireplaces and whirlpool tubs.

DAY 2

Morning

BREAKFAST: Take advantage of the Maricopa Manor's breakfast-in-a-basket policy, in which breakfast is delivered to the door of your suite at the requested time, to be eaten in your suite, in bed, or in a common area with other guests.

Near South Mountain Park, you'll find the **Mystery Castle** (800 East Mineral Road; 602–268–1581). Phoenix long has attracted dreamers, and Boyce Luther Gulley was one of the dreamiest. A Seattle businessman whose doctor told him in 1927 that he was dying of tuberculosis, Gulley abandoned his wife and daughter and took off, resurfacing in Phoenix three years later. Convinced his death was imminent, he apparently decided to spare his family the trauma of watching him die and didn't contact them again. But he never forgot that his little daughter had asked her daddy to build her a castle, and he also lived longer than he apparently thought he would; over the next fifteen years, he set about building his own brand of castle, one that's a testimony to recycling. After Gulley's death sixteen years after his disappearance, his attorney contacted his wife and daughter, who moved into the castle and opened it for tours.

Nearby in the northern part of Tempe you'll find the **Arizona Historical Society Museum** (Papago Park, Galvin Parkway at Van Buren Street; 480–929–0292), which has numerous short-term, long-term, and changing exhibits, in addition to a research library and archives. Among recent exhibits were a look at Central Arizona history from 1860 to 1912, the story of agriculture in

Arizona, an examination of how Arizona was changed by World War II, and a traveling exhibit on the history of Negro League Baseball.

Also in Papago Park is the **Desert Botanical Garden** (480–941–1225), which invites visitors to travel its paths through more than 145 acres of the world's arid land plants. Among the themed pathways are the Plants and People of the Sonoran Desert, the Desert Discovery Trail, and the Harriet K. Maxwell Wildflower Trail.

Oh, but there's still more in **Papago Park** (602–256–3220), including a golf course, fishing lagoons, picnic areas, hiking trails, and the Hole-in-the-Rock peek-through landmark.

LUNCH: Just across the Salt River near University Drive you'll find **Crocodile Cafe** (525 South Mill Avenue, Tempe, AZ 85281; 480–966–5883), which has indoor seating plus patio tables if you want to absorb the life-in-a-college-town feel lent by nearby Arizona State University. Specialty calzones and pizzas (including a three-section pizza), sandwiches, and burgers are among the favorites there. Moderate.

Afternoon

Back to Papago Park, where you'll find the **Phoenix Zoo** (455 North Galvin Parkway; 602–273–1341). One of the largest nonprofit zoological parks in the country, the zoo is home to more than 1,300 animals, including many threatened or endangered species. The zoo is divided into the Tropics Trail, home to elephants, orangutans, and the rainforest environment of the spectacled bear; the Africa Trail, with its lions and tigers and rhinos (oh, my!); the Discovery Trail, with its kids' farm, playground, and butterfly garden; and the Arizona Trail, with native plants and animals including mountain lions and coyotes.

If you're the type who likes things hot, another spot to consider is the **Hall of Flame Museum of Firefighting** (6101 East Van Buren Street; 602–275–3473), which displays the world's largest collection of firefighting equipment, representing three centuries.

If you're a sports nut and your timing is right, you may be able to catch an **Arizona Diamondbacks** baseball game at Bank One Ballpark (401 East Jefferson Street; 602–514–8400). The **Phoenix Suns** play basketball at America West Arena (201 East Jefferson Street; 602–379–7878); the **Phoenix Coyotes** (602–379–7800) play hockey there as well. And the **Arizona Cardinals** play football at Sun Devil Stadium (3115 South Mill Avenue; 602–379–0102 or 800–999–1402).

DINNER: The **Melting Pot Fondue Restaurant** (8320 North Hayden Street, Suite 103, Scottsdale, AZ 85258; 480–607–1799) is a unique, soup-to-nuts fondue experience. Try any of a variety of cheese fondues for an appetizer, followed by meat or seafood (or both) entrees prepared in oil or fat-free broth, with a design-your-own chocolate fondue for dessert. Only the salads aren't served fondue-style. Moderate.

LODGING: Maricopa Manor Bed and Breakfast Inn (see above).

DAY 3

Morning

BREAKFAST: Have breakfast-in-a-basket at the Maricopa Manor, or head to Scottsdale and **First Watch** (4422 North 75th Street, Scottsdale, AZ 85251; 602–265-2092). Watch out for those bigger-than-a-dinner-plate blueberry pancakes; even one is enough to fill up the average eater. Other breakfast selections include First Watch's signature Crepeggs, which combine crepes with scrambled eggs, and omelets including the Bacado, which combines bacon, avocado, and Monterey Jack cheese. Inexpensive.

While in Scottsdale, take in **Rawhide** (23023 North Scottsdale Road; 480–502–1880), which is an 1880s Western town come to life, complete with a shooting gallery, panning for gold, hayrides, a petting zoo, burro rides, stagecoach or train rides, and craftsmen working in twenty antique buildings and shops. Oh, and of course Rawhide offers six-gun shootouts and stunt shows.

An attraction of quite a different type is **Taliesin West** (114th Street/Frank Lloyd Wright Boulevard and Cactus Road; 480–860–2700) which was Wright's winter home and architectural studio on 600 acres of desert at the foot of the McDowell Mountains. Various tours provide an introduction to life at Taliesin; there's even a desert walk on the surrounding grounds.

If you're a collector, take in the antiques and specialty shops of **Historic Downtown Glendale,** along the suburb's Glendale Avenue, Glenn Drive, and Palmaire Avenue.

LUNCH: The Quilted Bear (in the Lincoln Plaza Shopping Center, 6316 North Scottsdale Road, Phoenix, AZ 85253; 480–948–7760) serves sandwiches, salads, and more in a nice light garden atmosphere complete with signature stained-glass "quilted bear." Moderate.

Afternoon

Then it's time to head home. Follow Lincoln Road west to I–17, turn north and retrace your steps to return to Las Vegas.

THERE'S MORE

Arizona State Capital Museum, 1700 West Washington Street; (602) 542–4581. Artifacts and memorabilia from early Arizona.

Deer Valley Rock Art Center, 3711 West Deer Valley Road; (623) 582–8007. Short trail leads to rocks covered with more than 1,500 petroglyphs; exhibits explain their history and meaning.

Dolly Steamboat Excursion, Canyon Lake; (480) 827–9144. Tours on replica paddle-wheel steamer.

Phoenix Art Museum, 1625 North Central Avenue; (602) 257–1222. More than 14,000 works, plus more than twenty temporary exhibitions each year, as well as a fashion-design collection, Thorne Miniature Rooms, and the Artworks Gallery interactive area for children.

Pioneer Living History Museum, 3901 West Pioneer Road; (623) 465–1052. More than twenty buildings including a blacksmith shop, dance hall, church, and miners' cabins present a depiction of local life in the 1880s. Costumed interpreters and staged shootouts on weekends bring things to life.

Waterworld Safari, 4243 West Pinnacle Peak Road; (623) 581–8446. Water slides, wave pools, and a lazy river.

SPECIAL EVENTS

Goodyear, Arizona

June. Cool Corn and Melon Celebration, celebrating harvest with tastings of corn and melon, Duncan Family Farms; (623) 853–0111.

Phoenix, Arizona

January. Fiesta Bowl Parade, downtown, plus football game in Sun Devil Stadium in Tempe; (480) 350–0900.

March. World Championship Hoop Dance Contest, with more than forty Indian hoop dancers gathering for one of the few competitions in the country, Heard Museum; (602) 252–8840.

May. *Cinco de Mayo* Festival, Mexican-themed street celebration with music and dancers, including major acts, Patriot's Park, downtown; (877) CALL–PHX or (602) 254–6500.

July. Fabulous Phoenix Fourth, celebration that draws as many as a quarter-million people, State Capitol; (877) CALL–PHX or (602) 254–6500.

October. Arizona State Fair, two and a half weeks of traditional agriculture, livestock, crafts, and collectibles, State Fairgrounds; (602) 252–6771.

December. Fiesta of Light Electric Light Parade with more than one hundred floats sporting upward of one million lights, downtown; (602) 534–3378.

Las Noches de las Luminarias, with paths at Desert Botanical Garden lined with more than 7,000 luminarias; (480) 481–8188.

ZooLights, with more than 600,000 lights decorating the Phoenix Zoo, some in animal shapes; (602) 273–1341.

Queen Creek, Arizona

April. Country Thunder USA, four-day festival drawing as many as 30,000 fans per day to see major country stars; (480) 966–9920.

Scottsdale, Arizona

March. National Festival of the West, four-day event commemorating the American West with rodeo, cowboy poetry, music, movies, and costumed participants, Rawhide Western Town; (602) 996–4387.

November. Thunderbird Balloon Classic, drawing more than 130 balloons and thousands of spectators; (480) 978–7790.

OTHER RECOMMENDED RESTAURANTS AND LODGINGS

Phoenix, Arizona

Arizona Biltmore Resort and Spa, 24th Street and Missouri Avenue; (800) 950–0086 or (602) 955–6600. Landmark resort with architecture inspired by Frank Lloyd Wright.

Arizona Biltmore Resort and Spa

Embassy Suite Phoenix–Biltmore, 2630 East Camelback Road; (602) 955–3992. Lush atrium with koi ponds and five-story Southwestern murals.

The Felsen House, 1008 East Camelback Road; (602) 277–1119. German cuisine.

Mystery Mansion Dinner Theater, 3950 East Campbell Avenue; (480) 994–1520. Specially designed mystery dinner theater.

The Pointe Hilton Tapatio Cliffs Resort, 11111 North Seventh Street; (602) 866–7500. Grounds feature The Falls, three and a half acres of pools and waterfalls.

Scottsdale, Arizona

Maria's When in Naples, 7000 East Shea Boulevard, No. 1010; (480) 991–6887. Specializing in homemade pasta.

Sanctuary on Camelback Mountain, 5700 East McDonald Drive; (800) 245–2051 or (480) 948–2100. Fifty-three acre resort on Camelback Mountain with infinity-edged resort pool, tennis, hiking trails, fitness center.

Tempe, Arizona

Aunt Chilada's, Pointe South Mountain Resort, 2021 West Baseline Road; (602) 431–6470. Mexican fare served in cantina atmosphere.

FOR MORE INFORMATION

Greater Phoenix Convention and Visitors Bureau, One Arizona Center, 400 East Van Buren Street, Suite 600, Phoenix, AZ 85004-2290; (877) CALL–PHZ or (602) 254–6500; www.phoenixcvb.com.

Scottsdale Chamber of Commerce, 7343 Scottsdale Mall, Scottsdale, AZ 85251-4498; (480) 945–8481 or (800) 877–1117.

Prescott and Jerome

A LOOK AT LIFE IN THE TERRITORY

2 NIGHTS

Historical spots • Pine forests • Old mines
Indian artifacts • Romantic inns

Prescott, Arizona, is nearly surrounded by the pinewoods of the Prescott National Forest. That's key to two things that would make it attractive to most Las Vegans: It's green and—at 5,346 feet—generally cool compared to Sin City. And the presence of those pine trees means that Prescott has a lot of interesting old wooden buildings just waiting to be explored.

Of course, the pine forests weren't the only thing that brought early settlers to Prescott. There was gold in them thar hills—enough gold to prompt Pres. Abraham Lincoln, ever wary of the need for cash for his struggling troops, to declare Arizona a territory in 1863, with Prescott the territorial capital. The capital later was shifted to Tucson, then back to Prescott, before being permanently located in Phoenix in 1889.

Today, Prescott—that's pronounced "PRES-kit," according to most residents and even a commemorative poster—remains proud of its heritage as the territorial capital, and while its lovely location has brought much growth to the town as a retirement community and vacation destination, the historical aspects have been well preserved.

Near Prescott is Jerome, an old copper-mining town that was nearly swallowed by the depths of the Depression. Perched precariously on the side of a mountain, much like an Alpine village, Jerome is a little more rustic than Prescott, a little more colorful, and remarkably well preserved, with few major changes in its buildings over the past several decades. Jerome has so much

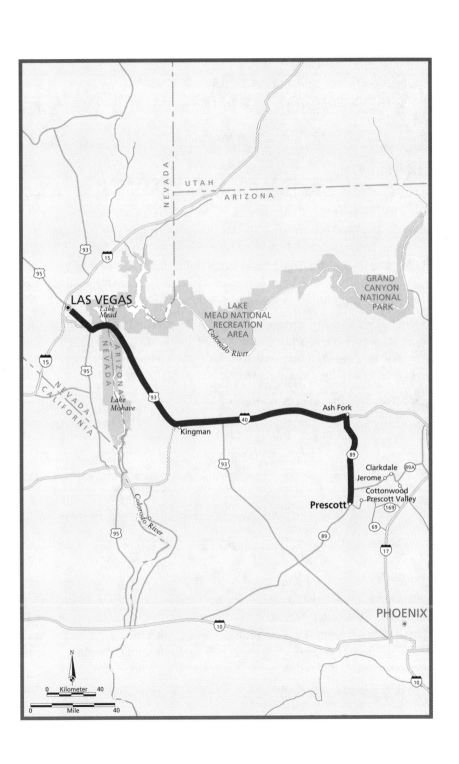

charm, in fact, that a quarter-million visitors find their way there each year, nearly overwhelming the population of just 400.

Together, the two make a fascinating and cooling weekend getaway.

DAY 1

Afternoon

Prescott is about 242 miles from Las Vegas, for a trip of about three to three and a half hours. Head south on U.S. Highway 93, through Boulder City and over the Hoover Dam, picking up Interstate 40 East in Kingman, Arizona.

From Kingman, take I–40 for about 96 miles to exit 146 and Arizona Route 89. You'll be on AZ 89 for about 50 miles. Just stay on the highway and you'll find yourself on Gurley Street, the main drag through Prescott, which runs past the landmark Court House Square.

DINNER: For a casual dinner in a 1905-vintage building that's been fully restored, stop at the **Gurley Street Grill** (230 West Gurley Street, Prescott, AZ 86301; 520–445–3388), which serves everything from salads and burgers to roasted chicken pot pie and pistachio fried chicken. Moderate.

LODGING: The **Pleasant Street Inn** bed and breakfast (142 South Pleasant Street, Prescott, AZ 86303; 877-226-7128 or 520–445–4774; rates from $85 to $135), right off Court House Square in downtown Prescott, has four rooms in a house that was built in 1906 and moved to its current site (and remodeled) in 1990. The common area has a fireplace, as does the upstairs Pineview Suite; the downstairs Terrace Suite has a private covered deck. Rates include full breakfast including homemade breads, plus beverages throughout the day.

DAY 2

Morning

BREAKFAST: Have breakfast at the Pleasant Street Inn. Or, for a taste of the country, drive east on Arizona Route 69 (an extension of Gurley Street) 17 miles to the **Hungry Bear** at Young's Farm in Dewey (AZ 69 and Arizona Route 169; 520–632–7272) for farm-fresh favorites like build-your-own omelets, frittatas, biscuits and gravy, and pancakes. Or try the H. B. Benedict, two poached eggs on a croissant with ham, hollandaise sauce, and herbed potatoes. Inexpensive.

Miner in Jerome

After breakfast, travel west on AZ 69 to AZ 89 North to Arizona Route 89A to the old mining town of **Jerome.** About 30 miles from Prescott, Jerome is even more historic—and even more scenic, perched on the side of a mountain with nearly all of its buildings looking for all the world like they're about to let go and slide down the slope at any second (and a few actually have).

The route to Jerome winds through Prescott Valley and then up the side of a mountain and back down, with steep turns and sheer drop-offs. But it's a scenic road, and it's possible to spot a number of remnants of old mining operations. Just be sure that if you're the one looking, you're not the one driving.

AZ 89A winds into Jerome through a trio of steep hairpins. Follow Main Street and then make a left onto Hull Street and you'll find a public parking area. Park your vehicle and wander the little Victorian-era town, checking out its galleries and unique shops. **Ghost Town Gear Adventure Equipment** (415 Hill Avenue; 520–634–3113), for example, isn't a shop you'd find in the environs of Las Vegas.

Nature's Landscape Gallery (501 School Street; 520–649–1186) has lots of fine-art photography, featuring landscapes of the West. Interesting galleries and shops in the Main Street district include the **Jerome Artists Cooperative Gallery** (502 Main Street; 520–634–5642) and **Nellie Bly II** (130 Main Street; 520–634–7825) and its sister shop, **Nellie Bly.**

After an hour or so of shopping and browsing, drive about a mile—or walk, if you're feeling energetic—to the **Gold King Mine and Ghost Town** (follow the signs from Jerome; 520–634–0053) in what once was the Jerome suburb of Haynes. The area was developed after ambitious miners looking for more of the copper that had been found near Jerome were unsuccessful—and hit gold instead. Old mining equipment and trucks are part of this attraction that claims to be stuck in the "Mountain Stranded Time" period.

The **Mine Museum** (200 Main Street; 520–634–5477) in Jerome depicts the process of pulling millions of dollars worth of copper from the steep hillsides around Jerome.

Also of historical interest is the **Jerome State Historic Park** (State Route 89A; 520–634–5381), which is the site of the **Douglas Mansion,** an adobe-brick building that dates to 1916. This was the home of the family of James S. "Rawhide Jimmy" Douglas, who owned the Little Daisy Mine and United Verde Extension Mine, and also was used to house visiting officials and investors. Its wine cellar, billiard room, and steam heat are testimony to the high life of Jerome's copper kings before their fortunes crashed.

Today, the museum highlights the histories of both the Douglas family and Jerome itself, and has a model of the mining tunnels under the town. Picnicking is allowed on the grounds, so if it's a nice day, consider picking up lunch in town before you stop by the park; the picnic area has a great view.

Other Jerome landmarks you won't want to miss include **Sliding Jail,** so named because the jail, built on clay in about 1928, slid 2,500 feet down the hill between 1928 and about 1940. The jail now rests in the appropriately named **Sliding Jail Park.**

LUNCH: The Flatiron Cafe (416 Main Street, Jerome, AZ 86331; 520–634–2733), sells such delights as grilled panini, smoked salmon quesadillas, black bean hummus lahvosh, plus fresh juices and espresso. Moderate.

Afternoon

After lunch, follow AZ 89A northeast of Jerome to Clarkdale and the **Verde Canyon Railroad** (300 North Broadway; 800–293–7245 or 520–639–0010;

www.verdecanyonrr.com). This excursion train makes a four-hour round trip through red cliffs, ancient Indian ruins, vintage trestles, and a deserted ranch (the turnaround point); passengers might be lucky enough to see a bald eagle soaring above or a deer scampering next to the train.

As dusk approaches, wind back along AZ 89A through Jerome and return to Prescott.

DINNER: Zuma's Woodfire Cafe (120 North Montezuma Street, Prescott, AZ 86301; 520–541–1400) specializes in pecan-woodfired pizzas, plus seafood, steak, pasta, salads, and sandwiches and offers fireside patio dining and live music. Moderate.

LODGING: The Pleasant Street Inn (see above).

DAY 3

Morning

BREAKFAST: Have breakfast at the Pleasant Street Inn, or stop by the **Waffle Iron** (420 East Sheldon, Prescott, AZ 86301; 520–445–9944), which specializes in Belgian waffles. Inexpensive.

Now it's time to really get a feel for the history of Prescott, courtesy of the **Sharlot Hall Museum** (415 West Gurley Street; 520–445–3122; www.sharlot. org).

Actually, your education in Arizona history will be courtesy of the phonetically named Sharlot herself, because if there hadn't been a Sharlot, there wouldn't be a museum. She was an Arizona pioneer—and "poet, historian and independent thinker," according to the museum—who in 1927 had the foresight to recognize that Arizona life as she had known it was rapidly disappearing, and the strength of spirit to set about preserving it for generations to come.

Her museum today comprises about three and a half acres on the edge of downtown Prescott. Sprinkled around the grounds are the original territorial governor's "mansion," a log building constructed on the site in 1864 from local Ponderosa pines; the home of pioneer John C. Fremont when he was fifth territorial governor of Arizona; Fort Misery, the oldest log building in the territory, constructed in 1864 and rebuilt on the site (at the behest of Sharlot Hall) in 1934; a building showcasing early modes of transportation; the Bashford House, a painted lady that houses the museum shop and a few exhibits;

the Sharlot Hall Building, which houses various exhibits (including a new one focusing on the lives of Native Americans in territorial Arizona and approved by a local tribe); and several others.

American Indian Art and Culture also is the focus in the **Smoki Museum** (147 North Arizona Street; 520–445–1230), which opened in 1935 and is designed to resemble a Hopi pueblo. The Smoki Museum is known for its collection of pre-Columbian and contemporary artifacts, including baskets and pottery from a number of Arizona tribes and a collection of Hopi kachinas. Oil paintings and photogravures of Native American life round out the collection.

For a little bit of back-to-nature activity, head west on Gurley Street until it becomes Thumb Butte Road and follow the road to **Thumb Butte** 4 miles west of town. There you'll be able to park in a paved lot and hike to the top of the butte for some panoramic views of Prescott. Thumb Butte is part of Prescott National Forest (520–771–4700), which encompasses 1.2 million acres in the center of the state, including two mountain ranges.

LUNCH: The Palace (120 South Montezuma Street, Prescott, AZ 86303; 520–541–1996) is a historic restaurant and saloon specializing in steaks and seafood, plus such local favorites as pistachio chicken and stuffed Idaho trout. The Palace is on Whisky Row, once a row of raucous bars but now a strip filled with gift shops and souvenir shops—as well as a rowdy spot or two. Moderate

Afternoon

Whiskey Row follows along one side of Prescott's **Court House Plaza,** site of a fascinating timeline of Arizona history—inscribed in and painted on the pavement—and the impressive bronze Bucky O'Neill monument, a tribute to Teddy Roosevelt's Rough Riders and one Bucky O'Neill, who organized the Rough Riders and was the first volunteer in the Spanish-American war.

Court House Plaza is the site of another memorial, dedicated to Mike, the community dog, who died in 1960 and apparently was buried with honors. That Mike's grave should claim so prominent a place is testimony to the kind of charming, homey place Prescott is.

Time to head back to Las Vegas. Retrace your earlier route for a three-and-a-half-hour trip home.

THERE'S MORE

Cottonwood, Arizona

Clemenceau Heritage Museum, 1 North Willard Street; (520) 634–2868. Exhibits dedicated to the history of the Verde Valley.

Prescott, Arizona

Antelope Hills Golf Course, 1 Perkins Street; (520) 776–7888. Full-service facility with thirty-six holes of golf.

Granite Basin, Prescott National Forest, 12 miles northwest of Prescott; (520) 771–4700. Recreation area with ten-acre lake, fishing, camping, and hiking.

Heritage Park Zoo, 1403 Heritage Park Road; (520) 778–4242. Showcases exotic and native animals.

Phippen Museum, 4701 Highway 89 North; (520) 778–1385. Artifacts and works by prominent Western artists.

Prescott Downs, 828 Rodeo Drive; (520) 527–4590. Live horse racing May through September.

Prescott Valley, Arizona

Yavapai Downs, 10401 Highway 89A; (520) 445–7820. Live horse racing May to September.

SPECIAL EVENTS

Jerome, Arizona

May. Paso de Casas (home tour); (520) 634–2900.

Historic Jerome Walking Tours; (520) 634–2900.

Prescott, Arizona

April. Arizona Designer Craftsmen Juried Exhibition; (520) 776–2031.

Southwestern Artists Spring Fling show; (520) 445–1891.

May. Whiskey Row Marathon; (520) 445–7721.

Late June–July 4. World's Oldest Rodeo; (520) 445–3101 or (800) 358–1888.

July. Prescott Indian Art Market; (520) 445–3122.

August. Arizona Cowboy Poets Gathering; (520) 445–3122.

September. Fair on the Square; (520) 778–2193.
Yavapai County Fair; (520) 445–7820.

October. Fall Fest in the Park; (520) 778–2193.
Folk Music Festival; (520) 445–3122.
Shakespeare Festival; (520) 443–1868.

November. Holiday Light Parade; (520) 771–5852.

December. Christmas Parade and Courthouse Lighting; (800) 266–7534.

OTHER RECOMMENDED RESTAURANTS AND LODGINGS

Jerome, Arizona

Jerome Brewery, 111 Main Street; (520) 634–8477. Pizza, salads, sandwiches, appetizers, and fresh-brewed beer.

Jerome View Inn, 894 Hampshire Avenue; (520) 639–2824. Bed and breakfast originally built in 1925 of hand-poured concrete.

The Surgeon's House Bed and Breakfast, P.O. Box 998; (520) 639–1452, (800) 639–1452; www.virtualcities.com/ons/az/r/azrb601.htm. All rooms and suites have private baths; terraced gardens.

Prescott, Arizona

The Hassayampa Inn, 122 East Gurley Street; (520) 778–9434 or (800) 322–1927. Grand hotel with golf and romance packages available.

Hotel Vendome, 230 South Cortez; (520) 776–0900 or (888) 468–3583. Quaint hotel on the National Register of Historic Places.

Machu Picchu Peruvian Restaurant, 111 Grove Street; (520) 717–8242. Peruvian cuisine in an old Victorian house.

Murphy's, "an establishment of good taste," 201 North Cortez; (520) 445–4044. Known for steaks and seafood. Specialties at dinner include Mongolian-marinated pork chops and mesquite-grilled salmon.

Prescott Brewing Company, 130 West Gurley Street; (520) 771–2795. Traditional and nontraditional pub fare in a restaurant/brewery.

Prescott Resort, Conference Center and Casino, 1500 Highway 69; 520–776–1666. Hilltop resort with spectacular views. Limited casino gambling in separate building.

The Rose Restaurant, 234 South Cortez; (520) 777–8308. Fine dining with continental cuisine; outdoor dining in season.

FOR MORE INFORMATION

Jerome Chamber of Commerce, 310 Hull Street, Drawer K, Jerome, AZ 86331; (520) 634–2900; www.jeromechamber.com.

Prescott Chamber of Commerce, 117 West Goodwin Street, Prescott, AZ 86302; (800) 266–7534 or (520) 445–2000; www.prescott.org.

HISTORICAL
ESCAPES

HISTORICAL

Boulder City and Lake Mead

FUN AT THE DAM AND LAKE

2 NIGHTS

*Watersports • Recreation • Historic Boulder City
Hoover Dam*

It's a truly symbiotic relationship: The pasts, presents, and futures of Lake Mead and Boulder City, Nevada, are inextricably linked: One wouldn't exist were it not for the other, and it's doubtful either could thrive on its own.

The history of Lake Mead goes back to the turn of the last century. The mighty Colorado River had long wreaked havoc in the region, and in 1902 President Theodore Roosevelt authorized engineers to find a way to tame it.

And not a moment too soon. While the engineers were working, the Colorado had a few ideas of its own. From 1905 to 1907, it broke into the Imperial Valley and created the Salton Sea, a saline lake in the Sonoran Desert. In 1916, it flooded the Yuma Valley.

During the next decade or so, study continued, with Congress passing bills to try to stanch the flooding. Finally, in June 1929, the Colorado River Compact was signed and the Boulder Canyon Project Act was a reality.

Again, not a moment too soon. If you'll recall, something else happened in 1929: Black Monday occurred in October, ushering in the Great Depression. And to make matters worse, the Dustbowl of the Midwestern and Southern plains had left farmers betrayed by their own land and desperate to find ways to feed their families.

The Boulder Canyon Project couldn't have come at a more fortuitous time: Jobs would be available at last. Entire families packed up their belongings, tying them on the roofs and even the sides of their flivvers, and made

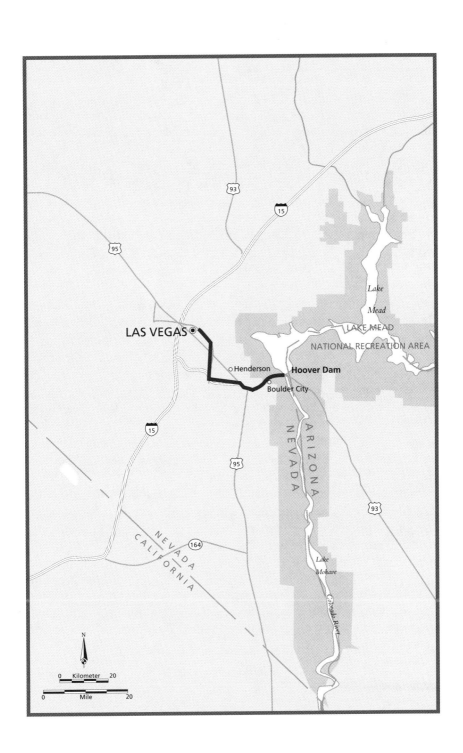

LAS VEGAS

93

15

95

Lake
Mead

LAKE MEAD

NATIONAL RECREATION AREA

○ Henderson

Hoover Dam

○
Boulder City

15

95

NEVADA

ARIZONA

164

NEVADA

CALIFORNIA

Lake
Mohave

Colorado River

93

N

0   Kilometer   20

0   Mile   20

their way west. They descended on Las Vegas, waiting for the work to begin, then made their way to the site of the future dam, some 30 miles away, and established a makeshift camp they dubbed Ragtown.

Conditions were worse than deplorable. Ragtown was near the dam site in Black Canyon (Boulder Canyon was the original site—hence the name—but a fault was discovered in the canyon) and during the summer, heat radiating off the canyon walls led to heatstroke and even death for numerous dam workers and members of their families. The river, which the workers nicknamed the Red Bull, didn't help much; residents liked to say the water was "too thick to drink and too thin to farm."

But many of the luckiest Ragtown residents—initially, those who worked for the federal government and the Six Companies confederation that was building the dam—soon were able to move to Boulder City, a federal government–established town that now calls itself the country's first planned community. Boulder City, on the edge of the dam site, housed 4,000 workers during construction, giving them and their families a real community to live in, with real houses instead of the makeshift tents at Ragtown.

Boulder City was only supposed to last as long as the dam construction, but when the project was completed in 1935—forming Lake Mead in the process—many residents demonstrated an interest in staying on, perhaps because they had no other place to go. At any rate, the federal government, which still owned the city, shifted its function, making Boulder City a base to agencies involved in the dam's water and power operations. In 1958, the feds established an independent municipal government in Boulder City and handed off the townsite and utilities to the residents.

But beyond its actual presence, the dam has cast a long shadow over the city. Because the government didn't want its workers raising havoc drinking and gambling, the latter was outlawed in Boulder City, and things remain that way today; this is the only place in Nevada where gambling is not legal.

Today, Boulder City is a peaceful, thriving city of more than 15,000 residents who like to brag that their hometown is clean and green. And the memories of the dam workers' descendants remain strong, so various historical spots in the area are dedicated to the days when 5,000 men worked in a 4,000-foot canyon as they tamed the Red Bull.

Hoover Dam draws tourists from around the world, who travel to see what's still regarded as an engineering marvel. And Lake Mead has become a prime spot for fishing and boating.

It's not far from Las Vegas, and it's a prime spot for a quick escape.

Hotel Plaza in Boulder City

DAY 1

Afternoon

Boulder City is only about 30 miles from Las Vegas and takes only forty-five minutes to an hour to reach, depending on traffic and what part of the Las Vegas Valley you're coming from. Simply drive south on U.S. Highway 93 right into Boulder City; drive a little longer and you'll find yourself at Hoover Dam.

DINNER: As you drive into town, bear right onto Nevada Highway (instead of taking the US 93 bypass). Turn right onto Wyoming Street, then left onto Avenue C to Hotel Plaza. **Carlos' Mexican Cafe** (561 Hotel Plaza, Boulder City, NV 89005; 702–294–6640) has the combination plates you'd expect, plus a few offbeat selections, such as fish tacos with either salmon, halibut, crab, or prawns; fajitas with prawns, halibut, or salmon; broccoli-and-pine-nut or zucchini-and-pine-nut enchiladas; avocado-and-cheese tacos; and some nice light chocolate-spiked flan for dessert. Moderate.

ESCAPE ONE

HISTORICAL

LODGING: Right across the plaza you'll find **The Historic Boulder Dam Hotel Bed and Breakfast** (1304 Arizona Street, Boulder City, NV 89005; 702–293–3510; rates from $99 to $149), which recently was renovated to its 1930s glory. In its heyday, all of the greats came through: Bette Davis slept here, and so did Harold Lloyd, Will Rogers, Boris Karloff, Shirley Temple, James Cagney; heck, even Fibber McGee and Molly (Mr. and Mrs. Jim Jordan). Today it has twenty-two pastel rooms and suites.

DAY 2

Morning

BREAKFAST: Just around the corner from your hotel you'll find **The Coffee Cup** (558 Nevada Highway, Boulder City, NV 89005; 702–294–0517). The Coffee Cup is a blast from the past, a convivial little place where the locals/tourists mix is as smooth as a milkshake. Go for a classic egg platter, or pancakes hot off the griddle. For something a little homier, dig into a plate of biscuits and gravy. Inexpensive.

The Boulder City/Hoover Dam Museum (1305 Arizona Street; 702–294–1988) tells the story of the dam and the Boulder City community as only its loving residents could; the museum was the culmination of a city-wide effort to raise funds to pay for its exhibits, some of which are interactive.

Museum backers pride themselves on telling the "human side" of the dam story; they leave it to the museum at Hoover Dam to provide the technical stuff. And they've succeeded admirably; even children will be able to get some picture of what the dam meant, and still means, to these people, and the sacrifices they had to make to survive in this harsh region, eventually making it their own.

The interactive features of the museum mostly involve moving parts of exhibits to listen to voices or see pictures or more elaborate displays. But in the section titled "5,000 Men in a 4,000-Foot Canyon," visitors see a model of a high-scaler—one of the men who worked high on the canyon walls, knocking off loose rock so the concrete could be poured—at the top of a two-story mural, and can try their hands at positioning a model of one of the huge concrete buckets.

Even the museum ticket is interactive; visitors get to punch it at several locations, at one spot even voting for their choice of names: Hoover Dam or Boulder Dam.

Afterward, spend some time strolling through **Downtown Boulder City,** which is pretty much centered on Nevada Highway and Arizona and Wyoming Streets. In the neighborhood, you'll find City Hall, the Chamber of Commerce, and the library. You'll also find a number of galleries, including the **Boulder City Art Guild Gallery** (1305 Arizona Street; 702–293–2138), which displays members' works, primarily paintings; **Fire and Water Gallery** (555 Hotel Plaza; 702–294–4177), which has handmade glass and ceramics; and **Brent Thomson Art and Framing** (1672 Nevada Highway; 702–293–4652), which carries prints and paintings, including local landscapes.

Gift shops in the area include the workshop and store of **Begay Indian Jewelry** (1311 Nevada Highway; 702–293–4822); **Burk Gallery** (1305 Arizona Street; 702–293–4865), which has collectibles and jewelry; and **Craft Cottage** (1326 Wyoming Street; 702–294–4465), which carries needlework and craft supplies.

LUNCH: The Happy Days Diner (512 Nevada Highway, Boulder City, NV 89005; 702–293–4637). True to its name, the Happy Days is straight out of the 1950s, down to the red-vinyl stools at the counter and the vintage soda fountain. Lunches include sandwiches, burgers, soups, and salads; to combine a couple, try a chiliburger with cheese. Inexpensive. While you're in the area, you might want to consider a stop for a beer at the **Backstop Sports Pub** (533 B Avenue, Boulder City, NV 89005; 702–294–8445), especially if it's raining. The Backstop promises a free drink to anyone who comes in on any day the sun doesn't shine in Boulder City. Of course, that's a very rare occurrence.

Afternoon

You've seen depictions of **Hoover Dam** and the project that created it; now it's time to see the whole dam thing. (Yes, you'll find that dam puns abound in the area, and that started long before Chevy Chase's *Vegas Vacation*.) It's a popular place; more than a million people tour the dam each year, and millions more drive across it on the main route between Las Vegas and Arizona.

The U.S. Department of the Interior Bureau of Reclamation offers a Discovery Tour, which is designed to enable guests to plan their own visits. Tours include entrance to the visitor center, access to all exhibits, a twenty-five-minute film, and scheduled talks by dam guides. Tours are $10.00 for adults, $4.00 for ages 7–16.

Lake Mead National Recreation Area (702–293–8907 or 702–293–8990; www.nps.gov/lame) offers a plethora of recreational opportunities, including touring by car, backpacking, biking, bird watching, camping, hiking, nature walks, stargazing, and wildlife viewing. Watersports include boating, fishing, kayaking, scuba diving, snorkeling, swimming, and whitewater rafting. Boat rentals are available at several spots, including **Las Vegas Bay Marina** (702–565–9111); houseboats can be rented at **Forever Resorts** houseboats (800–255–5561).

Another option is to take a cruise on the lake. **Lake Mead Cruises** (702–293–6180) offers breakfast and dinner cruises, dinner-dance cruises, and midday excursion cruises. Narration is provided, so passengers learn more about the lake and dam project, and the boat at times cruises close enough to the hillsides around the lake that you might even see a desert bighorn sheep on a slope.

DINNER: Pete's (1300 Arizona Street, Boulder City, NV 89005; 702–294–PETE or 702–294–0475) is a young, downtown restaurant that has become a local landmark. Appetizers include smoked-salmon pizzas and homemade coconut shrimp; entrees include pecan-crusted chicken with cider sauce, cedar-roasted salmon, or wild mushroom lasagna. Moderate.

LODGING: The Historic Boulder Dam Hotel Bed and Breakfast (see above).

DAY 3

Morning

BREAKFAST: Drive to Lake Mead and follow the shoreline road to the north end of the lake. You'll be rewarded with breath-taking lake views, plus desert vistas where it seems there's no one else on earth. Continue along to Nevada Route 146—Lake Mead Drive—and the **Hyatt Regency Lake Las Vegas Resort** (101 MonteLago Boulevard, Henderson, NV 89011; 702–567–1234) for a buffet breakfast in the resort's **Cafe Tajine.** The buffet has all of the standard stuff—eggs, seafood, meats, chafing-dish entrees, pastries, and desserts— but is more luxe than most. And this resort was the site of the filming of *America's Sweethearts,* starring Billy Crystal, Catherine Zeta-Jones, Julia Roberts, and John Cusack, so it's kind of a hoot to spot places you saw in the movie.

Then it's time to head back to Las Vegas, content in the knowledge that the Boulder City/Lake Mead area is so close to home, you can visit anytime you like.

THERE'S MORE

Black Canyon River Raft Tours, 1297 Nevada Highway; (702) 293–3776. Explore the Colorado River by raft.

Boulder Bowl, 1504 California Avenue; (702) 293–2368. Open bowling available.

Boulder City Golf Course, 1 Clubhouse Drive; (702) 293–9236. Eighteen-hole championship layout.

Lake Mead Air, Boulder City Airport; (702) 293–1848. Fly over Colorado River, Hoover Dam, and Lake Mead.

St. Jude's Ranch for Children, U.S. Highway 93/95, just south of Boulder City; (702) 293–3131. Spanish-style mission overlooking Lake Mead; tours available. Gift shop.

Skydive Las Vegas, 1401 Airport Road No. 4; (702) SKY–DIVE or (800) U–SKYDIV. Skydiving for students and experienced jumpers.

SPECIAL EVENTS

March. Hoover Dam Weekend Dance, for square and round dancers. Two-day event concluding with street dance atop Hoover Dam. Garrett Middle School, 1200 Avenue G; (702) 293–2034.

May. Folk Art Festival, Bicentennial Park and Wilbur Square; (702) 293–2034.

Spring Jamboree and Craft Show. Two-day crafts event with classic car show, kiddie carnival, and business fair, Bicentennial Park; (702) 293–2034.

July. Boulder City Damboree, old-fashioned Fourth of July fun plus parade, band contest, food and games booths, and fireworks, Central Park; (702) 293–2034.

September. Chautaqua, historical figures portrayed with audience interaction, Bicentennial Park; (702) 293–2034.

Wurstfest, with bratwurst, beer, music, and auction, Bicentennial Park; (702) 293–2034.

Rattlin' Rails handcar races; (702) 293–2034.

October. Art in the Park, among largest arts and crafts shows in the West. Bicentennial Park; (702) 293–2034.

December. Parade of Lights, annual parade with up to fifty decorated boats, Lake Mead Marina; (702) 293–2034.

OTHER SUGGESTED RESTAURANTS AND LODGINGS

Best Western Lighthouse Inn, 110 Ville Drive; (702) 293–6444. Some rooms have views of Lake Mead.

Brody's, 524 Nevada Highway; 702–294–8480. Coffee house that also sells sandwiches and snacks.

El Rancho Boulder Hotel, 725 Nevada Highway; (702) 293–1085. Spanish-style motel with landscaped grounds.

Evan's Old Town Grille, 1129 Arizona Street; (702) 294–0100. Specialties include rack of lamb and prime rib; outdoor dining available.

Super 8 Motel, 704 Nevada Highway; (702) 293–4344. Indoor pool and spa; themed suites.

Tiffany's, 1305 Arizona Street; (702) 294–1666. Featuring Italian specialties.

FOR MORE INFORMATION

Boulder City Chamber of Commerce, 1305 Arizona Street, Boulder City, NV 89005; (702) 293–2034; www.bouldercitychamber.com.

HISTORICAL

Pasadena
EVERYTHING'S COMING UP ROSES

2 NIGHTS

Architectural landmarks • Museums
Old California grandeur • Romantic inns

Most cities would like the world to see a rosy picture of themselves, but no city has been more successful at achieving that than Pasadena, California.

Pasadena has much to its credit, but it's roses that most people associate with this city in the San Gabriel Valley, which every New Year's Day presents its Tournament of Roses Parade for millions of TV viewers and the thousands more who line the parade route. And Pasadena manages to hold much of that interest throughout the day with the famous Rose Bowl college football game, at which the national championship often is decided.

But Pasadena's roots are long and deep. The area originally was occupied by the Tongva tribe and then the Hahamongna tribe, at least the latter of which had a reputation for being both moral and religious. Then Father Junipero Serra arrived in 1771 to "save" the Hahamongnas from themselves, eventually assimilating them into the Spanish culture, with even their storied Chief Hahamovic marrying a Spanish woman and retiring peacefully in San Gabriel. California passed from Spanish to Mexican rule before eventually becoming a state in 1849.

Oh, but the invasions weren't quite over. A group of friends in Indiana decided to flee to the much more hospitable climate in the San Gabriel Valley, purchasing land in 1873. They promptly subdivided it, and by 1875 they named their little settlement Pasadena, from the Chippewa word for valley, although various interpretations also have translated the word to mean crown

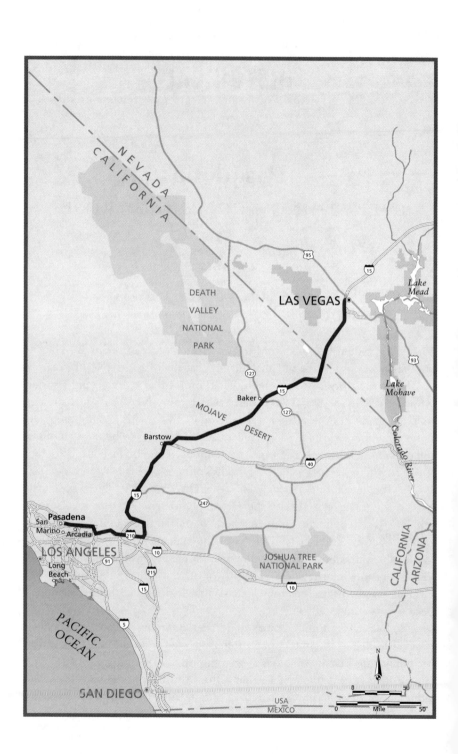

or key of the valley. Hence, both a crown and a key are incorporated into the city's very simple official seal.

Those early Pasadena residents had ranching and agriculture in mind, but progress was unstoppable; things just kept building in this most hospitable climate and lovely environment. The first schoolhouse was built by 1875, a library by 1884. By the late 1880s, advancements in rail travel to the area had made Pasadena quite the fashionable winter resort.

The city was incorporated in 1886, and improvements just kept coming. The Valley Hunt Club, mindful of the city's image as a premier place to escape the Eastern winters, decided to present a festival in 1890 to entertain all of those visitors and included a parade of carriages decorated with flowers. By 1898, the Tournament of Roses Association was sponsoring the parade, and the rest, as they say, is history.

Despite setbacks that also had long-lasting effects on the rest of the country—the Depression (from which the booming tourist economy never quite recovered) and World War II—Pasadena's fortunes steadily improved. Commercial development continued and so did cultural development; museums and educational institutions sprang up, including the California Institute of Technology, which manages the Jet Propulsion Laboratory.

Today, the grand old houses of Pasadena, a city of more than 140,000, are being preserved and are gaining attention nationwide for their architecture; the historic center of town has been revitalized as Old Pasadena. There are plenty of daylight activities and a burgeoning nightlife—all of which makes for a super quick escape.

DAY 1

Afternoon

Pasadena is only about 250 miles from Las Vegas, for a drive of about four hours, making an afternoon departure possible.

Drive south on Interstate 15 for about 215 miles to Interstate 10 West, then follow I–10 for about 15 miles to the California 57 South/Orange Freeway South/Interstate 210 West exit toward Santa Ana/Pasadena. Then take the I–210 West exit toward Pasadena.

Follow I–210 West for about 23 miles to the Fair Oaks Avenue South exit, and turn left onto Fair Oaks Avenue. Then turn right onto West Colorado Boulevard and look for One Colorado Boulevard and Hugus Alley.

DINNER: Johnny Rockets (52 Hugus Alley at One Colorado Boulevard, near the intersection with Fair Oaks Avenue, Pasadena, CA 91103; 626–793–6570) is a blast out of the 1950s and 1960s; you'll feel like Jan and Dean are right around the corner, ready to burst into song about the "Little Old Lady From Pasadena." Burgers are king here, and some of the best are the No. 12, with its Tillamook Cheddar and "red red sauce," and the Route 66, with mushrooms and onions and Swiss. Other sandwich choices include grilled breast of chicken, egg salad, or a classic BLT. Don't forget a shake or malt; Johnny Rockets makes them the old-fashioned way, and, usually, the server will give you what's left in the shaker. Inexpensive.

LODGING: The Ritz-Carlton Huntington Hotel and Spa (1401 South Oak Knoll Avenue, Pasadena, CA 91106; 626–568–3900; www.ritz-carlton.com; rates from $245 to $420) is one of those grand old hotels that they just don't build anymore, and it's tucked into a residential neighborhood in Pasadena. The company recently restored this old Pasadena landmark to its twentieth-century splendor, and you'll feel that sense of history as you stroll its broad hallways. Even better are the twenty-three acres of lush grounds, including a Japanese garden and the Picture Bridge, a pedestrian bridge with historic paintings on its interior eaves.

DAY 2

Morning

BREAKFAST: The Original Pantry (877 South Figueroa Street, Los Angeles, CA 90017; 213–972–9279) isn't in Pasadena, but it's only about 11 miles away—a drive of about fifteen minutes—and it's well worth the short trip. The Original Pantry's been in business since 1924, and for good reason; it serves up down-to-earth, homemade food in ample portions. At breakfast, that means lighter-than-air pancakes, chili-and-cheese omelets, rich cinnamon rolls, danishes, and muffins and all of the all-American breakfast favorites you'd expect. Inexpensive. Eat hearty, because Pasadena has many fascinating museums, and you'll want to take in as many as you can.

   The Norton Simon Museum (411 West Colorado Boulevard; 626–449–6840) is a good place to start. The museum showcases the collection of industrialist Norton Simon, covering more than 2,000 years of Western and Asian art. Simon began collecting works by Degas, Renoir, Gauguin, and Cezanne in the 1950s, expanding into Old Masters and Modern works in the

Ritz-Carlton Huntington Hotel and Spa forecourt

1960s and Indian and Southeast Asian art in the 1970s. The museum, which opened as the Pasadena Art Museum in the 1960s, has recently been extensively remodeled to showcase the collection.

Close by is the **Gamble House** (4 Westmoreland Place; 626–793–3334), a National Historic Landmark owned and operated by the University of Southern California and a sterling example of the American Arts and Crafts movement. Built in 1908, it was the home of David and Mary Gamble, he of Procter and Gamble. The house contains its original furnishings, and its features include hand-rubbed teak and mahogany woodwork. So unique is the Gamble House that it has been used to add the right touch of atmosphere to several movies; for example, it was the home of Doc, the character played by Christopher Lloyd, in *Back to the Future*.

Also in the vicinity is the **Pacific Asia Museum** (46 North Los Robles Avenue; 626–449–2742), which is dedicated to the culture of Asia and the Pacific islands, focusing on history and art; exhibits change twice each year and student art also frequently is showcased. The main building surrounds a koi pond and Chinese Imperial Palace garden.

The **Huntington Library, Art Collections, and Botanical Gardens** are just over the border in San Marino (1151 Oxford Road; 626–405–2100). If you don't get to many museums in the Pasadena area, be sure to visit this one. The Huntington is a 150-acre oasis of indescribable beauty, and it has something to appeal to most interests. Spend some time wandering through the botanical gardens, with gorgeous accents such as ornamental bridges spaced throughout; the gardens showcase more than 14,000 species of plants. But be sure to allot yourself plenty of time for the three art galleries and the library, where you'll find a fantastic collection of art, rare books, and manuscripts. The Huntington's collections include Thomas Gainsborough's *The Blue Boy* from 1770, Sir Thomas Lawrence's *Pinkie* from 1794, and Rogier van der Weyden's *Madonna and Child,* which dates to the fifteenth century.

LUNCH: Linger at the Huntington a while longer for lunch or tea at the **Cafe and Tea Room** in the center of the botanical gardens. The Tea Room overlooks three acres of roses; specialties there include traditional tea and scones served at the table plus a buffet array of finger sandwiches and pastries. In the Cafe, you'll find salads, sandwiches, hamburgers, hot dogs, soups, and pastries. Expensive.

Afternoon

Want to get a little wild? Drive back into Los Angeles to Griffith Park at the intersection of the Ventura and Golden State Freeways and the **Los Angeles Zoo** (5333 Zoo Drive; 323–644–6400). The 113-acre zoo was born in the 1960s after Los Angeles residents taxed themselves to build it. Today, it has 1,200 animals of 350 species living in various environments, including a tropical rainforest and a saltwater habitat.

If you'd rather stay in Pasadena, consider making the rounds with **Rose City Tours** (626–356–0066), which offers a variety of sightseeing and special-interest tours during the day or evening. One possibility is the Best of Pasadena and Stroll in Old Town tour, which takes in all of the city's most noted sites; other tours pass by popular filming locations.

If you're in town during college football season and you've planned ahead, you might be able to see the UCLA Bruins play in the **Rose Bowl** (626–577–3100). If you're in town April through September, you might catch a game by the **Los Angeles Galaxy** (626–432–1540) Major League Soccer team.

DINNER: **Gordon Biersch Brewery Restaurant** (41 Hugus Alley at One Colorado, Pasadena, CA 91103; 626–449–0052) has great home-brewed beers and the food to go with them. For starters, there are the crispy artichoke hearts tossed with Parmesan and served with lemon aioli or chili and ginger-glazed chicken wings; entrees include peppered ahi tuna with tomato chutney or meatloaf with beer-mustard gravy and garlic mashed potatoes. Moderate.

LODGING: The Ritz-Carlton Huntington Hotel and Spa (see above).

DAY 3

Morning

BREAKFAST: Have Sunday brunch in the elegant **Terrace Room** at the Ritz-Carlton Huntington Hotel and Spa, where Ritz touches include finely pre-pared seafood, meats, and breakfast dishes and fresh-baked pastries. Expensive.

With more than 600 Pasadena buildings listed on the National Register of Historic Places, you'd almost be remiss in not taking an architectural tour of the city; seven such routes are spelled out on the Web site of the Pasadena Convention and Visitors Bureau, www.pasadenacal.com. One of the routes, "Victorian Triumphant," takes in the neighborhoods on and around Orange Grove Boulevard; "Craftsmen Bohemia" will lead you past the Arts and Crafts masterpieces in the vicinity of Arroyo Boulevard.

If you'd rather go shopping, there's plenty of that available in Pasadena, too. **Old Pasadena,** bordered by Arroyo Parkway, Pasadena Avenue, Walnut Street, and Del Mar Boulevard, has more than 130 specialty shops and boutiques, as well as eighty restaurants. **One Colorado,** a plaza located within Old Pasadena, is home to branches of nationally known retailers, plus specialty shops and restaurants. The **Pasadena Playhouse District,** centered on Col-orado Boulevard and El Molino Avenue, is known for its bookstores and antiques and specialty shops, and South Lake Avenue between California and Colorado Boulevards has more than 600 top retailers.

LUNCH: **McCormick and Schmick's** (111 North Los Robles Avenue, Pasadena, CA 91101; 626–405–0063) is known for its seafood, and that's exactly what you'll find there (with a few alternatives for those who just can't stand the stuff). Appetizer offerings might include rock shrimp popcorn with Cajun remoulade or a smoked-salmon quesadilla; entrees might include Ore-gon rockfish tacos or McCormick's meatloaf; note that the menu changes daily. Moderate.

Afternoon

Then it's time to make the return trip to Las Vegas, retracing your steps from I–210.

THERE'S MORE

Arcadia, California

Santa Anita Park, 285 West Huntington Drive; (626) 574–RACE. Thoroughbred racing from October to mid-November and from late December to April.

Los Angeles, California

Los Angeles Dodgers, Dodger Stadium, 1000 Elysian Park Avenue; (323) 224–1–HIT. Major League Baseball from April through September.

Los Angeles Lakers, Staples Center, 1111 South Figueroa Street; (213) 480–3232. NBA regular-season action from October through April.

Pasadena, California

Kidspace Museum, 390 South El Molino Avenue; (626) 449–9143. Interactive museum with exhibits in the sciences, arts, and humanities.

Pasadena Historical Museum, 470 West Walnut Street; (626) 577–1660. Includes Fenyes Mansion, Beaux-Arts style house built in 1905, and the Finnish Folk Art Museum.

Tournament House and Wrigley Gardens, 391 South Orange Grove Boulevard; (626) 449–4100. Mansion built between 1908 and 1914 once was owned by chewing-gum magnate William Wrigley, now is headquarters for Tournament of Roses Association. Open for tours on certain days; call for schedule.

San Marino, California

El Molino Viejo, 1120 Old Mill Road; (626) 449–5450. First water-powered grist mill in Southern California; changing exhibits relating to California history.

HISTORICAL

SPECIAL EVENTS

January. Pasadena Tournament of Roses Parade, with elaborate floral floats; (626) 449–4100.

February. Black History Parade and Festival, Jackie Robinson Center; (626) 791–7983.

March. Spring Home Tour, sponsored by Pasadena Heritage; (626) 441–6333.

April. Bungalow Heaven Home Tour, sponsored by the Bungalow Neighborhood Association; (626) 585–2172.

Pasadena Spring Fine Art and Crafts Fair, with more than 125 artists from around the state, Central Park; (626) 797–6803.

May. *Cinco de Mayo* Celebration; (626) 744–4463.

June. South Lake Avenue Classic Car Show, sponsored by the South Lake Business Association; (626) 792–1259.

July. Old Pasadena Jazz Fest, showcasing various headliners; (818) 771–5544.

August. Garfield Heights Evening Home Tour, sponsored by the Garfield Heights Landmark District; (626) 794–8999.

September. Latino Heritage Festival, on Colorado Boulevard in the heart of the Playhouse District, celebrating music and culture of South and Central America and Mexico; (626) 797–6803 or (626) 744–0340.

A Taste of Old Pasadena, showcasing area restaurants; (626) 795–2455.

November. Craftsman Weekend, sponsored by Pasadena Heritage; (626) 441–6333.

OTHER RECOMMENDED RESTAURANTS AND LODGINGS

Los Angeles, California

Millennium Biltmore, 506 South Grand Avenue; (213) 624–1011. Historical landmark in Spanish/Italian Renaissance style.

Pasadena, California

Celestino, 141 South Lake Avenue; (626) 795–4006. Italian cuisine.

Kathleen's, 595 North Lake Avenue; (626) 578–0722. Long-established restaurant that's popular with locals; emphasis on California cuisine.

Saga Motor Hotel, 1633 East Colorado Boulevard; (626) 795–0431. Bed-and-breakfast with heated pool in a garden setting.

South Pasadena, California

Artist's Inn Bed and Breakfast, 1038 Magnolia Street; (626) 799–5668. Victorian farmhouse with porch and rose gardens; rooms decorated in art themes.

Bissell House Bed and Breakfast, 201 Orange Grove Avenue; (626) 441–3535. Victorian house with leaded-glass windows and antiques.

Oak Tree Inn, 1315 Fair Oaks Avenue; (323) 682–2882. Cantonese and Mandarin cuisine.

Shiro, 626 Mission Street; (626) 799–4774. Japanese-inspired seafood.

FOR MORE INFORMATION

Pasadena Chamber of Commerce and Civic Association, 865 East Del Mar Boulevard, Pasadena, CA 91101; (626) 795–3355.

Pasadena Visitors and Convention Bureau, 171 South Los Robles Avenue, Pasadena, CA 91101; (626) 795–9311; www.pasadenacal.com.

Flagstaff

WHERE COLLEGE KIDS AND NATURE LOVERS CAN GET THEIR KICKS

2 NIGHTS

Ponderosa pines • Black bears and bald eagles
Route 66 • Old West meets college town

Because of its proximity to the south rim of the Grand Canyon to the north and the tourism region around Sedona to the south, Flagstaff, Arizona, often is as seen as a jumping-off point for trips to other places.

But veteran Las Vegans know Flagstaff as a place to escape the summer heat. During July, when mid-afternoon temperatures in the Las Vegas Valley have an alarming tendency to climb well into three digits, the average high in Flagstaff is a perfectly pleasant 82 degrees.

And Flagstaff is more than a place to cool off; it's also a prime spot to chill out. The town of about 46,000 people is surrounded by the Coconino National Forest, the largest contiguous ponderosa pine forest in the world, which offers camping and hiking and the possibility of sighting wildlife including black bears and American bald eagles.

It was one of those ponderosa pines, in fact, that gave Flagstaff its name. Early explorers discovered a lone tall ponderosa pine in an otherwise open valley, stripped it, and put it to use flying the flag during centennial Fourth of July celebrations in 1876. Later, wagon trains passing through on their way to the California promised land used the flag staff—and Flagstaff—as a landmark.

Today, Flagstaff continues to celebrate its history as an Old West landmark. More recent history is reflected in the stretch of historic Route 66 that runs

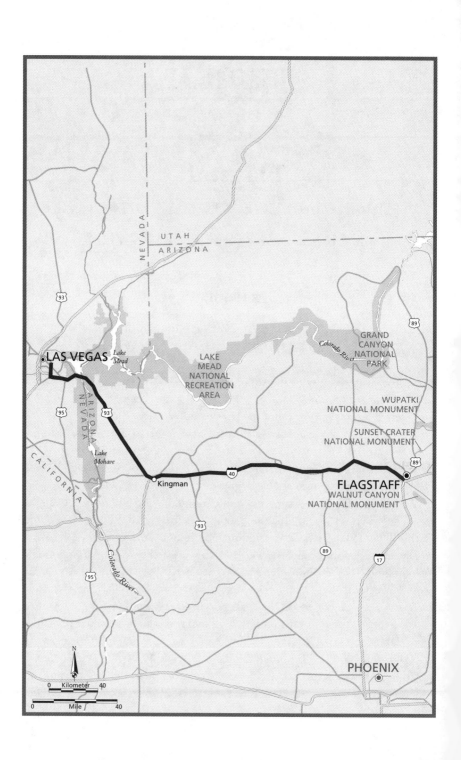

LAS VEGAS

NEVADA
UTAH
ARIZONA

93

LAKE MEAD NATIONAL RECREATION AREA

Lake Mead

Colorado River

GRAND CANYON NATIONAL PARK

89

WUPATKI NATIONAL MONUMENT

SUNSET CRATER NATIONAL MONUMENT

95

ARIZONA
NEVADA

93

Lake Mohave

CALIFORNIA

40

Kingman

89

FLAGSTAFF
WALNUT CANYON NATIONAL MONUMENT

Colorado River

95

93

89

17

N

0   Kilometer   40

0   Mile   40

PHOENIX

right through the center of town and is lined with appropriately colorful shops, restaurants, and bars. Flagstaff also is the home of Northern Arizona University, founded in 1899, bringing a cozy college-town feel and sports and cultural opportunities.

Add to that facilities for alpine and Nordic skiing during the winter, and Flagstaff stacks up as a prime place for a quick escape.

DAY 1

Afternoon

Flagstaff is about 251 miles from Las Vegas—mostly on interstate highways, for a trip of about three and a half hours—which makes it a great spot for a Friday afternoon departure.

From Las Vegas, head south on U.S. Highway 93 about 80 miles to the area of Kingman, Arizona, and pick up Interstate 40 East. Drive for about another 145 miles and you'll find yourself in Flagstaff.

DINNER: Follow I–40 to the Milton Road interchange and take the road north to **Buster's Restaurant and Bar** (1800 South Milton Road, Flagstaff, AZ 86001; 520–774–5155). Buster's serves everything from simple starters such as cheese and fruit to elaborate entrees such as Veal Buster (which incorporates crabmeat, asparagus, and béarnaise sauce), with steaks, prime rib, and seafood in between. Moderate.

LODGING: After dinner, follow Milton Road north to where it makes a sharp right and becomes Route 66, watching for Leroux Street on your left. Turn left onto Leroux and proceed to **The Inn at 410 Bed and Breakfast** (410 North Leroux Street, Flagstaff, AZ 86001; 800–774–2008 or 520–774–0088; www.inn410.com; rates from $135 to $190). The inn, in a 1907 Craftsman house, is just blocks from historic downtown Flagstaff and has nine antiques- and Southwestern-furnished rooms.

DAY 2

Morning

BREAKFAST: Have breakfast at the Inn at 410, or go 1 block over and south to **La Bellavia Restaurant** (18 South Beaver, Flagstaff, AZ 86001; 520–774–8301) for breakfast offerings that include trout and eggs, seven-grain

French toast, nine variations on eggs Benedict, or Swedish oat pancakes filled with fresh apples, bananas, or blueberries. Moderate.

Flagstaff's first white settlers were sheepherders in the 1870s; the arrival of the railroad brought workers and an 1880s tent camp that grew into a town. That relatively brief history is celebrated in **Old Downtown Flagstaff**, where many of the buildings date to the late nineteenth and early twentieth centuries, and a walking tour is a good way to take it all in.

The tour begins at the **Flagstaff Visitor Center** (1 East Route 66; 520–774–9541 or 800–842–7293; www.flagstaffarizona.org). That's convenient, because the Visitor Center sells tour maps and also offers free pamphlets and booklets.

Follow the tour along historic Route 66 and the neighboring streets and you'll see thirty-seven points of interest, including such spots as the 1898–99 **Weatherford Hotel,** which was made in two sections and retains a visible seam, and the 1888 **Berry Building,** built of brick with stucco added in the 1930s.

Oh, but Flagstaff's historical collection offers lots more. Off Milton Road on Riordan Road is the **Riordan Mansion State Historic Park** (409 Riordan Road; 520–779–4395), the 1904 home of lumbermen Timothy and Michael Riordan. Brothers who married sisters, the Riordans were known for their contributions to Flagstaff, both socially and economically.

The two families, who had eight children between them, were close, and so decided to build their homes as a mansion divided by a common room. Built in the Craftsman/Arts and Crafts style popular in the early part of the twentieth century (and created by the designer of Grand Canyon National Park's famed El Tovar Lodge), the forty-room, 13,000-square-foot mansion has siding of log slabs, arches of volcanic stone, and hand-split wooden shingles. If kids get a little antsy touring the house, take them to the park's visitor center, where there's a "touch table" for youngsters and you can pick up a map for a self-guided tour of the mansion's grounds.

Another historical option is the **Arizona Historical Society Pioneer Museum** (2340 North Fort Valley Road, reached by going northeast on Beaver Street from Route 66 and turning left onto U.S. Highway 180/Fort Valley Road; 520–774–6272). The museum, in the old Coconino County Hospital, has a collection of local artifacts that include Flagstaff's second motorized fire truck (an American LaFrance dating to 1923), a 1929 locomotive and a Sante Fe caboose. It also has a number of seasonal exhibits; the most popular is an annual winter exhibit, "Playthings of the Past."

Flagstaff

LUNCH: At **Tia Juanita's Mexican Food** (2320 North Fourth Street, Flagstaff, AZ 86004, off Route 66 east of downtown; 520–527–9386), the house specialties include such authentic-sounding dishes as coliflor y huevo (cauliflower dipped in egg and sauteed in garlic butter) and nopales y huevo (prickly-pear cactus with scrambled eggs and red chili) and the more whimsical chicken fried steak enchilada style. Inexpensive.

Afternoon

OK, here's a tip for finding a special place you won't see in any guidebook (except this one) and on few maps: **Grand Falls** is east of Flagstaff, on Navajo land. It's a favorite for NAU students, who shared the directions with us. The falls are impressively large and very scenic. One caveat: Grand Falls is fed by the Little Colorado River, and the water flow over it is more of a trickle than a gush, so don't expect anything of Niagara-like proportions.

To reach Grand Falls, continue east on Route 66 to the turnoff for Camp Townsend/Winona Road and make a right. Continue 8 miles to Leupp Road, turning left onto Leupp. Continue 15 miles to signs marking the boundaries of the Navajo Nation, then turn left at the first cattle guard onto a dirt road (you'll see a sign for a church, as well). Follow the dirt road (which is at times bumpy; an SUV or other heavy-suspension vehicle is best for this) for another 15 miles or so, until the road dead-ends at the river; by this time, you'll be able to hear the falls. You can't spot the falls from the road, so turn around and take the first dirt road to the right, which was marked with a discarded muffler when we were there. (Trust us on this!)

The area around the falls is mostly desolate, but a surprising number of visitors of all ages had found their way there on the morning we visited. And while the Navajos don't advertise the falls, they don't seem to mind visitors; a number of shelters have been built around the rim. For optimum viewing, get out of your car and walk around the rim. But be careful; the drop-offs are steep—and long. Be especially cautious if there are small children in your party.

The **Sunset Crater National Monument** (520–526–0502) is 15 miles north of Flagstaff off U.S. Highway 89, which branches off Route 66 east of downtown. The crater began to form during a volcanic eruption an estimated 900 years ago. Today, the cinder cone rises 1,000 above the surrounding area, and you'll see black streams of hardened lava and a rim of red cinders around the cone.

Some 7 miles east of Flagstaff off I–40 is the **Walnut Canyon National Monument** (Walnut Canyon Road; 520–526–3367). It's thought that the ancient peoples sensed the coming eruption of the volcano and moved to other areas, including Walnut Canyon. The canyon itself is a lovely gorge cut by a stream over many centuries. But walk down the paved path and you'll instantly be transported back to a time when ancient pueblo dwellers built their homes in the steep walls of the canyon.

They found natural shelters in the canyon's limestone, and most situated their dwellings facing south and east to take advantage of the sun's heat. In the visitor center is a collection of artifacts depicting the living and farming practices of the pueblo builders.

DINNER: Back in Flagstaff, the **Cottage Place Restaurant** (126 West Cottage Avenue, Flagstaff, AZ 86001; 520–774–8431; www.cottageplace.com) is tucked into a little neighborhood south of the corner where Route 66 meets Milton Road. Operating in a 1909-era Flagstaff residence, the Cottage Place offers such entrees as Cottage Place Cassoulet, risottos, Chateaubriand, beef, veal, lamb, poultry, and seafood dishes. Moderate.

LODGING: The Inn at 410 Bed and Breakfast (see above).

DAY 3

Morning

BREAKFAST: Have breakfast at The Inn at 410, or **Brandy's Restaurant** north of downtown (1500 East Cedar Avenue, No. 40, Flagstaff, AZ 86004; 520–779–2187). Brandy's is a sister restaurant of Bellavia; try the Cafe Aloha with steamed coconut cream along with your Eggs Brandy, poached eggs on a bagel with hollandaise sauce. Moderate.

The **Lowell Observatory** (1400 West Mars Road; 520–774–2096; www.lowell.edu) is 1 mile west of downtown; look for the brown directional signs. The observatory was founded in 1894, and some of the most well-known discoveries there have included founder Percival Lowell's observations about Mars and the discovery of Pluto in 1930.

While research continues at the observatory, it's open to the public as well, with daytime guided tours and nightly viewings.

The **Arboretum at Flagstaff** (4001 South Woody Mountain Road; 520–774–1442; www.thearb.org) is off Route 66/Business 40 southeast of downtown. The arboretum, situated in 200 acres of pine forest, has a wildflower meadow, children's garden, herb garden, display gardens, natural trails, visitor center, and more. Hours are seasonal and the arboretum is closed from mid-December until the end of March.

LUNCH: Down Under New Zealand Restaurant (6 East Aspen Avenue, No. 100, Flagstaff, AZ 86001; 520–774–6677) in Heritage Square downtown specializes in New Zealand–style fare including venison, lamb, and vegetarian dishes. Moderate.

Then it's time to head back to Las Vegas, across I–40 west to US 93 North.

THERE'S MORE

Arizona Snowbowl and Flagstaff Nordic Center, Snowbowl Road off US 180; (520) 779–1951. Alpine and Nordic skiing, snowboarding, and snowshoeing. Scenic skyride in summer.

Elden Hills Golf Course, 2380 North Oakmont Drive; (520) 527–7999. Ponderosa pine–lined holes.

Elden Pueblo, US 89 1 mile north of Flagstaff Mall; (520) 527–3475. Ongoing archeological project open to the public during summer Dig Days and other events; call for schedule.

MacDonald's Ranch, Highway 180 and Snowbowl Road; (520) 774–4481. Guided trail rides, hayrides, cowboy cookouts, and more through the Coconino National Forest, with views of the San Francisco Peaks.

Meteor Crater, off Interstate 40, 35 miles east of Flagstaff; (520) 289–2362. Crater caused by ancient meteor impact is 570 feet deep, nearly a mile wide, and more than 3 miles in circumference.

Museum of Northern Arizona, 3101 North Fort Valley Road; (520) 774–5213). Regional art and information on the cultures of the Hopi, Navajo, Pai, Zuni, and prehistoric peoples.

Old Main Art Gallery, Old Main, Knoles Drive and McMullen Circle, Northern Arizona University; (520) 523–3471. Exhibits of works by local, regional, and national artists.

Wupatki National Monument, 39 miles north of Flagstaff off Highway 89; (520) 679–2365. Trails lead to four pueblos built by ancient peoples.

SPECIAL EVENTS

February. Flagstaff Winterfest, with more than a hundred events including snowmobile drag races, skiing, children's activities, concerts, and cultural events; (520) 774–4505 or (800) 842–7293.

March. Arizona Ski and Golf Classic, with teams competing in golf tournament on Saturday and modified giant-slalom ski race on Sunday. Spectators welcome. Arizona Snowbowl; (520) 779–3019.

June. Chili Cook-Off, qualifying event for the World Championship Chili Cookoff; (520) 526–4314.

Pine County Pro Rodeo, plus barn dances and street dances. Coconino County Fairgrounds; (520) 774–3446.

July. Coconino County Horse Races, thoroughbred and quarterhorse racing. Fort Tuthill Downs; (520) 774–5130.

Flagstaff's Fabulous 4th Festivities, with parade, music, and more; (800) 842–7293.

August. Flagstaff Summerfest, a three-day celebration of arts and crafts with more than 200 juried artists from across the country. Fort Tuthill Coconino County Fairgrounds; (480) 968–5353 or (888) ART–FEST.

September. Annual Bed Race, plus parade and silent auction; (520) 523–1642.

Coconino County Fair, largest county fair in northern Arizona. Fort Tuthill Coconino County Fairgrounds; (520) 774–5130.

Late September–early October. Flagstaff Festival of Science, family-oriented learning experiences; (800) 842–7293.

November. Handel's "The Messiah." Northern Arizona University; (520) 523–5661.

Late November–early January. Annual Holiday Lights Festival, with more than 2 million lights; (520) 779–7979 or (800) 435–2493.

OTHER RECOMMENDED RESTAURANTS AND LODGINGS

Dierker House Bed and Breakfast, 423 West Cherry Street; (520) 774–3249. Vintage house with antiques-filled rooms.

El Metate Mexican Restaurant, 103 West Birch Avenue; (520) 774–5527. Mexican specialties including red or white menudo, quesadillas, and tamales, plus dirty shrimp.

Embassy Suites Flagstaff, 706 South Milton Road; (520) 774–4333. Two-room suites on edge of Northern Arizona University campus.

Galaxy Diner, 931 West Route 66; (520) 774–2466. Familiar favorites in a 1950s-style diner.

The Inn at NAU, Northern Arizona University; (520) 523–1616. Nineteen smoke-free rooms in country-inn atmosphere; two "green rooms" for those with allergies or environmental sensitivities.

Jeannette's Bed and Breakfast, 3380 East Lockett Road; (800) 752–1912 or (520) 527–1912. Victorian-style house with 1900–1930s decor, including clawfoot tubs.

Marc's Café Americain, 801 South Milton Road; (520) 556–0093. Crepes, rotisserie foods, and pasta.

Sakura Restaurant, Radisson Woodlands Plaza Hotel, 1175 West Route 66; (520) 773–9118. Sushi and teppanyaki.

FOR MORE INFORMATION

Flagstaff Chamber of Commerce, 101 West Route 66, Flagstaff, AZ 86001; (520) 774–4505; www.flagstaff.az.us or www.flagstaffchamber.com.

Flagstaff Convention and Visitors Bureau, 211 West Aspen Avenue, Flagstaff, AZ 86001; (520) 779–7645 or (800) 217–2367; www.flagstaffarizona.org. Visitors Center at 1 East Route 66, Flagstaff, AZ 86001-5754; (520) 774–9541 or (800) 842–7293.

Barstow, Victorville, and Apple Valley

CHILLING OUT IN THE HIGH DESERT

2 NIGHTS

Roy Rogers • Old West • Historical sites
Cozy bed-and-breakfasts • Skiing • Hiking

Wanna know how Western the Victor Valley/High Desert region of California is? Roy Rogers and Dale Evans chose to make their home there. It's what some of the region's residents choose to call the *other* Southern California.

Rogers and Evans lived in Apple Valley, California, a quiet, semirural community of ranchettes and equestrian estates that once was a playground for Hollywood refugees (Clark Gable and Carole Lombard reportedly frolicked here, on the Yucca Loma Ranch) but now focuses its energy on education and recreation. The Rogers-Evans museum is in nearby Victorville, California, where residents seem to get as excited about their mountain sunsets as they do about their golf courses and shopping malls. To the north is Barstow, California, a smaller city that's the intersection of several major highways and known as a key stepping stone on the road between Las Vegas and Southern California.

Actually, this region's been the path to Southern California for more than one hundred years. A settlement was established at present-day Victorville because the railroad came through there. In 1885 the community was known as Victor, for Jacob Nash Victor, a construction superintendent on the railroad. The name was changed to Victorville in 1901 because of some confusion that stemmed from the town of Victor, Colorado. Victorville was incorporated in 1962.

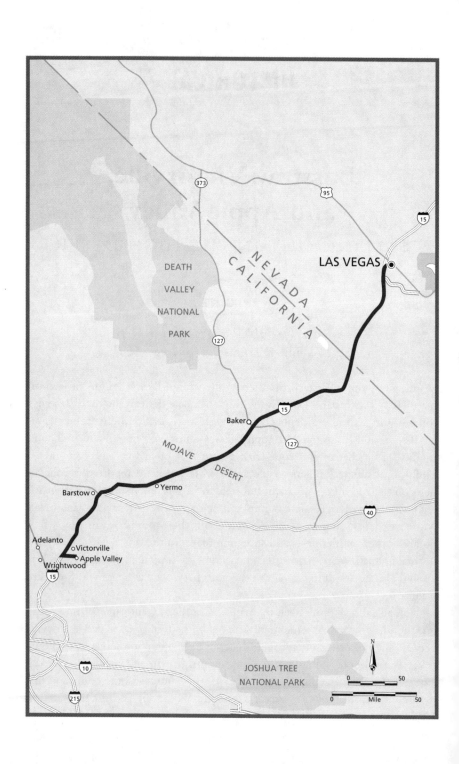

Barstow, too, owes its name to the railroad. While mining had begun in the region by the 1850s and white pioneers had begun settling along the Mojave River by the early 1860s, it was the railroad coming through in 1886 that really got things rolling. Barstow has long been a crossroads, it seems; the junction of the two railroad lines originally was named Waterman Crossing but was renamed Barstow in 1886 to honor William Barstow Strong, the tenth president of the Atchison, Topeka and Santa Fe Railway Company. The city was incorporated in 1947.

The first out-of-towners known to pass through what is now Apple Valley were Spanish missionary Father Garcias and explorers Jedediah Smith and, later (in 1884), John C. Fremont, who also explored much of Nevada. The area was named by settler Ursula Pates, who came to the valley about 1893, for the apples she saw growing by the river. Apple orchards flourished in later years, but then died out and the area returned to its original desert landscape. The town of Apple Valley was incorporated in 1988.

The region also is home to the San Bernardino National Forest and, farther north, the Mojave Desert National Preserve, so there's plenty for nature lovers as well. So instead of thinking of this area as merely a route to Southern California, plan to stop off for a quick escape.

DAY 1

Afternoon

The distance from Las Vegas to the night's lodging at Wrightwood is about 220 miles of mostly interstate—an easy drive of about three and a half hours—so you may have some time for sightseeing on the way: The **Mojave National Preserve** is a good spot for it.

Head south on Interstate 15 and cross the state line into California. There are three interchanges on I–15 that provide access to the preserve—the first is 10 miles across the border, the second is 13 miles farther, and the third is at Baker.

Park rangers suggest a scenic drive of at least an hour through the park's 1.6 million acres of Joshua tree forest, towering mountain peaks, dry lakebeds, pink sand dunes, and volcanic cinder cones. Remember, though, that this is, when all is said and done, the epitome of a desert climate, so if you're traveling in the summer, be sure to bring along plenty of water for both you and your vehicle.

The park is traversed by a number of roads, some of them paved and suitable for passenger cars, others—including the historic but decidedly rugged Mojave Road—best left to four-wheelers, and four-wheelers traveling in convoys, at that.

Other park activities include horseback riding, hiking, hunting, and viewing of the ever-present (but usually shy) wildlife found in the high desert.

From the ultimate natural environment, drive south along I-15 (about 94 miles from Las Vegas) to the ultimate kitschy one, with a stop at **Baker,** home of the **World's Tallest Thermometer,** which—in summer, at least—frequently reports what comes close to being the World's Highest Temperatures.

DINNER: Let's keep the kitschy theme going: **The Mad Greek** (6576 Baker Highway, Baker, CA 92309—watch for the billboards; 760–733–4354) is known for its fresh strawberry shakes and for its seasoned beef and lamb with pita bread, served up in an interior of Hellenic blue and white. If the weather's not too oppressive, have dinner on the air-conditioned enclosed patio. If it's chilly, try the Mad Greek's cappuccino bar. Inexpensive.

LODGING: Drive south on I-15 to California Route 138, then west on CA 138 to the turnoff for California Route 2 and the tiny town of **Wrightwood.** There you'll find the **Golden Acorn Bed and Breakfast** (5487 Morningstar Court, Wrightwood, CA 92397; 760–249–6252; rates from $100 to $125), an English-garden–themed spot in the San Gabriel Mountains.

DAY 2

Morning

BREAKFAST: Have breakfast at the Golden Acorn, or follow CA 2 to Big Pines, then Table Mountain Road to **Ski Sunrise** (760–249–6150), a resort with fantastic views and a restaurant that serves breakfast, lunch, and dinner. Inexpensive.

Feel like checking out the local scenery around Wrightwood? If it's winter, strap on a pair of skis or a snowboard (bring your own or rent them at **Wrightwood Ski Rentals,** 3496 Highway 2; 760–249–4751 or 1350 Highway 2, Suite D; 760–249–4742) and stay at Ski Sunrise, which has twenty-four trails, or head to **Mountain High** (24510 Highway 2; 760–249–5808; www.mthigh.com), which has forty-seven trails, five terrain parks, and two half-pipes.

World's Tallest Thermometer, Baker

If it's summer, hop on a mountain bike and take one of the three mapped-out trails in the Wrightwood area. Two of the trails are 4 miles round trip, although they vary in intensity; the other one is 6 miles round trip but great for beginners. Get maps at www.wrightwoodcalifornia.com. There are several variations of the three main trails, too, including a 13-mile loop.

Then travel east on CA 2 and south on California Route 38 to get back to I–15, where you'll head north to **Victorville.**

Roy Rogers and Dale Evans are Victorville's main claim to fame these days, it seems. Their **Roy Rogers–Dale Evans Museum** (15650 Seneca Road; 760–243–4547; www.royrogers.com/museum) is unlikely to be what you'd expect; it's not a typical museum, as the late Roy apparently was the first to admit.

Oh, the famous stuffed version of Roy's beloved horse Trigger is here, true enough, in all his glory, rearing on his hind legs because Roy figured that's how people remembered him.

But Roy was a big collector of ephemera, it seems; when other people had garage sales, Roy just packed the stuff up and put it in storage. Therefore, on a tour of his museum you'll also see his father's old tools, the car that brought the family from Ohio to California, photos, old scrapbooks, parade saddles, costumes, fan mail, and more. And more. And . . . .

For another aspect of the history of this part of the country, take the I–15 D Street exit and head east to the **California Route 66 Museum** (Route 66/D Street; 760–951–0436). Where do you think all of those dreamers were going as they traveled Route 66 all those years ago? California—and the better things that life seemed to promise them there.

Those hopes and dreams are reflected in this little museum, which has a collection of photographs and artifacts from the Mother Road, plus changing exhibits. There's a research library where you can learn more about the legendary strip of blacktop, and of course a gift shop with books and collectibles, including some exclusive to the museum.

LUNCH: The **Brass Pickle Sandwich Shop** (15329 Palmdale Road, Victorville, CA 92392; 760–241–3354) has lots of sandwich offerings, including the signature Brass Pickle, a cold sandwich of turkey breast, pastrami and provolone on sourdough bread. You'll find all the regular sandwiches, plus soups, chili, and salads. Moderate.

Afternoon

Would you like to learn more about Route 66 and the High Desert? Drive to nearby Apple Valley and the **Victor Valley Museum and Art Gallery** (11873 Apple Valley Road; 760–240–2111; www.vvmuseum.com). The museum features paintings of Route 66 scenes, mounted animals native to North America and assorted ephemera and bric-a-brac. Kids (preschoolers to sixth-graders) aren't left out; they enter the Imagination Station section of the museum through a doorway that looks like a miner's cave and then can explore an old schoolhouse, try their hands at panning for gold or connecting via an antique telephone switchboard, play hero with firefighting equipment, and dress up in police uniforms.

The **World War II Living Museum** at the Apple Valley Airport (21743 Cerrito Road; 760–954–4934) is a 3,000-square-foot hangar filled with artifacts and memorabilia from The Big One, including several aircraft.

Perhaps you'd prefer some back-to-nature time. The U.S. Forest Service's **Rim of the World Scenic Byway** is an extension of California Route 18, which passes right through the center of Victorville and Apple Valley and heads to the scenic **Big Bear Lake,** crossing the **San Bernardino Mountains** at **Onyx Summit.** You can follow the route for the 42 miles to Big Bear or on to Onyx Summit, or just for a little while—for as long as your schedule allows.

DINNER: Drive back into Victorville and the **Cask 'n Cleaver** (13885 Park Avenue, Victorville, CA 92392; 760–241–7318), an outpost of a small local chain that's known for its custom-cut Midwestern corn-fed beef, plus chicken and shrimp dishes including stir-fries. Moderate.

LODGING: The Golden Acorn (see above).

DAY 3

Morning

BREAKFAST: Today's a good day to explore all that **Barstow** has to offer, so retrace your route back across CA 2 to CA 38 East to I–15 North and try a local institution: **Bun Boy Barstow** (1981 West Main Street, Barstow, CA 92311; 760–256–8082), established in 1926. It isn't fancy by any stretch of the imagination, but breakfast offerings include such hearty fare as pork chops and eggs, chicken-fried steak and eggs, or a chili-and-bean omelet. Other options include Bun Boy's fluffy French toast or Belgian waffle—even a Belgian waffle sundae, with the crisp waffle topped with ice cream, strawberries, and whipped cream. Inexpensive.

Barstow's biggest landmark is **Calico Ghost Town** (3660 Ghost Town Road, Yermo, just off I–15 ten minutes north of Barstow; 760–254–2122 or 800–862–2542; www.calicotown.com). Calico actually was a silver-mining town between 1881 and 1896, but earned its "ghost town" appellation when the price of silver plummeted and the town emptied. Today, it's been revived as a tourist attraction; one-third of the town is original, the rest re-created. There's fun stuff, such as the requisite gun battles in the street, but educational elements, too, including historical information on the lives of the miners in the region during the era when silver was king, the twenty-mule teams that brought their huge loads of borax through the area, and a U.S. post office mail dog named Dorsey. There's a silver mine, gold panning, a blacksmith, and a narrow-gauge railroad, too.

LUNCH: Have lunch at **Lil's Saloon** at Calico Ghost Town, or try another Barstow institution: The **Idle Spurs Steakhouse** (690 Highway 58, Barstow, CA 92311; 760–256–8888) has been a ranch house since the 1950s and a restaurant since 1974. Lunch selections include a steak sandwich, of course, but also beef brochette, honey-dipped chicken, spareribs, fish, salads including shrimp Louis, or an avocado BLT on sourdough. Moderate.

Afternoon

Barstow's just a short hop from Las Vegas. Head north on I–15 and you'll be home in a few hours.

THERE'S MORE

Apple Valley, California

OK Corral Ostrich Farm, 21177 Glendon Road; (800) 224–4344 or (760) 961–9906. Petting zoo, plus more than 500 ostriches. Empty ostrich eggs (for craft projects) for sale.

Barstow, California

Factory Merchants Barstow, Interstate 15 at Lenwood Road; (760) 253–7342. Ninety-five stores including Adidas, Bally, Polo/Ralph Lauren, and Coach.

Western American Railroad Museum (WARM), 685 North First Street; (760) 525–5800. The museum has displays of railroad artifacts, memorabilia, and art in an old depot.

Helendale, California

Exotic World Burlesque Hall of Fame and Historical Museum, 29053 Wild Road; (760) 243–5261. "Home of the Movers and Shakers" with photos, films, library, etc.

Hesperia, California

Hesperia Golf and Country Club, 17970 Bangor Avenue; (760) 244–9301. Eighteen-hole course open to the public.

Victorville, California

Mavericks Stadium, Adelanto; (760) 246–MAVS (6287). Farm team for the Arizona Diamondbacks with season from April through mid-September.

Mojave Narrows Regional Park, 18000 Yates Road; (760) 245–2226. Horseback riding, paddleboat and rowboat rental, trout fishing, picnicking.

Mojave River Fish Hatchery, 12550 Jacaranda Avenue; (760) 245–9981. California Department of Fish and Game facility of sixty concrete ponds that produce up to 400,000 pounds of rainbow trout a year for stocking fifty Southern California lakes and streams.

SPECIAL EVENTS

Adelanto, California

January. Adelanto Grand Prix Motorcycle Race; (760) 246–5711.

Apple Valley, California

June. Presidio Arts Festival; (760) 247–6411.

July. Annual Freedom Festival; (760) 247–6411.

October. Happy Trails Roundup; (760) 247–6411.

Halloween Carnival and Haunted House; (760) 247–6411.

Barstow, California

February. Calico Civil War Re-enactment and President Day Week, Calico Ghost Town; (760) 254–2122.

March. Annual Roy Rogers Western Film Festival, Calico Ghost Town; (760) 254–2122.

September. Barstow Rodeo stampede; (760) 252–3093.

Victorville, California

May. San Bernardino County Fair; (760) 951–2200.

June. Annual Juneteenth Celebration; (760) 245–5551.

October. Annual Autumn Harvest Celebration; (760) 245–5551.

Wrightwood, California

February. Winter Carnival; (760) 249–4320.

June. Lilac Festival and Garden Tour; (760) 249–4320.

July. Mountaineer Days and Fourth of July Celebration; (760) 249–4320.

October. Chili Fest, Apple Fest, Mountain Challenge; (760) 249–4320.

December. Quilt and Home Tour; (760) 249–4320.

OTHER RECOMMENDED RESTAURANTS AND LODGINGS

Barstow, California

Best Western Desert Villa Inn, 1984 East Main Street; (760) 256–1781. Newly renovated guest rooms; pool and spa.

DiNapoli's Firehouse, 1358 East Main Street; (760) 256–1094. Italian entrees, pizza, pasta, subs, and salads.

California City, California

Silver Saddle Ranch and Club; (760) 373–8617. Riding, trap and skeet, golf, kayaking. Room, suites, bungalows, campsites.

Victorville, California

Amy's Mexican Restaurant and Seafood, 18768 Outer Highway 18 North, Unit 170; (760) 242–1474. Authentic mom-and-pop spot.

Best Western Green Tree Inn, 14173 Green Tree Boulevard; (760) 245–3461. Modern motel overlooking an eighteen-hole championship golf course.

Chateau Chang, 15425 Anacapa Road; (760) 241–3040. French, American and continental dishes with Asian touch.

Wrightwood, California

Oriole Lodge and Cottage; (760) 249–3873. Lodge with country French bedroom or cottage with sauna.

Pine View House; (760) 249–4348. Two suites in A-frame building in the pines.

Yermo, California

Peggy Sue's Diner, I–15 at Ghost Town Road exit; (760) 254–3370. Pizza, burgers, steaks, chili, soda fountain.

FOR MORE INFORMATION

Apple Valley Chamber of Commerce, 17852 Highway 18, Apple Valley, CA 92307; (760) 242–2753; www.avchamber.org.

Barstow Area Chamber of Commerce, 409 East Fredericks Street, Barstow, CA 92312-0698; (760) 256–8617; www.barstowchamber.com.

Barstow Mojave Desert Conference and Visitors Bureau, 2796 Tanger Way, Suite 106, Barstow, CA 92311; (760) 253-4782; www.barstowca.com.

Victorville Chamber of Commerce, 14174 Green Tree Boulevard, Victorville, CA 92392; (760) 245–6506; www.vvchamber.com.

INDEX

A

A & M Horse Drawn Carriage
    Rides, 185
Adele's, 183
Albert's Restaurant, 150
Alcatraz Brewing Company, 143
Alpine Meadows, 79
Alpine Pond Trail, 108
Amargosa Opera House, 8
American Pride, 162
Anaheim, 136
Anne Lang's Emporium, 132
Apache Stables, 195
Apple Valley, 251
Aquajito del Sol, 58
AquaLink, 162
Aquarium of the Pacific, 162
Arboretum at Flagstaff, 247
Arizona Cardinals, 204
Arizona Diamondbacks, 204
Arizona Historical Society
    Museum, 203
Arizona Historical Society Pioneer
    Museum, 244
Arizona Room, 195
Arnold Palmer Golf Academy, 17
Auto Log, 130

B

Backstop Sports Pub, 227
Balboa Fun Zone, 170
Balboa Inn, 169
Balboa Park, 150
Bar G Chuckwagon Cowboy
    Supper and Live Western
    Show, 86
Barstow, 253
Bay Shore Inn, 36
Bear Cloud Gallery, 58
Begay Indian Jewelry, 227
Berry Building, 244
Big Bear Discovery Center, 119
Big Bear Lake, 115
Big Bear Mountain Resort, 119
Big John's Steak 'n Pub, 23
Big Yellow Inn Bed and
    Breakfast, 108
Bike Zion, 89
Billy Reed's, 47
Bliss Mansion, 183
Bluff Park, 163
Bob's Root Beer Drive In, 67, 76
Bonnelli House, 36
Boo Bear's Den, 118
Boomtown Hotel and Casino, 68
Borax Museum, 6
Boulder City, 222
Boulder City Art Guild
    Gallery, 227
Boulder City, downtown, 227
Boulder City/Hoover Dam
    Museum, The, 226
Brandy's Restaurant, 247

Brass Pickle Sandwich Shop, 256
Brass Rail, 185
Brent Thomson Art and
    Framing, 227
Brian Head, 109
Brigham Young's Winter Home, 111
Bright Angel Coffee Shop, 196
Bright Angel Restaurant, 193
Bryce Canyon Lodge, 96
Bryce Canyon National Park, 94
Bryce Canyon Visitor Center, 96
Bucket of Blood Saloon, 186
Bullhead City, 31
Bumbleberry Inn, 89
Bun Boy Barstow, 257
Burk Gallery, 227
Buster's Beachouse Grill and
    Longboard Bar, 163
Buster's Restaurant and Bar, 243

C

C Street, 184
Cafe and Tea Room, 236
Cafe Tajine, 228
Calico Ghost Town, 257California
    Route 66 Museum, 256
Canyon Breeze, 56
Canyon South Course, 47
Canyon Trail Rides, 99
Canyon View, 131
Canyon View Information
    Plaza, 194
Canyon View Visitor Center, 194
Capistrano Beach, 172
Captain's Anchorage, 117

Carlos' Mexican Cafe, 225
Carollo's, 18
Carson City, 180
CasaBlanca Hotel-Casino, 15
Case de Pico, 149
Cask 'n Cleaver, 257
Catalina Express, 160
Catalina Island Company Discovery
    Tours Center, 161
Cedar Breaks National
    Monument, 108
Cedar Breaks Visitor Center, 108
Cedar City, 105
Cedar Creek Inn, 47, 172
Cedar Trail/Cedar Canyon
    Park, 110
Celebrities, 23
Chapel of the Holy Cross, 56
Chloride, 37
Chloride Old Jail, 37
Chloride Playhouse, 37
Chloride Post Office, 37
Chollar Mine, 186
Christmas Tree Pass, 34
Circus Circus, 68
Club Cappucino, 34
Coffee Cup, The, 226
Colonial Buffet, 160
Colorado River Museum, 35
Cottage Place Restaurant, 246
Court House Plaza, 216
Cowboy's Smokehouse, 96
Coyote Design, 17
Cracker Box, The, 182
Craft Cottage, 227
Crocodile Cafe, 204

Crown Point Restaurant, 186
Crystal Cathedral, 143
Crystal Cave, 128
C-Stop Pizza and Deli, 96

D

D. L. Bliss State Park, 78
Dana Point, 172
Dante's View, 6
Davis Dam, 34
Death Valley, 2
Death Valley National Park, 2
Delicatessen at Marketplace, 195
Desert Adventures, 47
Desert Botanical Garden, 204
Desert Hills Premium
    Outlets, 48
Desert Jeep and Bike
    Rentals, 56
Desert View Drive, 194
Desert View Watchtower, 195
Diamond Peak, 79
Disney's California
    Adventure, 140
Disney's Grand Californian
    Hotel, 139
Disneyland, 140
Dixie National Forest, 111
Don Laughlin's Riverside Resort
    Hotel and Casino, 33
Dory's Oar Restaurant, 79
Douglas Mansion, 214
Down Under New Zealand
    Restaurant, 247
Downtown Disney, 142

Dr. Priddy Meeks Cabin
    Museum, 110
Driftwood Gallery, 90

E

Ehrman Mansion, 79
1876 Territorial Enterprise
    Building, 186
El Rincon, 58
El Tovar Hotel, 193
Elmer's Pancakes and Steaks, 46
Emerald Bay, 78
English Village, 25
Environmental Realists, 58
Escalante Interagency Visitor
    Center, 99
Esteban's, 58
Evans American Gourmet
    Cafe, 77

F

Fairway Grill, 111
Fallen Monarch, 131
Fatali Gallery: Photography of the
    Southwest, 90
Fire and Water Gallery, 227
First Watch, 205
Fisherman's Village, 170
Fitzgeralds Hotel-Casino, 68
Five Crowns, 171
Flagstaff, 241
Flagstaff Visitor Center, 244
Flagstaff, Old Downtown, 244
Flamingo, 33

Flatiron Cafe, 214
Flying M Restaurant, 100
Forty Niner Cafe, 5
Fresh Market Square Cafe, 36
Fullerton Arboretum, 143
Fun Center, 26
Furnace Creek Golf Course, 7
Furnace Creek Inn, 4
Furnace Creek Ranch, 5
Furnace Creek Visitor
    Center, 6

G

Gamble House, 235
Gamlin Cabin, 131
Gardens on El Paseo, 48
Gaslamp District, 152
Gateway Restaurant and
    Lodge, 127
General Grant Tree, 131
General Sherman Tree, 130
Ghost Town Gear Adventure
    Equipment, 213
Ghosts and Legends Tour, 160
Glendale, Historic Downtown, 205
Gold Butte Back Country
    Byway, 17
Gold Door Gallery, 58
Gold Hill Hotel, 186
Gold King Mine and Ghost
    Town, 214
Gold Road Mine, 35
Golden Acorn Bed and
    Breakfast, 254
Golden Nugget Laughlin, 33

Gordon Biersch Brewery
    Restaurant, 237
Governor's Mansion, 183
Grafton, 90
Grand Canyon Imax Theater, 196
Grand Canyon National Park, 190
Grand Canyon Railway, 192
Grand Falls, 245
Grand Staircase-Escalante National
    Monument, 99
Grapevine Canyon, 34
Gurley Street Grill, 212

H

Hall of Flame Museum of
    Firefighting, 204
Hamburger Hamlet, 48
Happy Days Diner, 227
Hard Rock Cafe, 153
Harrah's Laughlin, 34
Heavenly Tram, 78
Heidi's Family Restaurant, 69
High Sierra Water Ski School, 79
Hilo Hattie - The Store of
    Hawaii, 143
Historic Boulder Dam Hotel Bed
    and Breakfast, The, 226
Hitching Post Restaurant, 57
Holiday Inn Big Bear Chateau, 117
Holiday Inn Hotel and Suites Old
    Town, 149
Holiday Inn Palm Mountain
    Resort, 45
Homewood Mountain Resort, 79
Honanki, 57

Hoover Dam, 224
Hopi House, 196
Horizon Outlet Center, 37
Hot Gossip, 78
Hotel del Coronado, 152
Hotel Queen Mary, 159
Hungry Bear, 212
Hungry Coyote, 99
Huntington Beach, 171
Huntingon Beach International
    Surfing Museum, 171
Huntington Library, Arts Collec-
    tions, and Botanical Gardens, 236
Hurricane Valley Heritage Park, 90
Hyatt Regency Lake Las Vegas
    Resort, 228

I

I Am One of a Kind, 58
Idle Spurs Steakhouse, 258
Inn at 410 Bed and Breakfast,
    The, 243
Inn by the Lake, 77
Inn on Oak Creek, 54
Inside Scoop, 16
Iron Mission State Park, 110
Island Mall and Brewery, 25

J

Jacob Hamblin Home, 111
Jake's on the Lake, 79
Jerome, 210
Jerome Artists Cooperative
    Gallery, 214

Jerome State Historical Park, 214
Jesse North Smith Home
    Museum, 110
Jetboat Tours, 27
Johnny Rockets, 234

K

Katherine Mine, 35
Kingman, 33
Kings Canyon National Park, 125
Kit Carson Trail, 183
Knott's Soak City U.S.A. Water
    Park, 142
Knott's Theme Park, 142
Kolb Studio, 196
Kolob Arch, 89
Kolob Canyon Visitor Center, 89

L

La Bellavia Restaurant, 243
La Fiesta Mexican Restaurant and
    Cantina 110
Laguna Beach, 172
Lake Havasu City, 21
Lake Havasu City Aquatic
    Center, 26
Lake Havasu State Park, 27
Lake Havasu Wildlife Refuge, 27
Lake Mead, 222
Lake Mead Cruises, 228
Lake Mead National Recreation
    Area, 18, 227
Lake Mohave Resort, 34
Lake Tahoe, 74

Las Vegas Bay Marina, 228
Laughlin, 31
Laughlin River Tours, 34
Lil's Saloon, 258
Locomotive Park, 36
Lodgepole Market and Deli, 130
Lodgepole Snack Bar, 127
London Arms Pub and
   Restaurant, 27
London Bridge, 21, 23
London Bridge Candle Factory, 25
London Bridge Resort, 23
Long Beach, 157
Long Beach, downtown, 163
Lookout Studio, 196
Los Angeles Galaxy, 236
Los Angeles Zoo, 236
Lost City Museum, 16
Lotions and Potions, 25
Louis' Basque Corner, 70
Lowell Observatory, 247
Luciano's, 70

M

Mad Greek, The, 254
Magic Mountain Recreation
   Area, 120
Maricopa Manor Bed and
   Breakfast Inn, 203
Marina Green Park, 163
McCormick and Schmick's, 237
Medieval Times Dinner and
   Tournament, 142
Melting Pot Fondue
   Restaurant, 205

Mermaid Inn, 26
Mesquite, 12
Mine Museum, 214
Mission de San Juan
   Capistrano, 172
Moapa Tribal Enterprises, 15
Mojave National Preserve, 253
Moro Rock, 128
Mountain High, 254
Mountain View Cafe, 109
Mountain View Museum, 110
Mt. San Jacinto State Park and
   Wilderness Area, 46
Mule trips, 195
Museum of Flying, 170
Museum of Photographic
   Arts, 150
Mystery Castle, 203

N

Nation's Christmas Tree, 131
National Auto Museum, 69
Nature's Landscape Gallery, 214
Nellie Bly, 214
Nellie Bly II, 214
Nevada Historical Society, 69
Nevada State Capitol, 183
Nevada State Museum, 182
Newport Beach, 169
Nicolinos Italian Restaurant, 26
19th Hole, 7
Ninibah, 58
North Shore Cafe, 119
Northstar-at-Tahoe, 79
Norton Simon Museum, 234

O

Oak Creek Canyon, 55
Oasis Golf Club, 17
Oatman, 35
Old Country Inn, 120
Old Pasadena, 237
Old Town Mexican Cafe, 150
Old Town San Diego State
 Historic Park, 149
One Colorado, 237
Onyx Summit, 257
Original Pantry, The, 234
Overton Beach, 18
Overton Beach Resort, 18

P

Pa'rus Trail, 89
Pacific Asia Museum, 235
Pacific Park, 170
Palace, The, 216
Palatki Ruin and Red Cliffs
 Rock Art Site, 57
Palm Springs, 42
Palm Springs Aerial Tram, 46
Palm Springs Desert Museum, 47
Panda Garden, 17
Panguitch Lake, 100
Papago Park, 204
Paradise Buffet, 15
Parawan, 110
Parkers' Lighthouse, 162
Pasadena, 231
Pasadena Playhouse District, 237
Peppermill Coffee Shop, 71

Peppermill Hotel Casino, 68
Pete's, 228
Phoenix, 200
Phoenix Coyotes, 204
Phoenix Suns, 204
Phoenix Zoo, 204
Pilgrim of Newport Historic Sailing
 Ship, 162
Pine Knot Coffee House and
 Bakery, 121
Pink Jeep Tours, 56
Pinnacle Peak Patio Steakhouse and
 Microbrewery, 202
Pioneer and Indian Museum, 90
Pleasant Street Inn, 212
Ponderosa Ranch, 80
Powerhouse Visitor Center, 36
Prado, The, 151
Prescott, 210
Prime Cut, 54
Prince of Wales, 152
Purcell Murals, 37
Purple Fez Cafe, 15
Pyramid Lake, 71

Q

Queen's Marketplace, 163
Quilted Bear, 205

R

Ralph Brennan's Jazz Kitchen, 139
Ramada Express Hotel and
 Casino, 33
Ramparts Trail, 109

Ranch and Gun Club, 17

Rapscallion Seafood House and Bar, 68

Rawhide, 205

Red Rocks State Park, 57

Redwood Canyon, 131

Rene, 58

Reno, 64

Reno Hilton, 68

Resort Boat Rentals, 26

Rhyolite, 9, 182

Rick's Cafe Catalina, 161

Rim of the World Scenic Byway, 257

Rim Trail, 195

Riordan Mansion State Historic Park, 244

Ritz-Carlton Huntington Hotel and Spa, The, 234

Rock Church Museum, 110

Ron Jon Surf Shop, 143

Rose City Tours, 236

Rotary Community Park, 26

Roy Rogers–Dale Evans Museum, 256

Roy's Newport Beach, 169

Royal Feaste, 107

Rusty's Ranch House, 107

S

San Bernardino National Forest, 119

San Diego, 147

San Diego Automotive Museum, 150

San Diego Chargers, 151

San Diego Museum of Art, 150

San Diego Natural History Museum, 150

San Diego Padres, 151

San Diego Zoo, 150

San Juan Capistrano, 172

Santa Monica, 170

Scotty's Castle, 8

Sea World Adventure Park, 150

Secret Garden Cafe, 54

Sedona, 52

Sedona Jeep Rentals, 56

Sedona, Uptown, 57

Sequoia National Park, 125

Sharlot Hall Museum, 215

Shep's Mining Camp Cafe, 37

Si Redd's Oasis, 15

Silver Reef, 111

Sir James Midtown Cyber Cafe, 26

Sir Winston's, 160

Ski Sunrise, 254

Slide Rock State Park, 54

Sliding Jail Park, 214

Smith Truckee River Walk, 69

Smoke Tree Stables, 47

Smoki Museum, 216

Snow Summit Mountain Resort, 119

Solid Muldoons, 184

Spa at CasaBlanca, 17

Spices Restaurant, 57

Spotted Dog Cafe, 89

Springdale Fruit Company, 86

Squaw Valley USA, 79

St. George, 111
Starboard Bakery, 160
Steakhouse at the Ramada
    Express, 34
Stillwell's, 119
Storytellers Cafe, 139
Sugar Bowl, 79
Sugar Pine Point State Park, 79
Sullivan's Cafe, 111
Sunrise Nature Center, 96
Sunset Crater National
    Monument, 246
Surfers' walk of fame, 171
Switchback Grill, 90

Tahoe City Marina, 79
Tahoe Paddle and Oar, 79
Tahquitz Canyon, 46
Tahquitz Creek Golf Resort, 47
Taliesin West, 205
Tallship *Californian,* 162
Terrace Room, 237
Thai Smile, 44
Thumb Butte, 216
Tia Juanita's Mexican Food, 245
Tiffy's Family Restaurant, 142
Tlaquepaque Arts and Crafts
    Village, 57
Tony P's Dockside Grill, 170
Topock Gorge, 27
Towne's Square Cafe, 35
Trading Post, 195
Treasures of the *Queen Mary,* 160
Tunnel Log, 130

Tusayan Museum, 196

Utah Shakespearean Festival, 107

Valley of Fire State Park, 16
V-Bar-V Ranch Petroglyph Site, 55
Venice, 170
Venice Pier, 170
Verde Canyon Railroad, 214
Victor Valley Museum and Art
    Gallery, 256
Victorville, 251
Vikingsholm, 78
Village, The, 121
Vineyard Room, 140
Vintage Marketplace, 47
Virgin River Gorge, 18
Virginia & Truckee Railroad, 186
Virginia City, 180
Virginia City cemeteries, 185
Virginia City Tram Tours, 185

W

Waffle Iron, 215
Walnut Canyon National
    Monument, 246
Weatherford Hotel, 244
Wilbur D. May Center, 70
Wild Island, 70
William Fisk's Steakhouse, 36
Wilma's Patio, 169

Windsor Beach, 27
Wingfield Park, 69
World War II Living Museum, 257
World's Tallest Thermometer, 254
Wrangler Steakhouse, 8
Wrightwood Ski Rentals, 254
Wrigley Memorial and Botanical
Gardens, 161
Wuksachi Lodge, 131
Wuksachi Village and Lodge, 127

Y

Yankee Tavern, The, 172
Yavapai Cafeteria, 196
Yavapai Observation Station, 194

Z

Zion Canyon Giant Screen
Theatre, 90
Zion Canyon Visitors Center, 87
Zion Factory Stores and
Promenade at Red Cliff, 18
Zion National Park, 84
Zion National Park Lodge, 86
Zion Park Gift and Deli, 88
Zion Rock and Gem, 90
Zuma's Woodfire Cafe, 215

ABOUT THE AUTHOR

HEIDI KNAPP RINELLA, a native of Cleveland and graduate of Ohio University, has been a newspaper journalist for more than 20 years in Ohio and Florida and currently with the *Las Vegas Review-Journal,* where she is restaurant critic and a staff writer in the features department. She has published one previous book. She and her daughters, Aynsley and Aubrey, and husband, Frank, live in Henderson, Nevada.